COLUMBUS'S OUTPOST AMONG THE TAÍNOS

KATHLEEN DEAGAN AND JOSÉ MARÍA CRUXENT

Columbus's Outpost among the Taínos

Spain and America at La Isabela, 1493–1498

Yale University Press
New Haven & London

Published with assistance from the
Louis Stern Memorial Fund

Designed by April Leidig-Higgins and set in
Centaur type by Copperline Book Services, Inc.

Printed in the United States of America by
Edwards Brothers, Inc.

Library of Congress Cataloging-in-Publication Data
Deagan, Kathleen A.
Columbus's outpost among the Taínos:
Spain and America at La Isabela, 1493–1498
Kathleen Deagan and José María Cruxent.
p. cm. Includes bibliographical references and index.
ISBN 0-300-09040-4
1. La Isabela (Dominican Republic)—Colonization.
2. Columbus, Christopher—Homes and haunts—
Dominican Republic—La Isabela. 3. Indians—First
contact with Europeans. I. Cruxent, José María. II. Title.
F1939.18 D43 2002   972.93'58—dc21   2001046771

A catalogue record for this book is available from the
British Library.

10 9 8 7 6 5 4 3 2 1

CONTENTS

To Eugenio Pérez Montás
and Rafaél Cantisano,
defenders of La Isabela,
whose visions for the future
made this work possible.

PREFACE

In December 1493, Christopher Columbus and his weary fleet of seventeen ships limped into the Bay of Isabela after nearly three months at sea. "I was at a point," wrote Columbus some years later, "from which I could no longer retreat or proceed with the ships, but had to unload them there and establish a settlement."[1] From this inauspicious beginning, the first European town in America was established, built on a dream of gold and wealth through trade. Columbus named it La Isabela, after the queen of Spain.

Although the settlement lasted for fewer than five years, it was a substantial and very Spanish medieval town during its lifetime. Its abandonment marked the end of the original Spanish model for colonizing America, and the emergence of a new strategy based on the social and physical realities of life in the "New World." Both the original idea and the ways in which it changed over the first decade of Spanish presence in America can be fully understood only by integrating the evidence from archaeology at La Isabela with documentary evidence from the Columbus era. Today the site of La Isabela is a Dominican national park where visitors can see the physical remains of the fifteenth-century

P.1. Aerial view of La Isabela. (Courtesy of Dirección Nacional de Parques, República Dominicana.)

town and learn about life there through the objects displayed in the site museum.

There is only one "first" site, and the opportunity to excavate and study the first European town in America (and the only place Christopher Columbus lived in America) was an exciting and occasionally daunting privilege for both of us. Although our ten years of collaboration at La Isabela were consistently rewarding in an intellectual sense, they were not without challenges. There was the ever-present anxiety of documenting this utterly singular, but physically ravaged, site as thoroughly as possible within the time and financial constraints with which we, like all archaeologists, were faced. The community's isolation, lacking fresh (let alone running) water, electricity, telephone, roads, postage, medical facilities, and public transportation presented unfamiliar challenges in organizing and implementing this complex program, particularly for José Cruxent, who lived year-round at La Isabela. Frequent changes in governmental administration of the site also created an ambient environment of political uncertainty.

But overriding the circumstances and routines of the research process was the exhilaration of learning things about Columbus's venture that had never been known before, and uncovering the physical remains of the settlement and material objects made and used by the first Europeans in America. A new, archaeologically informed understanding of

P.2. Conjectural reconstruction of La Isabela, ca. 1494. (Painting by Arthur Shilstone. Courtesy of *National Geographic* magazine.)

Columbus's colony emerged from that work, and we wanted to share it with as many interested people as possible in a nontechnical way. At the same time, however, we felt deeply responsible for the technical documentation of the site and wanted to provide a detailed explanation of our strategies and methods to our archaeological colleagues, who might wish to use our data in comparative studies.

These two aspirations, unfortunately, are nearly impossible to integrate in a single book. The technical details of archaeological sampling, excavation, and analysis are the basis for responsible archaeological interpretation and must be available for scrutiny. But they are also usually distracting to nonarchaeologists and in our case tended to detract from the flow of the larger story of Columbus's colonial project at La Isabela.

We have chosen to address this dilemma by writing two books. In this book, *Columbus's Outpost among the Taínos*, we present the new, materially based story of Columbus and La Isabela and explore its implications for understanding the emergence of Spanish-American society. We have based our account on the results of the historical-archaeological research at the site, but without detailing the technical archaeological evidence on which our conclusions are based. A companion volume, *Archaeology at La Isabela*, includes the contextual, spatial, statistical, and analytical data used in reaching our conclusions. It follows essentially the same format as *Columbus's Outpost*, and each volume has cross-references to the other. Each is intended to stand alone, although drawing on the conclusions of the other. Taken together, they offer the most detailed and comprehensive image of Columbus's La Isabela.

Historical archaeology is in some ways like a stereoscopic view of the past. Our premise is that, taken alone, neither the image of the past provided by written documents nor the image of the past provided by the archaeological record can provide us with a full or accurate view of social history. It is only when we overlay and articulate those images at the correct angle that the past emerges, like a stereoscopic view, in its full dimensions. In the chapters ahead we attempt to provide that overlay for Columbus's Isabeline project and its impact on colonial development in the Americas.

The setting free of the point where first converged the destinies of Europe and America will be of greatest historical interest.—Erwin Palm. 1945. Excavations at La Isabela, white man's first town in the Americas. In *Acta Americana* 3:298.

Chapter 1

Columbus and La Isabela

Christopher Columbus's departure from Cádiz in 1493 on his second voyage to America was a jubilant affair, in striking contrast to the sailing of his first expedition a year earlier. Instead of the three small, meagerly outfitted vessels that left in 1492 under a cloud of public skepticism, in the second fleet he commanded seventeen ships and more than twelve hundred eager men, infused with what Spanish historian Antonio Ballesteros Beretta has called the *ilusión indiana,* dreams of "the wild lands, the exuberant vegetation, the sweet climate, the fragrant flora, the landscape of marvels, the new animals . . . the tobacco and the thousand plants unknown to the Europeans . . . and the hopes they inspired of finding many more marvels."[1]

Columbus and his comrades planned and outfitted the second expedition in the spirit of these hopeful dreams, but they lacked any substantial knowledge of the Americas other than the often misconceived notions acquired during the brief shipboard sojourns of the first voyage. Their intent was to establish a royal *factoría,* or trading settlement, based on those of the Portuguese in West Africa, but one that would establish a hereditary governorship for the Columbus family. In Decem-

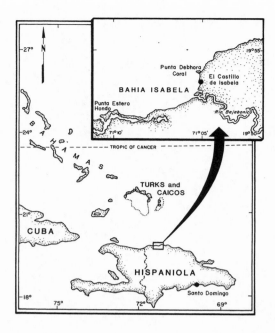

1.1. Location of La Isabela.

ber 1493 they settled on what is today the north coast of the Dominican Republic and called their town La Isabela, after the queen of Spain (figure 1.1). Just four years later, both La Isabela and their dream were in ruins.

La Isabela was the first intentional European colonial venture in the New World leading to permanent occupation. Norse settlements had been sporadically present before the sixteenth century in the northern reaches of the North American continent, but it was not until the Columbian voyages of exploration that the Old and New Worlds sustained regular and significant cultural and biological exchanges.[2] Those exchanges began at La Isabela in 1493 and had almost immediate (and enduring) impacts on the social, economic, religious, and political spheres of both Europe and the Americas. And as historian John Elliott has so elegantly illustrated, the human and environmental responses to these exchanges were profoundly influential on both sides of the Atlantic, producing the social, intellectual, and environmental changes that led to the development of the post-1500 modern world.[3]

The site of La Isabela provides the only direct physical evidence for the organization of this first, intrusive European colonial venture in the Americas. Even though the settlement itself was short lived, the material world of La Isabela reflects Columbus's and the Spaniards' expectations for America, and how they thought best to master the continent. The site offers a critical material baseline from which to assess not only the first European attitudes toward American colonization but also the nature of cultural change and exchange in the critical first decades of European entry into the Americas. For these and other reasons, La Isabela is an intensely important place for anyone interested in the encounter between Europe and the Americas.

Curiously, despite La Isabela's primacy and its seminal role in the creation of a Euro-American culture, the town itself has received little focused historical attention apart from the work of a handful of Spanish and Dominican historians.[4] La Isabela has generally been overlooked and insufficiently studied as a functioning community by modern historians, who have instead tended to relegate their treatment of the settlement to brief and disparaging comments about its poorly protected harbor, its unhealthy environment, its aridity, its infertile land, and its general unsuitability for colonial life.[5] The site of La Isabela has often been invoked as evidence for Columbus's poor judgment as a colonizer, and the underlying cause of the material poverty, hardship, illness, and hunger that led to the settlement's abandonment within four years.

While there is no doubt that La Isabela's residents suffered from hunger, sickness, and fatigue, modern archaeological research at the town site has revealed facets of the colony previously unknown to either historians or archaeologists, and these cast a new light on both the settlement strategy implemented by Columbus and the conditions of life in the town. The new information suggests that the plan for this first colony was, in fact, carefully and appropriately conceived, given the perceptions of America in 1493 and the experience of Spain in the late fifteenth century. The failure of the colony resulted less from the geographical and material conditions of life at La Isabela than from the inability or unwillingness of the first Spanish colonists to accommodate the material and social actuality of life in America. As combined historical and archaeological research in a number of sixteenth-century Spanish Caribbean towns has demonstrated, the experience of La Isabela taught the Spaniards lessons that led to a markedly different way of life after 1500, expressed in social, ideological, and material contours previously unknown in either Spain or America.

This book is concerned with the conditions and practices of life in fifteenth-century La Isabela, particularly those that shaped and directed subsequent Spanish colonial experience in the Americas. It is not about Christopher Columbus the man, as many volumes have already been devoted to the person and motives of Columbus.[6] Nor is it a recounting of the dramatic events that occurred during the first five years of Spanish presence in the Americas, although obviously both Columbus and those events provide an essential narrative structure for any consideration of La Isabela.

Instead, our intent is to recover, explore, and interpret the material expressions of life as lived by the earliest Europeans in America and to reveal how their experience influenced the transformation of Spain in the New World. We emphasize the material expressions of lived experience at La Isabela because, like most historical archaeologists, we believe that only material expressions reveal action and agency on the part of all actors in the past, including those who could not produce written or iconographic accounts. An understanding (however imperfect) of this "on the ground" agency is essential to the larger understanding of both the internal dynamics of the colonial venture and the true impact of the encounter between Europe and America in its historical, cultural, and ecological aspects.

Our view of the structure and organization of that encounter has been deeply influenced by five centuries of often distinguished historical scholarship. Yet, despite some notable exceptions, the scholarship has been largely restricted to the perspectives of the literate Spanish elites who controlled colonial policy and organization, and it has done relatively little to explore local circumstances in the earliest American colonies that provoked adjustments in the colonial structure itself.[7] This unbalanced focus evolved in part because of the nature of historical sources. Most documents were produced by members of a literate elite minority, usually to further in some way their own causes. The experiences and perspectives of the majority of people—the non-elite Spaniards and Americans who were willingly or unwillingly caught up in the early colonial arena—are not recorded primarily in written accounts but are found instead in the material expressions of local experience, that is, in the archaeological record.

This local experience was not trivial. It determined the outcome of the Columbian project and led within one decade to the recasting of Spain's approach to America as an imperial venture rather than a mercantile one. After the collapse of La Isabela, local non-elite experience and agency continued to provoke changes in the expressed structure of empire and, we believe, were at least as influential as the core imperial institutions in the genesis of a multicultural Spanish-American culture.

La Isabela was a consciously constructed experiment that failed, but changes in response to that failure (both locally in the Spanish Americas and at the imperial center in Spain) were central to the creation of a Spanish-American cultural tradition after 1500. Archaeological evidence from La Isabela offers us one of the few sources of information about the original configurations of the experiment, as well as the local circumstances that provoked the earliest changes in the colonial project. It allows us to examine the interplay between local experience and the structure of colonialism, which can lead us to a more refined understanding of such broad theoretical issues as ethnogenesis in the modern world, the transition from medieval to Renaissance patterns of society, and the interplay of hegemony and heterogeneity in the development of the diverse cultural mosaic of the post-1500 Americas.

Our interest in these questions has undeniably been influenced by the social and political circumstances of research at La Isabela, which took place in the context of the quincentennial observation of Columbus's voyages of discovery. That event provoked an exhausting amount of debate and confrontation in both the scholarly and the popular media, and as the place most tangibly associated with Columbus in America, La Isabela provided a focus for much of the debate.[8] Research at the site has unavoidably been colored by the diverse and often conflicting symbolic meanings attributed to La Isabela, which have inevitably led to a certain amount of not unhealthy intellectual tension. For example, among the many contested representations of La Isabela are the view of the settlement as the point of entry for the violent invasion of America by Europe versus the view of it as the point of entry of European science, technology, and literacy; as the point of introduction of Christianity to the Americas versus the beginning of forced conversion and eradication of Native-American belief systems; as the cradle of *hispanidad* and modern American society versus the nursery for the annihilation of Caribbean Indian society; as the initiation of large-scale slavery and class exploitation versus the introduction of capitalism (leading ultimately to democracy) and the incorporation of America into a world system; and even as the beginning of ecological destruction in the Americas versus the introduction of new animals and plants and techniques to increase food production.

It is not our intent to seek resolution of these contrasts in the meaning of La Isabela, as clearly they cannot be satisfactorily resolved except from individual perspectives constructed by experience. Archaeology rarely illuminates such questions of personal meaning in a way that is useful to the larger community of researchers. These questions have, however, colored the political context—and thereby the organization—of research at the site. While the intellectual research aspects of the program have been characterized by an acceptance of the ambiguities that are inevitable when admitting multiple perspectives, this has not necessarily been the case with many of the interests involved in the local and national communities.

From the perspective of the Dominican government and the local community, for example, the work at La Isabela was explicitly carried out in support of economic development through tourism. A principal objective of that tourism—as well as of the government-sponsored archaeology—has been to communicate to the global community an important symbol of national identity and source of considerable national pride.[9] We are both sympathetic and committed to this local perspective and have tried throughout the book to balance interpretations derived from archaeological material with those derived from contemporary consciousness. Other kinds of methodological tensions have been presented by the complexity of the project at La Isabela, and we have detailed these in chapter 3 of our companion volume, *Archaeology at La Isabela* (hereafter referred to as *Archaeology*).

We shall revisit many of the oppositions mentioned in the preceding paragraphs, treating them as acknowledged points of dialogue in our efforts to recover, explore, and interpret the material evidence of life as lived by the earliest Europeans in America. The first part of the book establishes a narrative structure within which to consider the documented circumstances that shaped life at La Isabela. In chapters 2 through 4 we consider the historical antecedents and cultural contexts of the settlement, and in chapter 5 we discuss the events that influenced what we know about La Isabela after its abandonment. Chapter 6 recounts the discovery of La Isabela's true configuration and assesses its role in the larger context of landscape. In the second part of the book (chapters 7 through 10), we examine the material expressions of life at La Isabela as revealed through the overlaying of archaeological and documentary information. The final chapter considers the impact of La Isabela on the subsequent imperial expansion of Spain in the Americas, at both structural and local levels, and reconsiders the questions raised earlier in this chapter.

Chapter 2

The Historical Setting

The fifteenth century was a period of unprecedented maritime exploration and economic expansion overseas by Iberian powers, not only in the Americas but also in Africa and Asia. Italian and Portuguese merchants expanded their markets throughout the then known world; Spanish internal expansion took place through the reconquest of Iberia from the Moors (the *reconquista*); and Spain and Portugal extended their domains by establishing colonies in the Canary Islands. The enterprise of La Isabela drew upon all these modes of expansion, combining elements from Columbus's own mercantile seafaring experience with the reconquest and colonial expansion of the Spanish Crown. The resulting union of elements and assumptions was unwieldy, and although it was appropriate to European experience, it ultimately proved unsuited to the circumstances of America.

European expansion in the fifteenth century was fueled by the fervor of the Iberian reconquista, the search for gold in Africa, and efforts to secure trade with Asia. It was made possible in large part by developments in shipbuilding technology and navigation (figure 2.1), and Portugal led the way in this endeavor, capturing Ceuta on the Moroccan

Libre de cõsolat tractãt dels fets maritims 7c.

2.1. A caravel of the Columbus era. (Libre de Cosolat. Barcelona: J. Luschner, 1502).

coast in 1415 and continuing throughout the fifteenth century to establish agricultural and trading entrepôts along the west coast of Africa.[1]

Portuguese strategies of expansion included not only conquest (as in Ceuta) but also the establishment of agricultural fiefdoms controlled by individual families (as in the Canaries and Madeira) and, most influential for La Isabela, trading ports or houses known as *feitorias* or *factorías*— factories—to facilitate long-distance trade. Trading settlements of this kind had been in place in Flanders since the mid-fourteenth century and were probably based on the even earlier Catalonian and Italian strategies to manage long-distance trade in the Mediterranean. The factorías were isolated trading communities established by individuals who were backed by private capital, without any presumption of political control of the territories in which they were established. They were, however, licensed by the Crown of Portugal, to which they owed one-fifth of any profits.

Artisans, craftsmen, and laborers—predominantly European—were employed in the factories and received wages. Columbus himself had spent the years 1476 to 1484 in the service of Portuguese traders, so there is no doubt that he was well-acquainted with the factory system and in fact drew on it as a model for the establishment of La Isabela.[2]

The Spanish experience in the Canary Islands also had a profound influence on the encounter with America, serving, as Felipe Fernández Armesto has suggested, as a conceptual "halfway house" between Spain and America.[3] The Canaries were an important source of material goods (and particularly plants and animals) for the Isabela colony.[4] Madeira and the Canaries (well known to medieval Europe as a source of slaves and dyewood) were among the earliest targets for fifteenth-century European mercantile expansion, and during his years as a seaman with the Portuguese fleets, Columbus himself came to know the islands and their economy.[5]

Although Castile had obtained a papal title to the Canaries by 1344, formal efforts to control them did not start until the beginning of the fifteenth century.[6] Between about 1402 and 1477 a series of primarily Franco-Norman adventurer-entrepreneurs (of whom the best known was Jean de Bethancourt) established settlements in the islands of Lanzarote, Fuenteventura, and Hierro and declared homage to the Crown of Castile. Norman presence was initially established by treaties with the native Guanche people, who apparently saw economic advantage in trade with the Europeans. Eventually, however, the Normans forcefully imposed a system of subjugation, dividing the islands and their people as spoils among the victors, in a practice known as *repartimiento*, which followed the precedent set by the Iberian reconquista. Ultimately a system of what were essentially feudal fiefdoms developed, with European families "owning" certain islands while swearing fealty to the Castilian Crown. They produced and exported sugar, wine, and wheat and also exported leather, dyes, and slaves to Europe.

Portugal contested the claims of Castile to sovereignty in the Canaries, but after the Treaty of Alcaçovas, which ended the War of Succession between Portugal and Castile in 1475, Portugal ceded all claims to the Canaries in return for uncontested rights in the Madeira islands.[7] Once rid of the Portuguese challenge, the Crown of Castile began a program of imperial conquest and colonization of those Canary Islands not already occupied by Europeans: La Gomera, Gran Canaria, La Palma, and Tenerife.

The conquest and colonization of the Canaries by the Spanish Crown was an undertaking substantially different in kind from earlier European invasions. It was a formal military conquest in which the Crown appointed *adelantados* (military captain-governors) who led largely self-supported military expeditions to the unconquered islands in order to claim them as possessions of Spain. Successful conquistadors were rewarded with allocations of land and the servitude of the native Guanche people. Ideally, the land would contain profitable natural resources and a sizable stable population that could be subjected to peonage. Religious evangelization was also formally incorporated as part of the imperial strategy, and it in fact helped justify conquest.[8] Franciscan missionary friars accompanied these expeditions with varied degrees of success. The imperial conquest of the Canary Islands also served as a crucible for many of the men who were later to figure centrally in the conquest of America, including Pánfilo de Narváez, Hernán Cortés, Francisco Pizarro, and Diego de Almagro.

After sustained resistance and dramatic population losses, the Guanche inhabitants of the Canaries were assigned to the victorious conquistadors who claimed their land, but they were nevertheless theoretically given the privileges of Castilian subjects so long as they adopted Christianity and accepted the sovereignty of Spain. Those who continued to resist, however, were considered appropriate candidates for enslavement.[9]

The status and privileges of Guanche chiefs were formally recognized, and intermarriage between Spanish men and Guanche women was not uncommon. Through their production and sale of agricultural products and livestock considered necessary by the Spanish, the Guanches were able to maintain an important independent role in the colonial economy, in contrast to the Taínos who were to encounter the Spanish in America.

By the time Columbus embarked on his first American voyage of exploration, Gran Canaria and La Palma were occupied and the invasion of Tenerife was about to begin. The pattern of private entrepreneurship, evangelization, and Crown control that emerged during the colonization of the Canary Islands would profoundly influence Spain's first attempt to settle in the Americas.

Spanish conquest and colonization of both the Canaries and the Caribbean also drew directly upon the experience of the reconquista— the recapture of Iberia from Muslim occupation. The completion of that process in 1492 had a huge impact on the organization and ideology of Spanish colonization overseas.[10]

Arab and Berber forces of the Umayyad and Abbasid dynasties had invaded and conquered most of the Iberian peninsula between A.D. 711 and 715, ending the Visigoth occupation of Spain, which had in turn followed the fall of Rome between the fifth and seventh centuries. Under the eight centuries of Muslim rule Eastern and Greek science, technology, and philosophy were reintroduced to Spain and Europe with a lasting influence on Spanish language, cuisine, agriculture, art, architecture, commerce, technology, and social practice. A richly diverse society developed, blending elements of Roman, Iberian, and Arab cultures, a society in which Muslims, Christians, and Jews coexisted and intermarried.[11]

Efforts to recapture Spain for Christendom began almost immediately after 715 and continued for eight centuries. Cast as a holy war, much of the military reconquest was undertaken through partnerships between the Crown and private individuals, who were awarded the title of adelantado and carried out their campaigns with little or no financial support from the monarchs. They were rewarded for success, however, by receiving hereditary family governorship of conquered territories, along with rights to the labor of the Muslim peasants who occupied them. This institution, known as repartimiento, was simultaneously a punishment for the vanquished and a reward for the victors.

Efforts were made by the Christian rulers to populate these newly won territories with Spanish Christian settlers, and commoners could acquire property through squatter's rights laws (the *presura*). Crown resources for military protection of these frontier areas were scarce, however, and the settlers eventually agreed to provide labor and tribute to military *hidalgos* (minor nobility) in exchange for protection from marauders and other enemies. This practice, known as the *behetría*, evolved in the Americas into the *encomienda*, an institution that gave Spanish settlers the rights to Indian labor and tribute, in exchange for instruction of the natives in Christianity.[12]

By the fourteenth century, Al-Andalus, the name given by the Muslims to their holdings in Iberia, was reduced to the principality of Granada, and this, too, finally fell in 1492 to the Catholic Ferdinand and Isabela, the crowned heads of Aragon and Castile. The fall of Granada not only united much of Iberia under Christian rule but also ushered in a new era of religious fervor, which included intolerance of non-

Christians and intense proselytizing promoted by Queen Isabela. It was in this context that the colony of La Isabela was conceived, and named for the queen; because of this connection, we have chosen to use the Spanish spelling of Isabela throughout.

Planning American Colonization

There is little doubt among either sixteenth-century or modern chroniclers that Columbus's determination to sail west across the Atlantic was grounded in his desire to find a quicker route to the riches of Asian commerce.[13] Columbus spent the decade of the 1480s trying to solicit the support of various European monarchs for his planned Atlantic exploration, and in 1492 he finally secured the sponsorship of Ferdinand and Isabela. The terms of their sponsorship were generous, assigning hereditary governing rights and economic benefits in the manner of the reconquista and the settling of the Canaries. The terms were outlined in the *Capitulations* of Santa Fe, entered into in April 1492.[14] They named Columbus "now and henceforth, their Admiral in all islands and mainlands that shall be discovered by his effort and diligence in the said Ocean Seas, for the duration of his life, and after his death, his heirs and successors in perpetuity, with all the rights and privileges belonging to that office." The *Capitulations* also named Columbus viceroy and governor-general of all lands he should discover, with the right to use the title Don.

These titles, extended to Columbus's heirs in perpetuity, carried with them the right to nominate the candidates for local government, to try cases, and to dispense punishment in the name of the sovereigns. Columbus was also granted one-tenth of all merchandise of any kind acquired through barter, purchase, or any other means, after the initial expenses were deducted. He was furthermore given the option of personally investing one-eighth of the total cost of fitting out the expedition, in exchange for receiving an additional one-eighth of the profits after expenses. Both of the important contemporary chroniclers of Columbus, his son Fernando Colón and the Dominican friar Bartolomé de Las Casas, make it clear that these were terms demanded by Columbus, to which the monarchs acceded.

It is evident from the *Capitulations* that the colonial venture intended to establish a Crown-controlled trading enterprise along the lines of the Portuguese factoría model, under the local administration and control of Columbus. The Columbian project, however, diverged from the earlier West African factories in that it was a Crown-financed economic venture in which Columbus could share a small part of the profits. This curious combination of private and monarchical rights and interests would not serve the colonies well, particularly in the view of those hidalgos who expected recompense for their participation in the manner of the reconquista—that is, with hereditary rights to land, labor, and production.[15]

The First Voyage

The 2,500 ducats requested by Columbus for the expedition was a relatively minor investment for the Catholic Kings in 1492, and much of the expense was in fact underwritten by Genoese merchants.[16] The small fleet of two caravels—the *Niña* and the *Pinta*—and one *nao*—the flagship *Santa María*—left Palos on 3 August 1492, put in at the Canary Islands for supplies, and set out westward across the Atlantic on 8 September. They first sighted land on 11 October 1492 in the Bahamas.

The events and encounters experienced on the expedition by its ninety participants have alrady been treated in exhaustive detail.[17] The basic accomplishment of that first expedition was to demonstrate that it was in fact possible to reach the land thought to be India by sailing a western route. Columbus's misplaced insistence that he had reached outlying islands of Asia certainly influenced the organization and composition of the second expedition, reinforcing his desire to establish a trading entrepôt from which to organize commerce with the Asian mainland that he believed must surely be nearby.

Despite his single-minded pursuit of Asia (*Cipango*), the Great Khan, and any other source of gold, Columbus found little precious metal during the first voyage, and most of that was acquired from the Taíno inhabitants of the Antilles in already worked fragments. Parrots, carvings, cotton, and ornamental items were also acquired through barter, often in a form of ritual exchange with Taíno caciques, or chiefs, who, as Samuel Wilson has argued, established a common diplomatic ground through elite exchange that was comprehensible to both the Taínos and the Spaniards.[18]

Columbus formed the opinion that the people of the islands he had reached were peaceful, timid, and guileless—childlike and incapable of seriously harming the Spaniards. As he wrote to his friend Luís de Santángel in 1493, "They have no iron or steel or weapons, nor are they fitted to use them, not because they are not well-built and handsome men, but because they are very marvelously timorous . . . incurably timid. It is true that, after they have been reassured and have lost their fear, they are so guileless and are so generous with all that they possess, that no one would believe it who has not seen it."[19]

In the same letter, Columbus concluded that the Taínos believed the Spaniards and their ships had come from heaven. "They are very firmly convinced that I, with these ships and men came from the heavens, and in this belief they everywhere received me, after they had overcome their fear. And this does not come because they are ignorant; on the contrary, they are of a very acute intelligence and are men who navigate all these seas, so that it is amazing how good an account they give of everything, but it is because they have never seen people clothed or ships of such a kind."

Columbus's conclusions were undoubtedly both shaped and reinforced by the disaster that befell the first expedition on Christmas eve 1492, when the *Santa María* ran aground on a sandbar and could not be saved. The wreck occurred in what is today the Bay of Limonade near Cap Haitien, Haiti, close to the principal town of the region's paramount chief, Guacanagarí.[20] Guacanagarí provided canoes and people to offload and guard the cargo of the *Santa María* for storage in his town, and they did this so quickly and diligently that not a single *agujeta* (lace tip) was lost. Furthermore, Guacanagarí gave two houses, "the largest and best in the town," to the Christians for the safekeeping of the goods, and he offered Columbus every sort of assistance and reassurance.

Because the remaining ships could not transport the crew of the flagship back to Spain, thirty-nine men were left at Guacanagarí's town with instructions to obtain gold, find its source, trade peaceably with the Indians, and build a fortified tower from the timbers of the wrecked *Santa María*. Columbus named the town and fortress La Navidad. Ever ready to shape events to his vision, Columbus concluded that the wreck of his flagship was a divine sign that he should establish a settlement there. "In truth it was no disaster, but rather great good fortune, for it is certain that had I not run aground there, I should have kept out to sea without anchoring at that place."[21]

Part of Columbus's enthusiasm for La Navidad no doubt stemmed from the successful trade that was concluded there with the Indians, which netted more gold than any other part of the voyage. As he wrote to the Catholic Kings, "Thus, Sovereign Princes, I realize that our Lord miraculously ordained that the ship should remain there, because it is the best place in all the island for forming a settlement and nearest to the mines of gold."[22]

During the ten days Columbus spent as Guacanagarí's guest, the two leaders apparently established a rapport that would endure for the subsequent seven years. Columbus left La Navidad on 3 January 1493, confident of the timid, tractable, docile, and harmless nature of the Indians. He in fact took a number of Indians back to Spain on the two remaining ships—some forcibly seized in the Bahamas as translators, others joining later either willingly or under duress. According to Las Casas only seven Indians survived the journey, while the Spanish court chronicler Andrés Bernáldez claims that ten Taínos arrived in Spain and that seven sailed back to America on the second voyage, although only two survived the return trip.[23]

Columbus, sailing in the *Niña*, arrived in Lisbon on 4 March and finally returned to Palos with great public fanfare on 15 March. He had sent an account of the expedition ahead to Ferdinand and Isabela, whose court was then at Barcelona, and they reconfirmed all the concessions granted during the previous year by the *Capitulations* of Santa Fe. They also issued orders to prepare for a second expedition and bade Columbus come to court.

He organized a highly visible overland procession from Seville to Barcelona accompanied by Taíno Indians, parrots, and other exotic items, and people thronged the roads to see him and the Indians pass.[24] Despite the absence of riches or visible evidence that Asia had in fact been reached, Ferdinand and Isabela received Columbus with great celebration and honor in April 1493. In the spirit of excitement over the disclosure of a hitherto unknown and exotic land to the west, along with dubious claims of untold riches to be had there, Columbus easily garnered support and volunteers for an immediate second voyage.

While the first voyage of exploration was essentially an exploratory economic venture intended to find a direct route to Asia and to establish a trade factoría, the second expedition, during which La Isabela was founded, was a significantly different undertaking. Columbus returned from his first voyage to a Spain caught up in the triumph and religious fervor of the glorious success of the reconquista.[25] He brought not only the news of a new-found world but also the revelation that it contained uncounted numbers of souls in need of Christian conversion. This news clearly enhanced the religious motive for a second voyage, and the goals of evangelization and conversion were as compelling (at least in Queen Isabela's eyes) as Columbus's original economic objective. The dual intent of the voyage is reflected in the instructions given to Columbus by Ferdinand and Isabela.[26] The instructions, issued on 29 May 1493, included eighteen specific items. The first and longest instruction unequivocally established the religious interests of the Crown:

> It has pleased God our Lord in His abundant mercy to reveal the said islands and mainland to the King and Queen, our Lords, by way of the diligence of the said Don Christopher Columbus, Their Admiral, Viceroy and Governor thereof, who has reported to Their Highnesses that he knows the people he found residing therein to be apt for conversion to our Holy Catholic Faith, since they have neither dogma nor worship. This greatly pleases Their Highnesses (since in all matters it is meet that Their principal concern be for the service of God, Our Lord, and the enhancement of the Holy Catholic Faith); wherefore, desiring the augmentation and increase of Our Holy Catholic Faith, Their Highnesses charge and direct the said Admiral, Viceroy and Governor, to strive by all means to win over the inhabitants of the said islands and mainland to our Holy Catholic Faith; and to aid him in this work Their Highnesses are sending thither the learned Father, Fray Buil, together with other religious the said Admiral is to take with him.
>
> The Admiral is to see that the Indians who have come to Spain are carefully taught the principles of Our Holy Faith, for they must already know and understand much of our language; and he is to provide for their instruction as best he can; and that this object may be better attained, the Admiral, after the safe arrival of his fleet there, is to compel all those who sail therein as well as all others who are to go out from here later, *to treat the said Indians very well and lovingly, and to abstain from doing them any harm, arranging that both peoples hold much conversation and intimacy, each serving the others to the best of their ability* [emphasis added].
>
> Moreover, the Admiral is to present them with things from the merchandise of Their Highnesses that he is carrying for barter, and honor them much, and if any person or persons should maltreat the said Indians in any manner whatsoever, the said Admiral, as Viceroy and Governor of Their Highnesses, is to punish them severely by

virtue of the authority vested in him by Their Majesties for this purpose, and since spiritual matters cannot long endure without the temporal, in other matters the said Admiral and Governor is to obey the following orders. . . . "

The remaining seventeen instructions are largely devoted to establishing the Crown's monopolistic control over virtually all aspects of commerce related to the expedition. Don Juan de Fonseca was appointed royal factor and representative with responsibility for assembling the fleet and supplies according to the wishes of Columbus. Royal auditors were also appointed for additional fiscal oversight both in Spain and in Hispaniola, and detailed instructions were given for inventories and audits to be carried out before leaving or returning to Spain and after arriving at or leaving Hispaniola. Item 14, for example, charges that "immediately upon arrival, God willing, the Admiral and Viceroy shall provide for the erection of a customs house for the storage of all the merchandise of Their Highnesses, including the merchandise to be sent from here, as well as that to be collected for return shipment. At the time the said merchandise is unloaded, it is to be deposited in the said house in the presence of the said representative of the Royal auditors who is to be there, and in the presence of another officer who is to be appointed by the said Admiral in his own behalf, so that two books may be kept, in which everything is to be written, and these are to be kept by the treasurer whom Their Highnesses send."

In keeping with the intent of the royal factoría, the majority of the instructions outlined measures designed to ensure that nobody but Columbus or another Crown representative could barter with the inhabitants of the Americas, and even then only in the presence of the royal accountant. "No person or persons among those who are to sail with the said fleet, of whatever rank or station they may be, may carry or be permitted to carry . . . any merchandise for barter on the said islands and mainland, for none save Their Highnesses are to engage in barter" (item 9). "All barter is to be carried out by the Admiral or the person he may designate in his place and by the treasurer of Their Highnesses in the Indies, and by no other person" (item 14).

Besides reiterating the measures that would protect the Crown's economic interests and control, the instructions also reconfirmed the titles, governing privileges, and financial incentives granted to Columbus in the *Capitulations* of Santa Fe, including the right to appoint magistrates, judges, and public officials in the name of the Crown in any towns established in the Americas (items 11–13). Columbus was also given command over all ships and their captains in the new colony.

The organization and provisioning of the fleet were carried out in Seville. The account books, books of registry, and *Libros de Armadas* for the outfitting of the expedition have not survived, nor has the portion of Columbus's journal that covers the second voyage itself, so information about the composition of the fleet and its supplies can be only partially compiled from fragmentary documentation. Seventeen ships were conscripted, including three carracks, two large naos, and twelve caravels, and the multiple objectives of the second voyage to America— commerce, conquest, colonization, and conversion—were reflected in the human and material composition of the expedition.

People and Supplies

Between twelve hundred and fifteen hundred people sailed with the expedition, and all but about two hundred were paid salaries by the Crown.[27] Las Casas asserted that "most of the recruits were peasants whose job would be to cultivate the land, to mine gold and to do anything else they were ordered to," which suggests that the systematic exploitation of the Indians as a source of labor was not yet conceptualized.

Regardless of what the expedition's organizers may have thought, most writers have concluded that the great majority of the expedition members joined not for the Crown salary or for work opportunities but in anticipation of wealth and social advancement. This was particularly true for the hidalgos—minor nobility—who had served the Crown in the reconquista and undoubtedly had the model of allocating lands and resources to successful conquerors freshly in mind. "There came too many caballeros, hidalgos and other men of worth, drawn by the fame of gold and the other wonders of the land. So many offered themselves that it was necessary to restrict the number of those who might go thither."[28] This excess of enthusiasm and imagination on the part of the nobility contributed significantly to the troubles that later plagued La Isabela.

Artisans and representatives of all the trades were part of the group, according to both Las Casas and Ferdinand Colón.[29] At least two physicians were present, including Dr. Alvarez Chanca, who left a detailed and lucid account of the founding of La Isabela and the events of the second voyage. Columbus's personal retainers and household members included ten squires and "another twenty men," who were all on the royal payroll.[30] One of these was the traitorous Francisco Roldán, who was to figure prominently in the ultimate downfall of Columbus.

At least seventeen notaries were commanded to accompany the fleet, one for each ship, as well as two royal scribes and at least three royal treasury officials.[31] Some twenty hidalgos serving as foot soldiers joined the expedition, as well as a contingent of twenty armed horsemen, or *escuderos*, from Granada known as the *Lanzas de Jinetas*. They were included by order of Isabela, presumably to help oversee Crown interests in the colony.[32] The Lanzas were members of the *Santa Hermandad*, a sort of national militia with powers to maintain internal security and law, controlled by the Crown and feared by the people (discussed further in chapter 8).

Most of the expedition members were from Andalusia, but there were also men from Catalonia, Galicia, Santander, Portugal, and Italy. Among them were individuals who were to become important in shaping the American colonies, including Juan Ponce de León of Florida and Puerto Rico fame, Pedro de Las Casas, who was the father of Bartolomé, Defender of the Indians, the renowned cartographer Juan de la Cosa, and Diego Columbus.[33]

At least twelve members of religious orders and the priesthood accompanied the group. They were led by a Catalan friar of the Franciscan Minim (or Minor) Order (Franciscan followers of San Francisco de Paulo) from the monastery of Montserrat named Fray Bernaldo Buil (also recorded as Boyl). He was a confidant of King Ferdinand and had served the sovereigns in a diplomatic role on other occasions.[34] On 25 June 1493, he was furthermore designated *vicario apostólico* (papal nuncio) to the Indies by a papal bull of Alexander VI. Buil accompanied the colonizing expedition to La Isabela as a representative of the Catholic Kings and the pope with the triple charge of initiating conversion of the American Indians, overseeing ministrations to the spiritual needs of the Spaniards in America, and keeping an eye on Columbus. Various authors have documented (or suggested) the identities of the twelve members of Buil's religious contingent (presumably selected by him). They included the Franciscan priests Juan de la Duela, Juan de Tisín, Antonio de Marchena, Rodrigo Pérez, and Juan Pérez, as well as a Fray Jorge, who is thought to have been the comendador of the Order of Santiago.

In addition to the Franciscans, the group included at least three secular priests who were not members of orders (one of whom may have been Pedro de Arenas and another Angel de Neyra), two Mercederians named Juan Infante and Juan Solórsano, and one Hieronymite friar, Ramón Pané, who became the first ethnographer of the American Indians.[35]

Most scholars have long averred that no women were present on the second voyage, but Spanish historian Consuelo Varela believes that she has located evidence of at least one woman, a María Fernández, who was present at the founding of La Isabela. The comments of Ferdinand Colón and the discovery of a European female in the cemetery of La Isabela also indicate that at least some Spanish women lived in the town at some point.[36] The names of other individuals known to have been on the second voyage or at La Isabela are included in the Appendix.

The seventeen ships of the fleet were well provisioned with all the items needed for the voyage and thought to be necessary for the establishment of the colony. Because none of the supply lists or ship registries have survived or been located, the archaeological record has been the most important direct source of information about the material composition of the fleet, which we discuss in the chapters ahead.

Las Casas provided a general description of the matériel, writing that the expedition brought "artillery and arms, wine, biscuit, wheat, flour, oil, vinegar, cheese, all kinds of seeds, tools, mares, several stallions, fowl, and several coffers of trade goods and merchandise to be given away to the Indians."[37] We also know from the account by Michel de Cuneo that many of the plants considered essential to the Spanish diet were brought — wheat seed, grapevine cuttings, chickpeas, melons, olives, fruit stones for planting, onions, lettuce, and radishes. Columbus reported to the sovereigns that the fleet carried "horses, mares and mules and all the rest, cuttings and seeds of wheat and *cevada* and all the trees and good fruits, all this in great abundance.[38]

More provisions were taken aboard in the Canary Islands. These included sugar cane, and long after La Isabela was no more than a memory this single introduction continued for centuries to shape the economic life of the Caribbean. As the final stop before the transatlantic voyage, the Canaries also provided much of the livestock for the colony, and the fleet took on cattle, sheep, fowl, goats, and pigs.[39] The eight pigs brought aboard there multiplied so rapidly in the West Indies that by 1499 Columbus would write that "one now sees innumerable pigs here, all of them descended from these eight, which I brought on the ships at my own expense except for the purchase price, which amounted to seventy maravedís each on the island of Gomera.[40]

Animals not intended for food also accompanied the expedition. Some were brought intentionally, such as the horses of the Lanzas de Jinetas, the *perros bravos,* or war dogs, that were so to terrorize the Taínos, and rat-catching cats. Others—such as the rats, mice, and insects stowing away in the holds—arrived unintentionally. Many other undesirable live passengers arrived in the bodies of the Spanish passengers, including the European germs, microbes, and viruses that were to devastate the native people of the Caribbean.

The fleet set sail from the Canary Islands on 12 October 1493, and sighted land in the Lesser Antilles on 4 November. After spending twenty-one days at sea and some twenty more reconnoitering the Lesser Antilles, Columbus was understandably anxious to reach La Navidad. When his ships arrived there on 28 November, they found the fort and the Indian town burned, and all thirty-nine of the Spaniards dead. Chief Guacanagarí, in whose town they had lived, claimed that some of the men had died of disease and some in fights with one another over gold and women. Others had left to explore the interior and died there, while the rest had been killed in an attack by Caonabó, a rival Taíno chief. Caonabó, he continued, had also burned Guacanagarí's own town when Guacanagarí himself tried to protect the Spaniards. The cacique recounted this from his hammock, to which he was confined after receiving a wound to the leg while trying to defend the Spaniards and his town. When the physician Chanca offered to treat it, however, he could find no evidence of a wound. Guacanagarí left the area with his entourage abruptly and somewhat surreptitiously shortly after his interviews with Columbus.[41]

The Spaniards were devastated and confused, particularly about Guacanagarí's role in the massacre. Many of the high-ranking members of the expedition, including Fray Buil, insisted that Columbus punish the cacique, but the admiral refused to do so, not only out of uncertainty as to Guacanagarí's culpability but also, wisely, "judging that this was not the moment to irritate the spirits of the native."[42] This decision was probably the only thing that preserved the fragile detente between the Spaniards and the Taínos that persisted over the next year. It also, however, sowed the first seeds of discord that were to grow steadily between Columbus and the high-ranking members of his expedition.

Columbus decided that La Navidad was not the best place for his colony after all, and after searching the ruins of the settlement for the gold the dead Spaniards were supposed to have accumulated (but finding none), the fleet left La Navidad on 7 December to look for a better settlement location to the east.

The tragedy at La Navidad was to have far-reaching consequences, not only for the establishment of La Isabela but also, more profoundly, for the growth of the mutual distrust that pervaded the attitudes of the Taíno Indians and the Spaniards toward each other from that time on.

Chapter 3

Reluctant Hosts:
The Taínos of Hispaniola

Columbus and his companions on the second voyage knew, of course, that they were not entering a cultural vacuum when they came to America. Originally hoping to find Asians subject to the Great Khan, they soon realized that the people they encountered were something very different. Between preconceived notions, and assumptions based on brief observations made during the first voyage, Columbus and his companions gravely underestimated the people they met.

"American Indians," the term by which the indigenous people of the Americas have been known in Western literature since 1492, had occupied the Western Hemisphere for tens of thousands of years before the arrival of Europeans. It was Columbus himself who initiated the use of that term in his mistaken assumption that he had reached the offshore islands of India, referring to them as *Yndios* and their islands as *las Yndias* in the journal of the first voyage.[1] Sixteenth-century Europeans and present-day writers alike refer to the native inhabitants of the Greater Antilles as *Taínos*, a word used by the people themselves to mean "good people" or "good men and not cannibals."[2] Most of what is known about the Taínos is based on the accounts and descriptions of a relatively few fifteenth- and sixteenth-century European observers, and an ever-increasing body of archaeological information.[3]

The Taínos were among the most densely settled and complex pre-state, sedentary societies in the Americas.[4] Estimates for the population of the Caribbean in 1492 have varied enormously, and the debate over the number of Taínos living in Hispaniola when Columbus arrived remains unresolved. Estimates based on documentary data have ranged from a hundred thousand to more than a million, but the increasing archaeological database on village size and distribution suggests that a figure closer to the higher estimates might be more accurate.[5]

Regardless of how many Taínos were living in Hispaniola when Columbus arrived, the stunning reduction in their numbers was the most shocking immediate repercussion of European contact. The events leading to this decline were set in motion at La Isabela, and they had profound consequences for the development of Euro-American society after 1500. The rapid alteration of Taíno population and cultural expression also had a profoundly limiting effect on our understanding of these people. One basic restricting factor was vocabulary; the utter newness of the Taínos to Europeans made it impossible for chroniclers to describe them except by analogy to what they already knew, which led to their casting (and consequently obscuring) the initial characterizations of Taínos in European, biblical, and classical terms. Their observations were interpreted in ways that made sense to fifteenth-century European Catholic ideology and cultural vision.[6] Given these caveats, let us attempt to summarize the ethnohistorical and archaeological information relevant to understanding the people of Hispaniola who met Columbus on the first and second voyages. We shall emphasize the original words of the chroniclers themselves rather than modern interpretations of them.

Most researchers agree that the cultural ancestry of the Taínos can be traced to the Arawakan-speaking Ronquinian Saladoid people living along the Orinoco River in South America, whose culture was closely related to the Cedrosan-Saladoid culture of the northern South American coast.[7] By about 1000 B.C., these Ronquinian Saladoid people were living in large settled towns, cultivated manioc and corn, and made elaborate painted pottery. It is thought that they subsequently migrated into the Caribbean, reaching as far as eastern Hispaniola by about 250 B.C., continuing their traditions of agriculture and pottery making, as well as producing elaborate carved stone and shell pendants and figurines thought to have had ritual significance.[8]

In the Caribbean the Saladoid people encountered the islands' original inhabitants, who are referred to in the archaeological literature as "Archaic." These people did not make pottery or practice farming but ultimately adopted them through interaction with the Saladoid newcomers, who in turn undoubtedly adopted or developed new practices through interaction with the Archaic people.[9]

After about 250 B.C., the Saladoid people appear to have greatly diminished or ceased their geographic expansion, and by about A.D. 600 appear to have developed a new style of cultural expression in response to local conditions and populations. This new tradition is known archaeologically as Ostionoid. The Ostionoid tradition was marked by larger populations and the expansion of settlements into a wider range of ecological settings than in earlier periods. Ostionoid peoples practiced agriculture in raised mounds, or *conucos*, and developed an elaborate and distinctive artistic expression in pottery, bone, shell, and stone. Many Ostionoid towns contained planned open spaces for courts in which to play ceremonial ball games or to conduct other ritual functions.[10]

The Taínos of the Greater Antilles represented the last stage of the Ostionoid cultural tradition. By about A.D. 1100 or 1200, the Ostionoid people of Hispaniola lived in a wider and more diverse geographic area than did their predecessors; their villages were larger and more formally arranged, farming was intensified, and a distinctive material culture developed. This culture was marked by an extraordinary elaboration and refinement of ritual and artistic traditions in pottery, bone, shell, wood, and other media (figures 3.2, 3.3, and 3.9). Social stratification is thought to have become more intense and rigid during the period after A.D. 1100, but this process was attenuated by the arrival of Columbus.[11]

Throughout most of the Greater Antilles, this stage of intensification and elaboration after 1100 is known as "Taíno." The Taíno people, as characterized by archaeologists, were not a unified society, and they have been categorized into subdivisions according to the degree of elaboration in their artistic and social expression (see figure 3.1). The Central, or "Classic," Taínos are identified with the most complex and intensive traditions and are represented archaeologically by Chican Ostionoid material culture. They occupied much of Hispaniola, Puerto

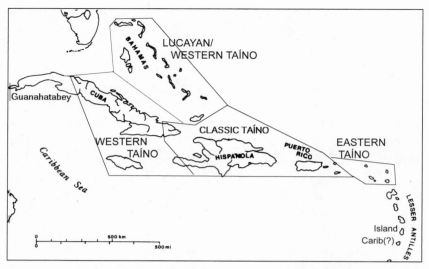

3.1. Distribution of Taíno groups at the time of contact. (Following Rouse 1992:6.)

Rico, and possibly eastern Cuba, although even within these areas there were groups of Taínos not considered Classic, such as the Macorijes (who produced Meillacan Ostionoid pottery) and Ciguayos of Hispaniola, discussed below. The Western Taínos occupied central Cuba, Jamaica, and parts of Hispaniola and the Bahamas, and they are also associated archaeologically with the Meillacan Ostionoid material tradition. The Eastern Taínos are thought to have lived in parts of the Virgin Islands and the Leeward Islands of the Lesser Antilles.[12] As many archaeologists have emphasized, however, the Taínos were but one of the recognizable cultural groups in the Caribbean at the time of contact. They co-existed and interacted with other Ostionoid peoples and perhaps even Saladoid-influenced Archaic peoples, such as the Guanahatabey of Cuba and the Caribs of the Lesser Antilles.[13]

Most of the ethnographic information available to us pertains primarily to the Central Taínos and the Macorijes, since it was with them that Columbus and the people of La Isabela interacted most intensively. As in any encounter between a literate and a nonliterate group, the ethnographic observations available to us are dramatically skewed to comments by Spaniards about Taínos. No doubt the Taínos had an equally complex set of observations, assumptions, and attitudes regarding the Spaniards, but because these were not recorded in written or vi-

3.2. Chican ceramics: white-slipped and molded water-bottle fragments. (Photo: James Quine.)

sual sources generated by the Taínos themselves, they are rarely accessible to us. Our basis for understanding Taíno-Spanish interaction and exchange is therefore severely compromised.

The Spaniards were fascinated by the absence of clothing among the Indians of Hispaniola, and Columbus used the adjective *desnudos* some thirteen times in his *Diario* of the first voyage.[14] He reported to Ferdinand and Isabela that "the people of this island . . . all go naked, men and women, as their mothers bore them, although some women cover a single place with the leaf of a plant, or with a net of cotton which they make for the purpose."[15]

The Spanish insistence on being covered with heavy woolen and leather clothing in the tropical heat must have been thoroughly perplexing to the Taínos. It has been claimed that the Spaniards were seldom, if ever, able to ambush the Taínos, because the Indians could easily detect them by their smell.[16]

Many of the Spaniards' descriptions of the Taíno compared them to the native Guanche people of the Canary Islands. Columbus wrote to Ferdinand and Isabela that the inhabitants of America were "of the color of the Canary Islanders, neither black nor white." Michel de Cuneo adds that "both sexes are of an olive complexion like those of the Canaries," and Bernáldez reports that "their color is ruddy and nearer to white than black."[17]

Other descriptions commented on cranial deformation among the Taínos, a practice supported by archaeological evidence from both Haiti and Cuba.[18] Bernáldez records that "they all have large foreheads and faces, round heads, as narrow from temple to temple as from the forehead to the neck; they have straight black hair, bodies of medium size, their color is ruddy and nearer to white than black." Cuneo writes that "they have flat heads, and the faces tattooed. Of short stature, as a rule they have very little beard and well-shaped legs, and are thick of skin." As in all things, beauty is in the eye and attitude of the beholder. Columbus's initial response, as recorded in his *Diario*, was one of reserved admiration: "They were very well built, with very handsome bodies and very good faces. Their hair is coarse almost like the hairs of a horse's tail and short; they wear their hair down over their eyebrows, except for a few strands behind, which they wear long and never cut. . . . [They are] all of a good height, very handsome people . . . all have very broad foreheads and heads, more so than has any people that I have seen up to now. Their eyes are very lovely and not small. . . . Their legs are very straight, none are bow-legged. They are not fat, but have very good figures."[19]

Michel de Cuneo, infamous for his self-congratulatory account of raping a captive Indian woman, observed Indian women closely: "The women's breasts are round and firm and well-shaped. When they have given birth, they immediately carry their infants to water to wash them and wash themselves; nor does childbearing give them folds on the belly, but it always stays well-stretched, and so do the breasts."

Bartolomé de Las Casas noted that "In this island of Hispaniola, I say it is true, that there were men and many women of such fine appearance [disposition] and composure in their gestures that though they would be somewhat dusky [in color], especially the women would be seen and praised in Spain for their good and eminent beauty by all those that would see them."

On the other hand, the historian Gonzalo Fernández de Oviedo y Valdés, who was in Hispaniola during the early sixteenth century, wrote disparagingly of Taíno women: "To be truthful there was a great lack of such women from Castile. And though some Christians married important Indian women, there were a great many others who for no reason would take them in matrimony, because of their incapability and ugliness."[20]

3.3. Taíno lapidary work: stone beads, ornament, and small celts. (Photo: James Quine.)

The Taínos, like the Spaniards, used a variety of personal adornments.[21] Body paint was apparently common and noted by many chroniclers, including Columbus: "Some of them paint themselves black . . . and others paint themselves white, and some red, and others what they find." Dr. Chanca's comments about Taíno personal decoration are typically ethnocentric and considerably more negative: "The decoration of men and women among them is to paint themselves, some with black, others with white and red, becoming such sights that to see them is good reason for laughter. Their heads are shaved in places and in places have tufts of tangled hair in such shapes that it cannot be described. In conclusion, whatever there in our Spain they might wish to do to the head of a madman, here the best of them would regard as a great honor."[22]

The Taínos practiced face and body piercing as part of personal adornment, using ear plugs, nose ornaments, and labrets (lip plugs) made of stone, bone, wood, shell and gold. Some of these can be seen in figure 3.3. They also made and wore finely carved beads, pendants, and amulets of stone, shell, bone, or gold. Fray Pané reported that some of the stone ornaments known as *cibas* were tied about the neck and

arms, and these probably had ritual significance. They may have functioned as protection or as supplication to the spirits in the manner described by Peter Martyr D'Anghiera: "The Indians call these images
zemes, of which the smallest of them, which represent little devils, they
wear in front when they go to fight enemies; attached by cords which
you see. They think that they obtain from these the rain when it is lacking, and the sun when they need it."[23]

Caciques also wore metal ornaments known as *guanines* in the ears,
"which they perforate when they are small." The metal was an alloy of
gold and copper, probably obtained through trade with South America.[24]

Although the majority of Taíno people in the Greater Antilles appeared to have spoken the same language, there were at least three languages spoken in Hispaniola. According to Las Casas, at the time of
contact "there were three distinct languages in this island, which were
mutually unintelligible; the first was of the people we called the Lower
Macorix [*Macorís de Abajo*], and the other of the people of Upper Macorix [*Macorís de Arriba*], which I described in chapters 2 and 3 as the
fourth and sixth provinces. The other language was the universal one for
all of the land, and was the most elegant and contained the most words,
and was the sweetest in sound." The Upper Macorix language was spoken in the northeastern section of the island, corresponding to the area
from the coastal mountains east of Puerto Plata eastward through the
Samaná peninsula.[25]

The Upper Macorix region was mountainous and, according to
Peter Martyr D'Anghiera, began about ten leagues west of La Isabela.
The people of this area included both those known archaeologically as
the Macorijes and those referred to by the chroniclers of the fifteenth
and sixteenth centuries as Ciguaias or Ciguayos.[26] In addition to speaking a different language, the Ciguayos were reported to have had different hairstyles and general appearance. They were also said to have been
much fiercer and more hostile toward the Spaniards than Taínos in the
rest of the island and to have made long-time enemies of other Taíno
groups in Hispaniola.[27]

Most researchers agree that the Taínos were politically organized into
hierarchical, nonegalitarian chiefdoms, each headed by an absolute paramount leader. They probably reckoned their descent through the
mother's line (matrilineally), and it is possible that some of the Taíno
groups—particularly among the elites—had avunculocal residence pat-

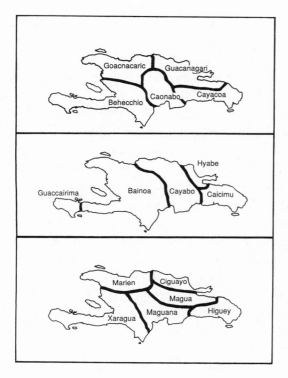

3.4. Hypothetical locations of Hispaniola chiefdoms, ca. 1493, proposed by Charlevoix 1730 (*top*), Vega 1980 (*center*), and Rouse 1948 (*bottom*). (After Wilson 1990:110.)

terns (residence and possibly inheritance through the mother's brother).[28]

Although debate continues about the names and boundaries of Hispaniola's regional political divisions in 1492 (because of ambiguities and contradictions in the primary sources), it is generally agreed that at least five coalitions of towns existed in Hispaniola at the time Europeans arrived. Figure 3.4 shows some of the suggested geographical schema for the major *cacicazgos*, or chiefdoms.[29]

Both residence and descent units are thought to have been organized hierarchically according to their importance in the hereditary sociopolitical system. Below the chiefs in the Taíno social system were the *nitaínos* and *naborías*, whom the Spaniards equated with nobles and commoners, respectively. Spanish chroniclers also implied that the naborías were slaves or of a low, servile class, although this seems to have been a later, sixteenth-century phenomenon.[30]

Taíno caciques could be either men or women (although male caciques were far more common than female), and they wielded a great deal of centralized political and ritual power. They were able to command labor, material goods, and possibly tribute. They lived in special houses, wore special garments, were carried on litters, and ate special food. The caciques, along with other members of elite lineages, practiced polygyny, and paramount chiefs were said to have had as many as twenty or thirty wives.[31]

The various noble clans of Hispaniola interacted regularly with one another through intermarriage, ritual gift exchange, official visits, and political alliances. They also engaged in warfare, which has been interpreted by some as indicating an emerging class-stratified society.[32] Although inter-chiefdom warfare took place among the Taínos of Hispaniola to resolve territorial or political disputes, the various Taíno chiefdoms did have a common enemy before the arrival of the Spaniards. The Island Caribs, a poorly understood group who lived in the Lesser Antilles, were apparently feared by Taínos throughout the Bahamas and Greater Antilles. The Taínos told the Spaniards on the first voyage that the Carib men were fierce warriors, who regularly raided Taíno settlements to capture and kidnap Taíno women as wives. They furthermore asserted that the Caribs were cannibals, an observation that horrified and fascinated the Spaniards. On the second voyage the fleet passed through the islands thought to have been inhabited by the Caribs, recounting many stories of cannibalism and cruelty. In the absence of conclusive archaeological evidence for cannibalism, it has been argued that this may have been a belief perpetrated by the Spaniards to justify enslaving the Indians of the Lesser Antilles.[33]

Gender relations among the matrilineal Taínos appear to have been egalitarian. Women were apparently responsible for much of the agricultural activity. Both Columbus and Cuneo observed that women did much, if not all, of the farming and other subsistence labor, Columbus noting that "it appears to me that the women work more than the men," and Cuneo that "the women do all the work. Men concern themselves only with fishing and eating."[34]

Taíno women served as *cacicas* and leaders, and they participated together with men in ritual worship of both male and female deities, which we discuss later. Women owned property and may have controlled access to military and political power through matrilineage. Representations of *zemis*—images of spirit protectors—include both males and females with exaggerated sex organs, and chastity appears not to have been particularly valued for either men or women.

Towns and Dwellings

Taíno settlements ranged from small hamlets to very large towns. In Hispaniola, Columbus's men (possibly exaggerating) claimed to have visited a town that was "of a thousand houses and of more than three thousand inhabitants," and in northern Haiti they described a town with more than "two thousand men and an infinite number of women and children." They also noted a number of hamlets "of seven or eight huts."[35]

Las Casas described Taíno towns and their houses:

The towns of these islands were not well laid out in streets. Beyond that, the house of the King or Lord of the town was in the principal place or location, and in front of the royal house in all of them was a large well-swept and well-leveled plaza, longer rather than square. In the language of these islands this was called *batey*, the penultimate syllable long, that is to say, the ball game, for they played ball as will be described later, if God wills. There were also other houses, near the said plaza, and if the town was very large, there were other plazas or ball parks of lesser importance. . . .

The inhabitants of this island Hispaniola and of the surrounding islands, and part of Tierra Firme up to the coast of París, and in many other parts, make their houses of wood and straw, in the form of a bell. These were very high and spacious, such that ten or more persons lived in each one. They drove in the big poles, as big as a leg or even a thigh, in a circle, half the height of a person, into the earth and close together; they were all joined together at the top, where they were tied with certain cord of roots which formerly were called *bejucos* [middle syllable long]. Upon these first poles . . . crisscrossed many other thin ones, tied well with roots. With these roots and the bark of trees of a black color, and other bark stripped off which remained white, they made lattice work with designs and foliage like paintings on the inside of the building, that would not appear unless they were of some other beautiful and painted material. Others were adorned with stripped reeds which appeared very white. There are very thin and delicate canes, and with these they did their handiwork and their gracious lattice work, thus painting, or appearing to paint, their houses. Beyond this they covered them with a very thin, beautiful, and pleasant-smelling straw, which type is mentioned above, the same which the cattle have destroyed in this island. I saw a house of

3.5. Taíno houses (as shown in Oviedo y Valdés 1851, volume 1, plate 1; courtesy of Irving Rouse).

this type, made by the Indians, which one Spaniard sold to another for 600 castellanos or pesos of gold, each peso having the value of 450 maravedís.[36]

The cacique's residence complex was often located on the plaza at the center of the town.[37] Peter Martyr D'Anghiera recounts a description of one such complex visited by Columbus's men in the province of Guacanagarí: "In the course of their explorations of this country the Spaniards perceived in the distance a large house, which they approached, persuaded that it was the retreat of Guacanarillo. . . . Upon measuring the large house which was a spherical form, it was found to have a diameter of thirty-five long paces; surrounding it were thirty other ordinary houses. The ceilings were decked with branches of various colors most artfully plaited together."[38]

The very large house was known as a *caney*, which apparently was a chiefly dwelling, a council house, perhaps a temple, and also a place to receive visitors. Common houses were referred to as *bohíos* (see figures 3.5 and 3.6). A cleared area often adjacent to the chiefly complex and used as a plaza, dance court, or ball-game field was noted by nearly all chroniclers of Taíno towns, and has been well-documented archaeologically.[39]

Taíno social and political complexity relied upon a system of intensive agriculture supplemented with abundant wild estuarine resources and interregional trade. The Taínos introduced Spaniards to a number of

3.6. "How the Indians make their alliances and marriages with each other."
Household conditions and items probably quite similar to those of the
Taínos. (Plate 113, *Histoire naturelle des Indes: The Drake Manuscript in the Pierpont
Morgan Library.* 1996. Second half of the sixteenth century. Courtesy of the
Pierpont Morgan Library.)

plants unknown in Europe before 1492, which have since been integrated as staples in many world economies. Among these were corn, manioc, *batata* (a kind of sweet potato), beans, peppers, arrowroot, peanuts, and cotton. They also introduced more than a hundred new fruits, including the now-familiar pineapple (*Ananas comosus* [L.] Merril), guava (*Psidium guajava* L.), and papaya (*Carica papaya* L.), as well as the less well-known star apple (*Chrysophyllum caimito* L.), custard apple (*Anona squamosa* L.), mamey (*Mammea americana* L.), and soursop (*Anona muricata linn*).[40]

The staple crop was manioc, a tuber also known in the region as cassava and yuca. The Taínos, in common with most of the native peoples of the Orinoco and Amazon River basins, had developed an ingenious method of making a durable, nourishing bread from these cyanide-containing roots. The tubers were shredded using a stone or coral grater and soaked in water. The manioc root mash was then put into a woven basketry tube or press with which to squeeze out the cyanide-containing juices. The resulting coarse flour could be mixed with water and grilled on a *burén*, a flat circular ceramic or stone griddle. The resulting "bread" is a high-calorie, portable food source and is still a staple of the current diet in much of the Caribbean (see figure 3.8).

The Taínos also cultivated corn, or maize, using the word *mahiz*, in common with the Indians of South America. Although the manner of planting (shown in figure 3.7) was similar to that in Central America, the Taínos apparently did not use stone metates for grinding but instead ate their corn in a form of soup or stew.[41]

The Taínos exploited a remarkably diverse array of estuarine and marine fishes, mammals, and invertebrates, using hooks and lines, nets, weirs, and baskets. They also captured and ate the hutia (*Isolobodon portoricencis*), a small rodent, as well as iguanas, birds, snakes, giant beetle grubs, and insects. This versatility did not commend them to the Spaniards, one of whom noted that "in addition to eating lizards and snakes, the Indians eat whatever spiders and worms they find in the earth, so that their bestiality is greater than that of any beast on the face of the earth."[42]

Many of their economic activities depended on water transport, and the Taínos were skilled seafarers, using the water both for fishing and for trading. Interisland trade, travel, and communication made use of large dugout canoes that were considered marvelous by the Spaniards for their workmanship, size, and beauty. It was claimed that some of these held as many as 150 people and were maintained communally. Columbus

La Maniere et facy de Jardiner et planter
Des Indiens.

L'indien faisans son Jardin semens plusieurs sortes
de graynes pour sa nourriture pour faire apparoistre
q[u']il est homme de grand trauail et aussy pl[us] complaire
a son amoureuse et suffisant pour nourrir femme et enffans
et la terre est si fructueuse q[u']elle porte du fruict en deux temps

3.7. "The manner and style of gardening and planting of the Indians." (Plate
121, *Histoire naturelle des Indes: The Drake Manuscript in the Pierpont Morgan Library.*
1996. Second half of the sixteenth century. Courtesy of the Pierpont Morgan
Library.)

3.8. Preparation of manioc and corn. (Girolamo Benzoni, *La historia del mondo nuovo*, 1565.) Translated by W. H. Smythe as *History of the New World by Girolamo Benzoni*. Hakluyt Society Publications, 21. London: Hakluyt Society, 1857.

reports that "they came upon a boathouse, very well arranged and roofed, so that neither sun nor water could do damage, and in it was another canoe, made of a single piece of timber like the others, of the size of a *fusta* of seventeen benches, and it was a pleasure to see its workmanship and beauty."[43]

Taíno traders traveled among the islands and to the South American mainland, exchanging cotton and cotton products, ground and polished stone beads and pendants, ornaments and tools of carved shell, bone, stone, and wood, tobacco, various foodstuffs, and exotic birds and feathers.[44]

Elite members of the Taíno chiefdoms exchanged scarce or luxury items to establish and solidify social and political relations in the governing class. The items presented to Columbus on his second voyage by the cacique Guacanagarí provide an idea of the nature of elite trade goods. Guacanagarí presented the admiral with "eight hundred small-figured white, green, and red stone beads," along with numerous objects of gold, wood carvings, and items of woven cotton and feathers. These included a wondrously elaborate belt, "which in the place of a purse bore a mask with two great ears of gold, as well as the tongue and nose; this belt was of very fine small stones, like pearls made of white fishbones interspersed with other colored ones. The manner of work was so closely sewn in cotton thread, and of such beautiful work in both front and back, although all in white, that it was a pleasure to see it, as if it had been made on a tapestry frame in the way that the embroiderers create the edgings of chasubles in Castile. And it was so hard and so strong that I believe without a doubt that an arquebuz shot could not pass through it, or only with difficulty; it was four fingers in width, in the manner of belts worked in embroidery or gold thread that are only used by Kings or great nobles in Castile."[45]

Most of these elaborate Taíno trade items surviving today—including cotton and bead belts, cotton and bead figures, and bead necklaces—have ended up in European museums, quite possibly through a system of elite exchange among the royalty of sixteenth-century Europe similar to that among the Taíno elites.[46]

Taíno subsistence as well as art, economy, and political hierarchy were inextricably interconnected with Taíno ritual and religion.[47] The most comprehensive first-hand account of Taíno ideology is that of the Hieronymite friar Ramón Pané, who lived for nearly four years among the Taínos of central Hispaniola with the explicit purpose of learning about the native religion. His account is to be taken with caution, however, as even during the contact period Pané was thought to be somewhat confused. Columbus himself said of Pané's report that "it contains so many fictions that the only sure thing to be learned is that the Indians have a certain natural reverence for the after-life and believe in the immortality of the soul."[48]

Las Casas was no more impressed by Pané, writing that "he was a simple-minded man, so that what he reported was sometimes confused and of little substance." He explains that "this Fray Ramón Pané did what investigating he could, depending on what he could grasp of the languages [of Hispaniola], of which there were three in this island; but he didn't know any except the one of a small province which earlier we called Macorix de Abajo, and that not perfectly, and of the universal language he didn't know much, like the rest, but more than the others. . . . The Admiral commanded this Fray Ramón to go to the Vega Real and the territory ruled by Guarionex, where he could work more fruitfully, since the people were many more, and their language universal for all the island; and thus he did, where he was two years, no more, and he did what he could according to his small abilities."[49]

Although Pané's original manuscript has not survived, Juan José Arrom's careful reconstruction and cross-referencing of the 1571 Italian translation with the reports of Ferdinand Colón, Peter Martyr D'Anghiera, and Las Casas has helped to clarify this first attempt by a European to organize and describe an utterly alien view of life. Pané records that "these Indians also know whence they came and where the sun and moon had their beginning, and how the sea was made, and of the place to which the dead go." He recounts several Taíno myths, including a partial origin myth which, although not making explicit allusion to migration, does bear similarities to many of those known from Amazonia or the Orinoco Basin.[50] Pané and Las Casas both report a supreme being named Yócahu Vagua Maórocoti, or Yúcahu Bagua Maóracoti, interpreted by Arrom as the "Spirit of Yuca / Master of the Sea / Conceived without male intervention" or the giver of manioc, from which the Indians made their staple cassava bread. Yócahu Vagua Maórocoti lived in the sky with his mother, who was known variously as Atabey, Yermaoguacar, Apito, or Zuimaco, and was the goddess of the moon, tides, and springs, as well as the protector of women in childbirth.[51]

Pané also recorded the Taínos belief that all aspects of their lives were governed by spirit beings known as zemis, which were sometimes associated with specific deities wielding specific powers, but which were also sometimes owned by individuals and embodied in physical objects. The zemi was a profoundly important representative of the spiritual world, governing social and ecological relations. Zemis could be male or female, and they were invoked to help women in childbirth, to bring rain, or give advice in war. They could also cause sickness, destroy houses, or wreak revenge on persons who failed to make proper offerings. Powerful ritual specialists known as *behiques* or *buhuitihus* intervened with the zemis and served as healing practitioners.[52] The Taínos regularly fashioned zemi images on their pottery, ornaments, and furnishings, reflecting the pervasive and important role of spirits in all aspects of Taíno life (figures 3.9 and 3.10).[53]

The Taínos believed that people lived on in another form after death and interacted with the living. The dead were only abroad at night and could be distinguished by the absence of a navel. Because of the continued existence of those who died, the Taínos revered and perhaps worshiped their ancestors. Columbus described the varieties of Taíno death

3.9. Pottery adornos from La Isabela, some representing zemis. (Photo: James Quine.)

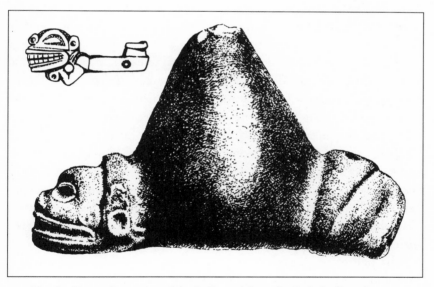

3.10. Zemis. *Top*, anthropomorphic shell zemi from La Isabela (length: 6 centimeters). (Drawing: P. D. Farrior). *Bottom*, stone three-pointer zemi, thought to represent the supreme deity, Yócahu. (After Rouse 1986, fig. 27c.)

and burial rites, which differed according to rank: "They bury the cacique in this way: they open the cacique up and dry him before a fire that he may keep whole. In the case of others, they preserve only the head. Others they bury in a cave and place bread and a calabash full of water above his head. The bodies of others they burn in the house where they have died; when they see them in the last extremity, they strangle them. This they do only with caciques. The bodies of some they throw out of the house, and others they set in a hammock, which is a kind of bed made of netting; they place bread and water beside the head, depart and never come to see him again. Some who are gravely ill they carry to the cacique, who decides whether they should be strangled, and his order is always carried out." Caonabó informed Columbus that after death the Taínos went to a valley "which every principal cacique believed to be in his country," where they lived on in pleasure and comfort.[54]

Taíno rituals also incorporated fasting, dancing, purging, bathing, chanting, and the ingestion of *cohoba*, an hallucinogenic powder made from the seeds of the tree *Anadenanthera peregrina* and inhaled through the nose. Sexual imagery is prominent both in Taíno cosmology and in Taíno art.[55]

Peter Martyr D'Anghiera recounts examples of the ritual Taíno songs and dances called *areytos*. The cacique beat a drum outside the central council house, and the men and women came in processions, singing and dancing areytos in honor of the zemi whose image was in the house. Before entering, each person thrust a long curved stick into his or her throat to provoke vomiting. "The [men] sprang to their feet and together with the women exalted in their areytos the power of the zemes, commemorating in song the great deeds of their cacique's ancestors. They afterwards gave thanks to the zemes for favors received, beseeching it to hear their prayers; and bending the knee they offered their gifts to the divinity."[56]

The ball game played by the Taínos was related to the great ball games of Central America and Mexico. There were two teams, sometimes of twenty to thirty players, who could be men or women, and they used a ball made with grasses and roots held together with the gum of trees. The ball could not be touched by the hands or feet but could be butted with elbows, shoulders, backs, or hips. If it went outside the boundary of the court, it was dead, and the other side scored.[57]

The Taínos had other competitive games, which frequently resulted in injuries and fatalities. During the visit of Bartolomé Columbus to Xaraguá in 1496, the Indians put on a show in which "squadrons of armed men with bows and arrows" began to have skirmishes in which they wounded their opponents, and according to Las Casas, "in a very short time, four of them were dead and many were badly wounded." The Spanish were shocked by the Taínos' indifference to the carnage, and it was Bartolomé himself who requested that the game be stopped.[58]

Taíno art, which is among the finest but least appreciated in the Americas, pervaded both sacred and secular life.[59] Artistic expression is evident not only in ornamental and ritual items of carved stone, bone, wood, and shell but also in house construction and the pottery used every day in Taíno households.

Taíno ceramics at the time of contact were often decorated in ways that are thought to have had symbolic importance.[60] The pottery is distinguished by zoomorphic and anthropomorphic figural appendages that served as ornament, symbolic communication, and handles for vessels. The applied elements occur in combination with various incised and punctated motifs, usually in geometric forms and abstract designs or in enclosed banded zones. Taíno potters also produced elaborately molded figural pots (figures 3.2 and 3.9).

As we saw earlier, the Taínos also sculpted and carved wood, stone, shell, and bone into zemi images, masks, and ornaments (figures 3.9 and 3.10). An important ritual form and central motif, persisting from pre-Taíno times, is found in the three-pointed carved stone objects interpreted by some as having been associated with the principal deity Yócahu Vagua Maórocoti, and by others as fertility or general mythic symbols (figure 3.10).[61]

The Spaniards took admiring note of Taíno skill in pottery making, weaving, stone carving, and gold work, and the Taínos were equally impressed by European items of glass, metal, cloth, or glazed ceramic, which were completely alien to them.[62] The initial interactions between the Spanish and the Taínos were grounded in exchange of these mutually valued goods, and they appear to have been generally amicable. Very quickly, however, mutual and lasting animosity was provoked on both sides by the events at and subsequent to La Navidad, as we shall see.

The Taínos at La Isabela

The region in which La Isabela was established seems to have been a Taíno cultural or geographic frontier of sorts, close to the border between the northern territories of Ciguayo (ruled at contact by Maya-bonex) and Marien (ruled by Guacanagarí or his superior chief) or possibly in a province known as Cayabo. Although the specific identity of the people who lived around La Isabela remains unclear, we do know from both documentary and archaeological sources that there were both Taíno and Macorijes towns near La Isabela in 1493.[63]

The Spaniards, as we shall see in the next chapter, interacted daily with the Indian inhabitants of the area and received a considerable amount of food from them during the early months of the settlement. "There come here constantly many Indians. . . . All come laden with *ages,* which are like turnips, very excellent for food; of these we make here many kinds of foodstuffs in various ways. It is so sustaining to eat that it comforts us greatly."[64]

This evidence is nevertheless ambiguous regarding the status of Indian occupation on the site of La Isabela itself when Columbus arrived. Las Casas says of Columbus that "he anchored in a large river port where there was an Indian village," and Ferdinand Colón says "he proceeded to anchor in front of an Indian village." Cuneo reports that "having established the said area for our residence, the inhabitants of the island, who are distributed from one to two leagues away from us, came to see us." Chanca records that "there come here constantly many Indians and with them caciques."[65]

Columbus himself did not comment about Indian settlements at the site of his new town, other than to voice concern about protecting La Isabela from destruction, which "one Indian with a burning faggot could bring about, setting fire to the huts, for they come and go constantly, night and day. On account of them we have guards in camp, while the settlement is unwalled and without defense."[66]

It could be persuasively argued that, given the experience at La Navidad, the Spaniards would have been reluctant to settle in the midst of an existing Taíno town, and there is no mention of Taínos being forced out of an existing village. The archaeological evidence from excavations at La Isabela indicates that there was at some time a Taíno occupation there, concentrated at the south end of the site in the area containing the Spaniards' church and cemetery. The enormous twentieth-century disturbances to the site, however, have made it impossible to determine confidently the chronological associations of the Taíno and Spanish occupations at the site, although the balance of evidence leans toward the interpretation that the Taíno occupation at La Isabela itself predates—and ceased before—Spanish arrival. (The evidence for this and other aspects of Taíno presence at La Isabela is detailed in chapter 2 of our *Archaeology* volume.)

The archeological record is considerably less ambiguous about the presence of Taíno settlements separate from, but in the vicinity of, La Isabela. Several Taíno sites that could have been occupied in 1492 have been located within a few kilometers of the Spanish town site. Two of the best-known sites, El Perenal and Bajabonico, were within the two-league area noted by Cuneo.[67]

Spaniards and Taínos lived in what was undoubtedly an uneasy but peaceful coexistence for the first few months after the establishment of the Spanish town. The initial system of exchange between the groups—Taíno gold and food for Spanish beads, metal items, and ceramics—became an institutionalized system of barter. Groups of soldiers authorized by Columbus went to Taíno towns with orders to barter for gold and food (but only in the presence of and controlled by Columbus's accountant), and abuses of the Taínos must have been common. Open hostility between the two groups had begun in earnest, however, by April 1494, as Spanish incursions into the interior of the island became more frequent and regular. Indian uprisings and attacks and Spanish counterattacks took place in 1494 and 1495, and Spanish retaliatory raids into Macoriz territory resulted in the first large-scale enslavement of American Indians by Europeans.[68] Although most of the confrontation took place away from La Isabela itself, we can speculate that the region around La Isabela was probably one of the first areas to lose its Taíno population, either from flight or disease. The deterioration of Spanish and Indian relations paralleled the decline of La Isabela, as we shall discover.

Chapter 4

"Hell in Hispaniola": La Isabela, 1493–1498

Beset by doubt, confusion, and surely some despair, Columbus's second fleet left the ruined fort of La Navidad in Guacanagarí's town on 7 December, and sailed eastward along the north coast of Hispaniola, looking for a more hospitable location in which to settle. The journey from La Navidad to La Isabela was terrible.[1] The westerly trade winds made sailing eastward tortuous—as Chanca noted, "The weather was contrary to us, so that it was more labor for us to go back thirty leagues than to come from Castile. As a result of the unfavorable weather and the length of the voyage, three months had already passed when we landed."[2] It took twenty-five days of indecisive tacking to sail the 160 kilometers against the wind and choose the site some twenty-eight miles west of present-day Puerto Plata that was to become La Isabela (figure 4.1).

Columbus and his men, as well as the animals, were ill and exhausted, food supplies were spoiled, and morale was undoubtedly at a nadir after the catastrophe at La Navidad and the subsequent disagreements among

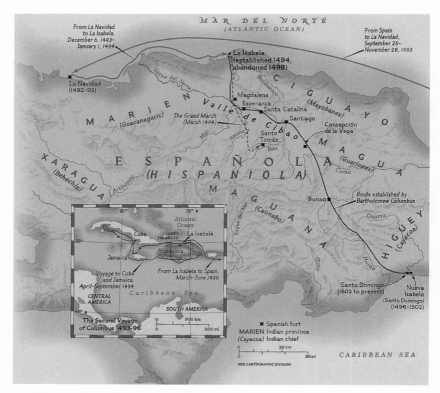

MAR DEL NORTE
(ATLANTIC OCEAN)

From La Navidad
to La Isabela,
December 6, 1493–
January 1, 1494

From Spain
to La Navidad,
September 25–
November 28, 1493

La Isabela
(established 1494,
abandoned 1498)

La Navidad
(1492–93)

Yaque del Norte

C I G U A Y O

MARIEN Valle
(Goacanagaric)

The Grand March
(March 1494)

Magdalena
Esperanza
Santa Catalina

(Mayobanex)

de Cibao
Santiago

Concepción
de la Vega

Santo
Tomás

MAGUA
(Guarionex)

XARAGUA
(Behechio)

ESPAÑOLA
(HISPANIOLA)

Artibonito

M A G U A N A
(Caonabo)

Bonao

Route established by
Bartholomew Columbus

Ozama

HIGUEY
(Cayacoa)

Yaque del Sur

Santo Domingo
(1502 to present)

Nueva
Isabela
(Santo Domingo)
(1496–1502)

Atlantic
Ocean

Cuba
AREA
ENLARGED
La Isabela

Hispaniola

Jamaica

Voyage to Cuba
and Jamaica,
April–September 1494

From La Isabela to Spain,
March–June 1496

CENTRAL
AMERICA

Caribbean Sea

SOUTH AMERICA

The Second Voyage
of Columbus 1493–96

500 km
500 mi

■ Spanish fort
MARIEN Indian province
(Cayacoa) Indian chief

30 km
30 mi

CARIBBEAN SEA

NGS CARTOGRAPHIC DIVISION

4.1. Hispaniola in the time of Columbus. (Map courtesy of *National Geographic* magazine cartographic division.)

the Spaniards about how to retaliate. With a rebellious company of more than a thousand men, contrary winds, and a threatening storm, Columbus simply could go no farther by the end of December 1493 when they sailed into the Bay of Isabela.

The site chosen by Columbus for his first city is located between latitude 19°53' and 19°58' 30" north and between longitude 70°01' and 70°05' west. The region is part of Hispaniola's Atlantic coastal plain, a narrow strip of alluvial soil between the sea and the northern edge of the Cordillera Septentrional mountain range. The Bay of Isabela is dominated by the region's principal river, the Río Bahabonico (also known as the Isabela River), which empties into the bay (figure 4.2). The most notable feature of the site is a rocky promontory that rises from four to five meters above the sea (figure 4.3). It is bounded on the west by the Bay of Isabela and on the north and south by *rías*, or lagoons, that in recent memory have been filled with salt water.[3] Today

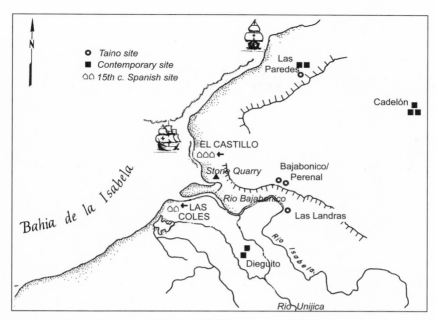

4.2. Locations of cultural and natural features surrounding La Isabela.

4.3. The rocky promontory on which Columbus's fortified town was established.

both the north and south rías have been partially filled in and covered by the road leading from El Castillo to Luperón.

The formal establishment of the town took place on 6 January 1494 (the Feast Day of the Three Kings, or Epiphany). Between arrival and founding, a chapel and some houses were hastily built, and the dedication of the city was commemorated by a mass celebrated by thirteen priests, led by Fray Buil.[4]

La Isabela has always been synonymous with misery, hardship, and failure. As we noted earlier, modern historians have generally blamed Columbus's choice of the site for that failure, assessing it as a poor selection in terms of strategic position and available resources.[5] Although much of the criticism of the site makes sense in the context of the modern landscape of the National Park of La Isabela, which is indeed arid and limited in its access to fresh water, there was no censure voiced by those chroniclers who were actually present at La Isabela. On the contrary, they consistently lauded the fine qualities of the site, emphasizing natural fortifications, nearby rivers, fertile land, abundant fish, and good building materials. Columbus, of course, recounted the advantages of the site in justifying his selection, but he was not alone in his praise (see sidebar 4.1).

SIDEBAR 4.1

Eyewitness and Other Fifteenth-Century Descriptions of the Site of La Isabela

The site . . . is above rock and at the shore of the sea, at the foot of a great plain, larger than that of Granada, and at fifty paces [*pasos*] there is a mountain of quarrying stone [*cantería*], better than that of which the church of Santa María in Seville is built; together with this, not very far, [is] a mountain of very fine limestone, the one and the other very well supplied with trees. . . . Here there is a very suitable place of high land, almost an island, at the foot of which arrived a large nao, and unloaded at the base of the wall. There is a powerful river, better than the Guadalquivir, a lombard shot from here, which we can carry into the town in the plaza by canals [*acequias*]. It passes through a great plain, going toward the southeast, and until today I have not been able to learn where it ends [*no e podido saver el cavo*]. . . . From the town to the west, for some two long leagues, it is all very beautiful beach, and at

the point [*cavo*], one of the best ports in the world, in which can fit
all the naos that there are.
—*Letter of Columbus to Isabela, reproduced in Varela (1987:734–35)*

He anchored in a large river port where there was an Indian village.
Despite the exposure to northwest winds, he decided leave the ships
there and go ashore because the riverbanks looked green and fertile,
and water could be brought to town by canals, thus making possible
the construction of water mills and other commodities. . . . The admiral thanked God for the amenity of the land and rightly so, too, for
the location is rich in stones, tiles and good earth for the making of
bricks, besides being very fertile and beautiful.
—*Las Casas I, LXXXVII (1985, vol. 1:363)*

He proceeded to anchor in front of an Indian village; and having
found a plain, with a ravine on one side, that appeared a suitable site
for a fortress, he went ashore with all his people, provisions and
equipment. There he founded a town to which he gave the name Isabela, in honor of the Catholic Queen. They believed it to be an excellent site for a town because it had a very large harbor, although
open to the northwest, and a lovely river a crossbow shot in width,
from which water channels could be led to the town, and beyond the
river extended a very charming plain, not far from which, according to
the Indians, were the mines of Cibao.
—*Ferdinand Colón in Keen (1959:121)*

The city of Isabela, which is growing beautifully, is next to an excellent port, that abounds in fish of succulent flavor, and which, as the
doctors have shown, cause the sick to recover their health . . . our people call this "Isla bella" ["beautiful island"], having given to the city
the name of "Isabela." This, in surpassing all others by virtue of its
strategic position and benign climate, will within a few years be very
populated, and filled and frequented by Colonists.
—*Guillermo Coma to Sylaccio in Gil and Varela (1984:199)*

The land is very rich for all purposes. Nearby there is one main river,
and another of reasonable size, not far off, with very remarkable
water. On the bank of one a city, Marta, is being built, one side being
bounded by the water with a ravine of cleft rock, so that no defensive
work is needed on that side. The other side is protected by a wood, so
thick that a rabbit could scarcely pass through it, and so green that

never at all will fire be able to burn it. They have begun to canalize a branch of the river, and the foremen say that they will bring this through the center of the town and that they will place it on mills and water wheels and whatever can be worked with water. They have sown many vegetables, and it is certain that they grow more in 8 days than they do 20 in Spain.
—*Dr. Chanca in Parry and Keith (1984:86–87)*

We came to another site, also in this island [Española], at an excellent port where we took land.
—*Michel de Cuneo in Morison (1963:213)*

He decided to build a city in the northern region on an elevated hill, because this site was located near a high mountain, very appropriate for building and making lime because of its stone quarries. In addition, extending from the slopes of this mountain is a vast plain of some sixty miles in length. . . . Many rivers of healthful water cross over this plain, the largest of all, which is navigable, empties at a distance of a half estáncia into a port that is located at the foot of the city. Such is the fertility of this valley, and such the kindness of its soil, *aprécialo por lo que cuentan.*
—*Peter Martyr D'Anghiera in Gil and Varela (1984:64)*

The divergence between fifteenth-century descriptions and twentieth-century interpretations of them is accounted for in part by hindsight and perspective—those chronicling the colony's establishment did so in a spirit of hope, and those analyzing it after the fact did so knowing the outcome. The fragmentary and incomplete accounts of La Isabela left to us by its contemporaries did not permit modern scholars to understand or properly evaluate the full scope of Columbus's settlement strategy until archaeological evidence revealed the missing pieces nearly five hundred years later.

All modern interpretations of La Isabela up to now have been predicated upon the assumption that the site at the town of El Castillo, which is on the limestone promontory designated today as the National Park of La Isabela, comprised the entire Columbian settlement. This is understandable, as the promontory corresponds very closely to the fifteenth-century eyewitness descriptions of La Isabela provided by Columbus and Chanca. Columbus writes, "Here there is a very suitable place of high land, almost an island, at the foot of which arrived a large nao, and unloaded at the base of the wall. There is a powerful river, better than the Guadalquivir, a lombard shot from here." Chanca speaks of "one side being bounded by the water with a ravine of cleft rock, so that no defensive work is needed on that side. The other side is protected by a wood, so thick that a rabbit could scarcely pass through it, and so green that never at all will fire be able to burn it."[6]

In 1987, however, Cruxent, while surveying the bay surrounding El Castillo, located a second, unequivocally fifteenth-century Spanish settlement across the bay from the National Park of La Isabela (figure 4.2).[7] We recount the details of the discovery and investigation of this second settlement—in an area known today as Las Coles—in chapter 6 and also in our *Archaeology* volume. It is important to note that the settlement at Las Coles provided the elements and resources that were not immediately at hand at the El Castillo site, including fertile agricultural soil, clays suitable for bricks and pottery, and an adjacent river.

The settlement at Las Coles may in fact have been the Ciudad Marta described by Dr. Chanca: "Nearby there is one main river, and another of reasonable size, not far off, with very remarkable water. On the bank of one a city, Marta, is being built." Chanca's mention of Marta has long been dismissed by historians as an error on the part of the physician, but the archaeological evidence suggests that he may have been referring to the settlement at Las Coles.

A limestone quarry was located between the two sites, today near the bank of the Río Unijica, also called Río Tablazo, which may have been even closer to the El Castillo site in 1493. The access to a river would have greatly facilitated transport of the quarried stone by water to the "well-situated rock," where the town's masonry buildings were constructed.

It is now apparent that Columbus's settlement strategy incorporated multiple nuclei with complementary features around the bay, including the fortified site at El Castillo, a service or agricultural settlement at Las Coles, the stone quarry between them, and perhaps others as yet undiscovered. Together, these constituted the setting for the sequence of events that took place at La Isabela between 1494 and 1498.

The Spaniards at La Isabela were almost immediately beset with problems. Food supplies brought with the fleet had spoiled on the extended voyage and were quickly depleted—particularly (and most alarmingly to the Spaniards) the wine, which Columbus claimed had leaked out of the casks during the voyage because of the poor work-manship of his suppliers.[8] Within a few days of their arrival most of the men fell sick, and many died. Columbus wrote to Ferdinand and Is-abela in January 1494 that he wanted to send more gold back to them and would have done so "if only the majority of the people here had not fallen ill." He added that "the country tries them for some space of time and after that they recover," and that "the cause of the illness, so general among all, is the change of water and air, for we see that it spreads to all one after another, and few are in danger."[9] Close quarters during the two months on board ship as well as new parasites in the local water probably provoked widespread dysentery and gastrointesti-nal ailments among the Spaniards.

Some historians have suggested that influenza communicated by swine and horses may have been responsible for much of the illness suf-fered by both Spaniards and Indians at La Isabela.[10] Others, including Oviedo and Las Casas, suggested that syphilis—the one contagious American disease to which the Europeans had no resistance—was a factor in the continuous disease experienced by the first European colonists.[11]

Despite his and his men's exhaustion and illness, Columbus insisted on immediately starting construction of the town. Most historical ac-counts of La Isabela have been based on the description provided by Las Casas: "He hastened to proceed to the building of a fort to guard their provisions and ammunition, of a church, a hospital and a sturdy house for himself; he distributed land plots, traced a common square and streets; the important people grouped together in a section of the planned township and everyone was told to start building his own house. Public buildings were made of stone; individuals used wood and straw for theirs."[12]

A somewhat more rhapsodic description was given by Guillermo Coma: "It will compete with any of the cities of Spain when its build-ings are finished and its walls are magnificently raised. They have done the houses, and are constructing the protective walls, which adorn the city and give secure refuge to its inhabitants. A wide street like a straight cord divides the city in two parts, this street is cut transversally by many other coastal streets [cortada . . . por otras muchas costaneras]. At the beach a magnficent castillo is being raised, with a high defense [elevada fortaleza].[13]

The expedition members were on short rations because of the food spoilage, and this greatly exacerbated their unhappiness at being forced to work on construction of the town.[14] Columbus, despite the urgent need to build the settlement, replenish food supplies, and rebuild the company's health and morale, wasted no time in beginning the search for the gold mines of Cibao. The day after the first mass at La Isabela, he sent two platoons of between fifteen and twenty men each under Alonso de Hojeda and Ginés de Gorvalán into the interior of the island to explore and search for gold. They returned from the interior on 20 January with news of gold "in so many places that a man hardly dares say it." It was one of the first hopeful moments for La Isabela, causing Cuneo to gloat that "with this he and all of us made merry, not caring any longer about any sort of spicery, but only of this blessed gold."[15]

Columbus was now able to write to Ferdinand and Isabela with promises of gold, and he did so immediately. The letter went with Antonio de Torres, a trusted ship's captain, who commanded a fleet of twelve ships that left La Isabela for the return trip to Spain in February 1494. Torres also carried news of the voyage and its discoveries, and requests for food, clothing, livestock, and other supplies for the colony.[16] Five ships remained at La Isabela as a means of escape in case of attack by Indians, and also to explore other islands.

The departure of the fleet under Torres must have significantly reduced the population of La Isabela. At minimum, there would have been a crew of about twenty on each of the twelve ships (240 people), and no doubt others unhappy with the conditions at La Isabela departed with them.[17] This would have left between eight hundred and twelve hundred (or fewer) people in the settlement after February 1494.

Meanwhile, the building efforts continued relentlessly. La Isabela was essentially unprotected during those first weeks—the stone buildings and defensive walls were not finished, the fields were not cultivated, and the town was made up of thatched huts filled with sick men unable to work. With the catastrophe of La Navidad undoubtedly still fresh in his mind, Columbus noted in the Torres memorandum that a single Indian torch could easily destroy the unprotected settlement. He pushed everyone who was still standing—including the outraged hidalgos—to work on the construction of the principal buildings, water mills, and town walls, as well as the planting of crops. Las Casas recounts that "everyone had to pitch in, hidalgos and courtiers alike, all of them miserable and hungry, people for whom having to work with their hands was equivalent to death, especially on an empty stomach."[18]

The use of the hidalgos' horses for agricultural and construction tasks was another point of contention. Columbus felt that the horses, having been paid for by the Crown, should be used for the work of the community. The hidalgos were deeply opposed to this position, insisting that they alone should use their horses, and that they should in fact be required to do only things that had to be done on horseback. (The symbolic importance of horses and the problems this caused for Columbus are discussed further in chapter 9.)

These hugely unpopular measures, combined with food shortages and illness, provoked mutinous resentment among the colonists, and the first open rebellion against Columbus took place in February 1494. It was organized by the frustrated and disappointed royal accountant, Bernal de Pisa, who was supported by Fray Buil. Columbus crushed the rebellion, jailed Pisa, and hanged several others, among them the Aragonese Gaspar Feríz. The episode intensified the hatred that Buil and other hidalgos had for Columbus, and according to Las Casas it was one of the principal provocations for his ultimate discredit in Spain.[19]

By March 1494 the building of the town was well under way, the general health of the people was somewhat improved, the rebellion had been quelled, and the fleet dispatched back to Spain. Feeling more secure, Columbus organized a major exploratory expedition to the Cibao. He took five hundred of the most able and healthiest men, including masons, carpenters, laborers, and hidalgos, as well as the things necessary both to extract gold and to build a fort that could be a base for exploitation of the region By all accounts this was an impressive entourage. The expedition, headed by Columbus, left La Isabela on 12 March "with colours flying, in rank and file, drums beating and trumpets sounding."[20] They marched twenty-seven leagues (about 160 kilometers) in this manner, undoubtedly to the astonishment of the Taíno inhabitants of the many towns through which they passed. The Indians were particularly alarmed by the horses, which appeared to them a horse and rider must have seemed like a centaur, half man and half beast.

At a bend in the Jánico River (about three kilometers from the present town of Jánico), Columbus built a small fort of packed earth and wood and named it Santo Tomás.[21] Leaving a contingent of some fifty men at Santo Tomás under the command of Pedro de Margarite, the party returned to La Isabela on 29 March, to find that disaster had struck again. Not only had another bout of illness swept the community, killing many of the remaining settlers, but a fire had destroyed some

two-thirds of the settlement as well. Columbus wrote that "after I proceeded to build this city, already filled with houses, a disaster of fire occurred, burning two-thirds, in the time and hour when I was away in the
Cibao.[22]

The situation at La Isabela had deteriorated dangerously. There was
almost no more biscuit, and Columbus immediately determined to
build a water mill to grind the wheat they had brought from Spain, so
that they could make bread. The closest appropriate place for these activities, however, was an inconvenient league away, which was probably
near the site identified today at Las Coles.[23] Columbus writes of "at
this river, which is here close to the city, as much as Santa María in
Seville is toward the river, and within one league to another river, not
so large as this, where I am now making the mills."[24]

The threats and punishments Columbus had to invoke to force the
sick and hungry colonists to work on the mills and rebuild the town
merely fueled the settlers' burgeoning hostility toward him. To make
matters worse, within a few days of returning from the *entrada* into the
Cibao, Columbus received word from Margarite at Santo Tomás that
Indians were all deserting their villages, and that Caonabó was preparing to attack the fort. He sent a reinforcement of seventy men immediately and then organized a contingent of four hundred more under
the command of Alonso de Hojeda. They included sixteen cavalrymen,
two hundred squires and crossbowmen, 110 musketeers, and twenty artisans. Hojeda was given orders by the admiral to lead them to the
Cibao, assume command of the fort, and turn over 350 men to Margarite. Margarite was then to march with the men into the heavily populated central plain of the Cibao, the Vega Real, "and spread terror
among the Indians in order to show them how strong and powerful the
Christians were." Hojeda and Margarite were also ordered by Columbus
to "see that the Spaniards got used to the native foodstuffs," which
must have considerably relieved the strain on supplies at La Isabela. Ferdinand Colón recorded that the intention of the expedition was to
"pacify that region, make the Indians respect them, and gradually grow
accustomed to eating Indian food, for the provisions from Castile were
daily in shorter supply."[25]

Columbus's instructions to Margarite, dated 9 April 1494, reflect the
contradictory approach to dealing with the Taínos that was soon to destroy any chance of coexistence. Columbus advised Margarite that "the
main thing you are to do is to take great care that no harm or injury is

done to the Indians, and that nothing is forcibly taken from them; but rather that they are treated with respect and protected, so that they do not rebel." He went on in the next sentence to mandate that "if you discover that any of them steal, you shall punish them by cutting off their ears and noses, as these are the parts of the body they cannot hide."[26]

Both Hojeda and Margarite took the charge of terrorizing the Indians seriously, and they almost immediately provoked a series of localized but violent confrontations with Taínos in the Vega Real.[27] The unstable situation was made even worse by Columbus's decision to embark on a voyage of exploration to Cuba and Jamaica just two weeks after sending Hojeda and Margarite into the interior.

Before he left, Columbus appointed a council in La Isabela to govern the colony in his absence. Diego Colón, his brother, was the head of the council, whose other members included Fray Buil, Pedro Fernández Coronel, the chief constable of the fleet, Alonso Sánchez de Carvajal, who was Columbus's business associate, and Juan de Luján, a member of the royal household. Columbus left with two caravels and one nao on 24 April 1494 and did not return until 29 September.

Little is known from documentary accounts about La Isabela during Columbus's absence, but it must have been populated by only a few hundred men. Of the original fifteen hundred, at least 240 had left with Torres and the fleet in February, about five hundred were in the interior, at least sixty must have gone with Columbus on his exploratory venture, and an unknown number had died. Food shortages nevertheless still plagued the reduced company, made even more desperate by increasing conflict not only with the Taínos but also among the Spaniards themselves.

Pedro de Margarite, for example, had been instructed by Columbus to explore and subdue the island, trading with the Indians for food. But according to Ferdinand Colón and others, he did not carry out his orders. Instead he went with his men to the Vega Real, some ten leagues from La Isabela, where he stayed, forcing the Taínos to supply his company with food and trying to undermine the authority of Columbus's governing council by writing insolent letters to them. Margarite abandoned his post in the summer of 1494, returning to Spain on the ships that had arrived in June of that year with the admiral's brother, Bartolomé.[28] As a consequence, the nearly four hundred men under Margarite's command were left to their own devices, prowling the countryside and preying upon the Indians, stealing their property and wives and inflicting so many injuries upon them that the Indians resolved to avenge themselves on any Spaniards they found. The deterioration of Taíno-Spanish relations quickly accelerated from that point onward. Two months after Columbus departed for Cuba, his brother Bartolomé arrived at La Isabela with two ships and desperately needed provisions. The ships returned to Spain without Bartolomé but a large number of disgruntled and influential Spaniards did leave, including Margarite, Fray Buil, several religious members, "and many others."[29]

Meanwhile, the men in the interior continued to roam the countryside, terrorizing the Indians. As Peter Martyr D'Anghiera observed, "It is a fact that the people who accompanied the admiral in his second voyage were for the most part undisciplined, unscrupulous vagabonds, who only employed their ingenuity in gratifying their appetites. Incapable of moderation in their acts of injustice, they carried off the women of the islanders under the very eyes of their brothers and their husbands; giving over to violence and thieving, they had profoundly vexed the natives."[30]

The Taínos, however, did not stand by passively. As Martyr D'Anghiera continues, "In many places when our men were surprised by the natives, the latter strangled them, and offered them as sacrifices to their gods."

The cacique Caonabó, who governed the Maguana region and had been implicated in the destruction of La Navidad, was particularly effective in attacking and provoking the Spaniards. By late 1494 he appears to have achieved an alliance among many of the caciques of the island, including Guarionex of Magua, Behechio of Xaraguá, Higuamaná of Higuey, and Mayobanex of Samaná, but excluding Guacanagarí, the cacique of the Marien province in which La Navidad had been located.[31]

Columbus finally returned to La Isabela from his explorations on 29 September 1494. Although he was delighted that Bartolomé had arrived, his pleasure was clouded by the deteriorating situation with the Taínos and the news that leading members of the colony had returned to Spain in anger and disgust, undoubtedly to defame him at court. He was furthermore very ill when he arrived back at La Isabela, and he remained bedridden until January 1495. Columbus named Bartolomé *adelantado* of the Indies, and he left much of the governance of the colony to him during the months of his illness.

The material conditions at La Isabela were somewhat improved in the winter of 1494, when Antonio de Torres arrived with a relief fleet of four ships with supplies, including food, wine, medicines, cloth, livestock, and hardware.[32] It is possible that women and other settlers arrived with Torres, as Ferdinand Colón wrote that in the spring of 1495 the Christians on the island "numbered only six hundred and thirty, most of them sick, with many children and women among them.[33]

Torres's four ships, however, brought considerably less in the way of provisions than had been requested by Columbus and approved by Ferdinand and Isabela earlier in 1494. The original request was for thirteen ships, and for the maintenance of a thousand people for a year.[34] The reduction of goods to what could fit in four ships may have been a response to news of La Isabela's depleted population and charges of mismanagement carried back in the summer of 1494 by Buil and Margarite.

Between December 1494 and April 1495 Columbus established two other forts between La Isabela and Santo Tomás, to guard the route into the Cibao and help control the region. The Magdalena fortress, under the command of Luis de Arriaga, an hidalgo and confidant of Admiral Columbus, guarded the crossing of the Yaque River some twelve leagues south of La Isabela. It was located near present-day Jacagua, in the province of the subchief Guatiguará (a subaltern of Guarionex), who promptly attacked the fort and killed forty Spaniards. The fortress of Concepción was erected at or near the village of Guaranico on the Río Verde, which was the capital of the cacique Guarionex (see figure 4.1). Juan de Ayala was placed in command.[35]

With the settlement bolstered by the fresh supplies Torres had brought, Columbus decided once his health had improved that he needed to display a show of force against the increasingly aggressive Taínos. In early 1495 he headed a punitive expedition against Guatiguará, the subchief who had allegedly attacked and slain the Spaniards at the fortress of Magdalena.[36] Although Columbus did not capture the cacique, he did seize more than fifteen hundred Indians and marched them to La Isabela, initiating the first open enslavement of Caribbean Indians. Their fate is chillingly recounted by Michel de Cuneo, who departed with the Indian captives for Spain in February 1495 on the homeward voyage of Torres's relief fleet: "We gathered into our settlement 1,600 people male and female of those Indians, of whom, among the best males and females we embarked on our caravels on February 17, 1495, 550 souls. Of the rest who were left the announcement went around that whoever wanted them could take as many as he pleased; and this was done. And when everybody had been supplied there were some

400 of them left to whom permission was granted to go wherever they wanted. Among them were many women who had infants at the breast. They, in order to better escape us, since they were afraid that we would turn to catch them again, left their infants anywhere on the ground and started to flee like desperate people."[37]

More than two hundred Indians died on the voyage and were thrown into the sea. The rest were sold as slaves in Seville.

The departure of the fleet further reduced the Spanish population of La Isabela, as a large number of other colonists who decided to give up the venture returned to Spain along with Cuneo and the Indians. Meanwhile, conflict with the Taínos escalated. At the end of February 1495 Caonabó and his forces marched against Magdalena and Santo Tomás, and they held Santo Tomás under siege for a month before withdrawing. Shortly after the siege, Caonabó was captured by Hojeda and sent to La Isabela in chains.[38]

The capture of Caonabó both alarmed and enraged the Taíno caciques, and they responded by organizing an allied insurrection in the Vega Real, allegedly planning to march against La Isabela with a force more than five thousand strong. Columbus, however, mounted a preemptive expedition against them, leaving La Isabela on 24 March 1495 with at least two hundred foot soldiers, twenty horsemen, and twenty dogs. He was accompanied by Guacanagarí, still his ally, and a number of Guancanagarí's Taíno subjects.[39] The Spaniards routed the Taíno forces, killing large numbers of them and capturing many others, including Caonabó's brother. This battle brutally and effectively brought the Vega Real under Spanish control, pacifying it to the extent that "a Christian could safely go wherever he pleased, and the Indians themselves offered to carry him pickaback, as they do nowadays at the post stages."[40]

Caonabó and his brother were to be sent to Spain as prisoners, since Columbus was unwilling to execute such important persons without the involvement of the monarchs. The Taíno nobles, however, died either on the voyage or chained in the ships that sank in La Isabela's harbor during the hurricane there in the fall of 1495.[41] Caonabó's widow, Anacaona, who was the sister of Behechio, the cacique of Xaraguá, returned to her girlhood home to govern with her brother.

The fortresses of Magdalena and Santo Tomás appear to have been lost or been abandoned during this period. Magdalena was replaced by a fort named Esperanza, farther upstream, and Concepción (established during or after the March 1495 expedition) served the defensive functions formerly provided by Santo Tomás.[42]

After his pacification of the Taíno alliance, Columbus imposed a harsh tribute payment on all the Indians of Hispaniola, payable every three months: "In the Cibao, where the gold mines were, every person of fourteen years of age or upward was to pay a large hawk's bell of gold dust; all others were each to pay one arroba (twenty-five pounds) of cotton. Whenever an Indian delivered his tribute, he was to recieve a brass or copper token which he must wear about his neck as proof that he had made his payment. Any Indian found without such a token was to be punished."[43] In other cases, labor and personal services were rendered in place of goods.[44]

The tribute was organized through the caciques, who were responsible for its collection and delivery. Obviously, therefore, the success of the system depended on the maintenance of the Taíno social hierarchy. Over the next two years, however, the Taíno population was drastically depleted through disease, warfare, and social disruption, and the caciques gradually became disaffected or were killed. By 1497, the tribute system had essentially collapsed.

The years 1495–1496 were to be the most devastating of all for the Taínos. They were burdened not only by the excessive tribute requirements but also by the continuing effects of population loss through diseases that the Europeans introduced. During the same period a famine gripped the island, making the Taíno's situation even more desperate. The reorganization of labor required by the tribute undoubtedly contributed to the decrease in food production by the Taínos, as did falling population levels. Many of the Spanish accounts, including those of Las Casas and D'Anghiera, attributed the famine to an intentional policy of resistance on the part of the Taínos, recounting that they burned their fields and destroyed their crops rather than let the Spaniards use them. Ferdinand Colón credited the famine to the wrath of God against the Indians, writing that He "visited them with such a shortage of food and such a variety of plagues that he reduced their number by two-thirds." The famine extended across the island, and was observed on the south coast as well as the central and northern parts.[45]

Whatever their origins, the famine and epidemics precipitated a dramatically steep decline in Taíno population in 1495 and 1496. Although the Spaniards at La Isabela undoubtedly also suffered from food shortages, they had their meager relief supplies to sustain them and took what food they could find from the Indians. Guarionex, for example, "whose territory had suffered less than the others, distributed some provisions among our people."[46]

Another disaster struck La Isabela in June 1495 when a hurricane sank three of the four ships which lay at anchor—probably the *San Juan*, *Cardera*, and *Gallega*. The *Niña* survived, and the colony's shipwrights set about constructing two caravels, modeled after the *Niña*, from the salvaged remains of the wrecked ships. This first ship built in the Americas was named the *Santa Cruz* but was generally called the *India* by her seamen.[47]

The Columbus brothers spent much of 1495 on expeditions to complete subjugation of the island. In October, while Christopher was away and Bartolomé was in command of La Isabela, a fleet of four ships under Juan de Aguado arrived at La Isabela carrying not only supplies and reinforcements but also orders from the Crown to investigate Columbus's administration of the colony. The reports of Buil and Margarite had evidently had their effect.

The detailed instructions given to Aguado by the Catholic Kings make it clear that they were fully aware of difficulties at La Isabela.[48] They included orders for better care and more equitable distribution of the storehouse supplies and specified the rations that were to be allotted to each man every two weeks. The monarchs also sent a master miner, Maestro Paolo, and four assistants, along with orders that they were to be treated with special consideration and care. Other settlers also apparently accompanied Aguado, and the Crown outlined a plan to send the "useless" people back to Spain to help conserve supplies.

Aguado, according to contemporaries, behaved with high-handed arrogance and undermined Bartolomé's authority in his brother's absence.[49] He interviewed the sick and disabled people at La Isabela (since, according to Las Casas, most of the healthy ones were out roaming the countryside looking for gold and food), and they assailed him with stories of misery:

> All of the people that have been in this island are incredibly discontented, especially those that were at La Isabela, and all the more for the force, the hunger and the illnesses that they endured, and they did not swear any other oath than "as God would take me to Castile"; they had nothing to eat other than the rations given to them from the

storehouse of the King, which was one escudilla of wheat, that they had to grind in a hand mill [atahona a mano] (and many ate it cooked), and one chunk of rancid bacon or of rotten cheese [queso podrido], and I don't know how many haba or garbanzo beans; of wine, it was as though there was none in the world [como si no lo hobiera en el mundo], and this was the allowance [sueldo] of the Crown. And the Admiral for his part ordered them to work hungry, weak, and some sick (in building the fortaleza, the Admiral's house and other buildings) in such a manner that they were all anguished and afflicted and desperate, for which reasons they complained to Juan Aguado and used the occasion to speak about the Admiral and threaten him to the King.[50]

Columbus, alerted to Aguado's arrival by his brother, hastened back to La Isabela and quickly decided that he had to go to Spain to defend himself against his many critics. Neither he nor Aguado was able to leave until the following year, however, because another hurricane struck La Isabela, in the fall of 1495, destroying Aguado's ships and stranding him on the island.[51] (It was on one of those ships that, Las Casas asserts, Caonabó was being held prisoner and drowned.) Nobody could leave until the ships being constructed to replace those lost in the hurricane of June that year were finished and outfitted.

While waiting for the new ships to be completed, Columbus sent the adelantado Bartolomé on an expedition to the southern part of the island to explore a region around the Río Haína thought to contain ancient gold mines. The group included not only soldiers under the command of Francisco de Garay and Miguel Díaz but also Maestro Paolo and his miners. The region proved to be much more productive even than the Cibao, and it was named San Cristóbal.[52] They sent news and gold samples back to the delighted Columbus at La Isabela in time for his departure.

The American-built caravels were finally ready in March 1496. Aguado and Columbus both sailed to Spain, Aguado with the newly built Santa Cruz and Columbus commanding the Niña. They were carrying some 220 Spaniards and thirty Indians, including (according to Ferdinand Colón) Caonabó and his brother.[53] Before he left, Columbus appointed his brother Bartolomé as governor and captain general of the island in his absence, and he appointed Francisco de Roldán, a capable but unlettered cavalry soldier (escudero) in Columbus's personal entourage as the alcalde mayor, or chief magistrate, of La Isabela.

Columbus had already begun planning to relocate the town even before he left. The adelantado Bartolomé accompanied the two departing ships as far as Puerto Plata, which they inspected as a possible site for the new city.[54] The area was rejected in favor of the south coast near the mines of San Cristóbal, and one of Columbus's last orders for the adelantado was to fortify a settlement in the San Cristóbal region. This was to mark the beginning of the city of Santo Domingo, and the end for La Isabela.

At the beginning of 1496, two years after it was established, La Isabela was still in a very precarious state. Whatever relief Aguado had brought in October 1495 was short-lived. There were probably about five hundred to six hundred Spaniards on the island, including some women and children. Probably no more than a few hundred of them lived at La Isabela, where the supplies from Spain were stored, where the only official church was located, and where water mills, pottery kilns, and forges were still being used to try to replicate a Spanish material lifestyle.

The complaints of scarce food and rationing, along with the departure of many settlers from the town to exploit Indian food sources in the countryside, imply that by the middle of 1495 or earlier there were few Indians in the vicinity of La Isabela able to provide food to the Spanish colonists.[55] After the first few months of 1494 there are no longer comments such as those of Chanca that "there come here constantly many Indians . . . all come laden with *ages* [yams] which are like turnips, very excellent for food," or of Columbus that the Indians "come and go constantly, night and day. . . . On account of them, we have guards in camp while the settlement is unwalled and without defense."[56] Many Taínos in the vicinity of La Isabela apparently abandoned their towns and fled the area quite early, while others undoubtedly died from epidemics.

Scarcity of food—and the illness it exacerbated—was the overriding theme of La Isabela as the town entered its third year of existence. Despite the euphoric accounts of virtually all the chroniclers about the extraordinary fertility of the land in the early months of the colony, the promise was not fulfilled. Efforts at European crop production and animal husbandry were apparently still unsuccessful. Cuneo suggested in 1494 that this had more to do with the attitude of the Spaniards than it did with the poverty of the land: "Although the soil is very black and good, they have not yet found the way or the time to sow, the reason being that nobody wants to live permanently in these countries."[57] The situation was no different two years later.

Rationing of food was still strictly enforced in 1496, even after Aguado's arrival with the relief ships, and hunger was the overriding complaint.[58] During the first half of 1496 there were also Spaniards garrisoned at the three fortalezas of Concepción, Bonao, and Magdalena, and these men were for the most part living off the Indians. Others were in the mining region of San Cristóbal. For many Spaniards (particularly those who were reasonably healthy) it seemed preferable to strike out on their own in the countryside, seizing food from the Indians.[59]

Relief came in early July 1496, when a fleet of three ships under Peralonso Niño sailed into La Isabela's harbor with supplies and news that the admiral had arrived safely in Spain. They brought wheat, wine, oil, dried pork, and dried beef, although some of the provisions were moldy and rotten. The ships also carried letters from Columbus, officially ordering, with the Crown's consent, the construction of a new settlement at Santo Domingo and the abandonment of La Isabela.[60]

As Las Casas records, "The Admiral wrote to his brother Don Bartolomé Colón that he should get to work at once and march to the south part of the Island, and with all diligence, search there for a port that could be settled, and if this should be found, move everything from La Isabela to it, and to depopulate [the city]; which, seeing the orders of the Admiral, he quickly left for the south, leaving harmony and order in La Isabela, and appointing his brother Diego in his place (as the Admiral had ordered); and with the healthiest people that there were, and the number that seemed right, he went directly to the mines of San Cristóbal. There, asking about the closest place at the sea, he was taken to the River Hocama (as the Indians call it, a very lovely river) that was populated throughout, and this is the city where now is Santo Domingo."[61]

Peter Martyr D'Anghiera recounts that (in 1496) "after diligently exploring the southern coast, he [Bartolomé] moved the settlement and founded a fortaleza on an elevated hill next to a very secure port, which he called fortaleza of Santo Domingo, since he arrived there on a Sunday. . . . In La Isabela he left only the sick people and some master shipbuilders in order to finish two caravels which had already been started, and the rest were moved at midday to Santo Domingo."[62]

In addition to the instructions for relocating La Isabela, the relief ships brought orders from the Crown to enslave (as prisoners of a "just war") those Indian caciques and their subjects who had killed or otherwise tried to harm the Christians. When Peralonso Niño's ships left La Isabela on 29 September 1496, there were three hundred Taíno prisoners on board. Far fewer arrived in Cádiz when the ship docked at the end of October, since many had died at sea and many others died soon after they disembarked.[63]

The process of relocating the Spanish settlement from La Isabela to Santo Domingo probably took place gradually during the second half of 1496, and by the end of the year the Spanish presence in La Isabela had obviously been reduced dramatically. The town remained occupied, however, well into 1497. As before, hunger and strict food rationing were facts of life, and sickness continued to plague the Spaniards in La Isabela.[64]

The first half of 1497 was chaotic, and the colony suffered a series of turbulent episodes. The precise timing of these events is somewhat unclear in the documents, but they appear to have occurred roughly in the sequence discussed below. With the construction of the new settlement at Santo Domingo under way, Bartolomé Colón visited the province of Xaraguá and the caciques Behechio and Anacoana, to make arrangements for tribute. To the relief of Behechio, it was agreed that it could be provided in cotton and food rather than gold, and several days of negotiations ensued.[65] This initial visit of the adelantado to Xaraguá probably took place early in 1497.

When Bartolomé returned to La Isabela, he found that three hundred people had died of various illnesses. This blow was exacerbated by continuing food shortages, particularly as no ships had arrived since those of Peralonso Niño some seven or eight months before.[66] Bartolomé decided to distribute the remaining sick among the fortresses of Esperanza, Magdalena, Santiago, Concepción, and Bonao, leaving the healthiest men and craftsmen at La Isabela. Among those left in the town were Diego Colón, governor of La Isabela in Bartolomé's absence, Francisco Roldán, the alcalde, and, as later events were to indicate, about a hundred men.

Bartolomé then went to Santo Domingo, but shortly after his arrival, word came that the Taíno caciques in the Vega Real were planning an insurrection organized by Guarionex, made more dangerous by the fact that they had by now acquired both Spanish firearms and the knowledge to use them.[67] Bartolomé decided to march against them with the soldiers from the fort in Santo Domingo, and he captured several of the

Taíno caciques, including Guarionex, in a surprise night-time raid carried out simultaneously on several Taíno towns near Concepción. The next day some five thousand Taínos came to Concepción to plead for the release of the caciques. Bartolomé acceded to their request, thereby gaining the alliance of Guarionex, the repacification of the Vega Real, and the continued production of cotton and cassava by the Taínos.[68]

After the capture of the caciques of the Cibao, Bartolomé returned to Xaraguá and the capital of Behecchio and Anacoana to verify that they had complied with their promise to gather the tribute. Finding that they had indeed done this, and receiving large quantities of cotton, cassava bread, carved items, *hutias* (small, guinea-pig-like rodents), and roasted fish, Bartolomé sent for a caravel from La Isabela, on which he loaded the tribute and returned with it to that beleaguered city.

Rebellion

La Isabela was in chaos when the tribute ship from Xaraguá arrived with Bartolomé. During the adelantado's absence, the alcalde Francisco Roldán had been conspiring against the authority of the Columbus brothers. Roldán complained that Bartolomé went to Xaraguá with four hundred men and remained there for four months, leaving the sick and weak scattered about the country. Other reasons alleged to have provoked Roldán's dissatisfaction included the endless hunger and food rationing, the suspicion that the admiral was never going to return, the punishment of one of Roldán's close companions by the adelantado after the man had violated Guarionex's wife, and Roldán's own desire to rise above his station.[69]

The uprising itself occurred in May 1497 and was precipitated by Diego Colón's order that the caravel that had just arrived in La Isabela with the tribute from Xaraguá should be pulled up on the beach so that it could not be commandeered by the disaffected men. Diego then sent Roldán to Concepción with a contingent of soldiers to help control Taíno resistance to the collection of tribute in the Cibao. Roldán went instead to the town of the cacique Marque, where he openly announced his rebellion. Some of the soldiers refused to participate and went on to the fort of Concepción. The rest—some seventy Spaniards, mostly commoners, but including a few hidalgos—returned with Roldán to La Isabela. The events of the rebellion provide some clues to the state of things at the settlement in the spring of 1497.

The rebels broke into the royal storehouse, the *alhóndiga*, and with the cry of *"Viva el Rey"* (to indicate that they were rebelling only against Columbus and not against the monarchs) they seized the precious supplies of food, arms, and ammunition. Roldán's force of about seventy must have exceeded the number of men remaining with Diego Colón at La Isabela, because Diego's force was unable to restrain Roldán, and were forced into the Casa Fuerte (Columbus's house), where they had to stay while Roldán controlled the town.[70]

Las Casas reports that "from Isabela, the rebels went to the ranch [*hato*] of the King's cattle and slaughtered all the cows they wished, though to kill a cow at that time was considered a great crime, because they were being kept for breeding. They then went on the herd of mares, which also belonged to the King, taking whatever mares, colts and stallions they felt like."[71] Apparently, animal husbandry was successfully in effect at La Isabela in 1497, even if farming was not. Las Casas suggests that Roldán had been planning the insurrection for some time, "for as soon as the Admiral left Isabela, Roldán (who was the supervisor of the workers) began to assemble large quantities of horseshoes and nails, more than had ever been needed before."

From the king's ranch Roldán and his forces went into the interior of the country, trying unsuccessfully to take Concepción but gathering more and more Spanish recruits and Indian allies with the intent of attacking the adelantado and seizing power. By Roldán's own account, he had by that time some four hundred or five hundred men in his force, although by the following year Columbus reported that Roldán's force was only about 120 strong.[72] Peter Martyr D'Anghiera attributed Roldán's recruiting success to his perversion of the men, "promising them instead of grasping a hoe, to hold the breasts of a maiden; instead of work, pleasure; in place of hunger, abundance; and in place of weariness and watchful nights, leisure."[73] Roldán and his forces spent the rest of 1497 roaming the island, seizing Indian food and women, looking for gold, and essentially establishing a separate European polity in Hispaniola.

Abandonment

The depopulation and abandonment of La Isabela were almost certainly completed during the second half of 1497, by which time construction of the new settlement at Santo Domingo was well under way and Roldán had already sacked La Isabela. When the next ships from Spain arrived in February 1498, they did not even call at La Isabela.

Bartolomé and Diego Colón, meanwhile, continued trying to collect tribute from the increasingly burdened Taínos around the island, a task that became more and more difficult during the months of late 1497 and into 1498. Guarionex, the paramount chief of the Vega Real and the most important tribute vassal, fled to the mountains, provoking retaliatory expeditions by the adelantado.[74]

In late February 1498, the embattled Bartolomé was relieved to get news that two caravels dispatched by Columbus under the command of Pedro Fernández de Coronel had arrived, not at La Isabela but at Santo Domingo. The ships carried relief supplies and ninety laborers who were intended to work in the mines and cut brazilwood.[75] More important, they brought news from the admiral that he was soon to embark from Spain with six more ships carrying settlers and provisions.

Efforts by Bartolomé and Pedro Fernández de Coronel to treat with the rebels failed, even after the news of the admiral's imminent return. Roldán and his men retreated to the province of Xaraguá, "where there was food" and where, according to Las Casas, "they found the paradise they were seeking, since there they had the liberty and licence required for the fulfillment of all their corrupt desires."[76]

By the time Christopher Columbus arrived in Hispaniola on 31 August 1498, there was no chance of salvaging the original dream. The factoría model had failed, no significant gold deposits had been found, the Indians were tragically depleted and suffering, the Spanish settlers were in conflict among themselves, and La Isabela was abandoned. By 1498, a new story had begun, with a different idea of colonization. La Isabela's only part in that story was as a cursed, abandoned town, falling into ruins and inhabited only by pigs and the mournful ghosts of dead caballeros.

Chapter 5

The Hand of Vandals
and the Tooth of Time:
La Isabela, 1500–1987

Although La Isabela remained abandoned after 1498, its location was never lost. The site was known and used intermittently by smugglers, woodcutters, fishermen, pig hunters, sailors, Columbus researchers, and treasure hunters for nearly five hundred years, until the village of El Castillo was established there in the mid-twentieth century.

Through those centuries the site itself suffered countless natural and human depredations that severely compromised its physical and archaeological integrity. The neglect of La Isabela during its first three centuries of abandonment and amnesia had a relatively benign impact on the site. It was ironically the recognition of La Isabela as a symbol of American history—and particularly the rediscovery of Columbus in the nineteenth century—that led to the most serious impacts on the site, and its near destruction. Understanding these post-Columbian uses and misuses of La Isabela has been critically important, not only for understanding the site's archaeological record but also for developing appropriate methods and strategies by which to recover and interpret it.

Bartolomé de Las Casas attributed La Isabela's continuing abandonment both to its isolated location and to the aura of misery and death that lingered there. By the early sixteenth century it was widely believed that the site was haunted by frightening and horrible ghosts. As Las Casas commented,

> In this island of Española it was advised by many that no one could dare to pass by La Isabela after it was depopulated without great fear and danger . . . for those who passed by there widely proclaimed that they saw and heard day and night . . . many frightening voices and horrible ghosts. . . . Once, some men being one day at some buildings of La Isabela, saw two files of men appear, like two choruses, who seemed all to be noble people of the palace, well dressed, wearing their swords and wrapped in traveling cloaks such as they then used in Spain; those to whom this vision appeared were amazed—how had such elegant strangers come to be brought there, without there having been know anything about them in the island?—They greeted and questioned them about when and from where they had come, they responded in silence, only taking their hats in their hands to return the greetings, they lifted their heads from their bodies together with the hats, leaving themselves beheaded and then they disappeared. Such a vision and perturbation left those who saw it almost dead, and upset and frightened for many days.[1]

The belief that La Isabela was haunted by spirits and ghosts was still strongly held by people of the region nearly four hundred years later, and it was repeated to explorer Frederick Ober by local woodcutters when he visited La Isabela in 1891.[2]

Las Casas had direct experience of La Isabela in the years after its abandonment, as the prior of the Franciscan monastery in Puerto Plata. In 1526 he began construction of the monastery: "I had a large stone carried [from La Isabela], which I had placed as the first stone of the monastery which I began to build there in memory of such antiquity." Many more of the dressed stones from La Isabela's buildings found their way to Puerto Plata, and throughout the nineteenth and twentieth centuries stones from the site were being transported to Puerto Plata for use in such buildings as the Masonic Lodge.[3]

Even though La Isabela itself was not occupied, there was some continued casual use of the area at the end of the fifteenth century. In 1499 Francisco Roldán, still living in Xaraguá with a hundred or so Spaniards but by then pardoned, asked Columbus "to grant him the lands in a certain place, near La Isabela, which are called the Ababruco, land of a certain cacique, and of the farms that were there, because he said that before the uprising they were his."[4] The admiral granted Roldán's request.

Las Casas, in recounting La Isabela's ghostly reputation, also noted that in the early years of the sixteenth century those "who were dwelling near there in the country" and those who came to hunt pigs there did not dare to visit the town. Clearly, there was some rural occupation of the area around La Isabela, particularly after the establishment of Puerto Plata in 1503. The occupants could have been disaffected Spaniards living on the land, mixed-blood people, black *cimarrones*— escaped slaves—or Indians.

The area around La Isabela was well-known in colonial times for the large number of feral pigs descended from those left when the Spaniards abandoned the town, and licenses to hunt them became a not insignificant source of income for the Crown. In 1503, for example, license fees for the hunting of pigs in "Isabela la Vieja" brought in 2,000 pesos. Spanish mine owners were accustomed to hunting a pig each week to feed the Indians working in their repartimientos. Las Casas reports an owner "himself eating two quarters and more, and tossing out the other two quarters for 30 or 40 Indians, to cook a piece each day, distributing to each Indian a little chunk the size of a nut."[5]

By the middle of the sixteenth century, the Bay of La Isabela had become a center for illicit trade between the Spanish occupants of the region and foreign corsairs. An incident in 1563 involving the English slave trader John Hawkins illustrates La Isabela's role in these activities.[6] Hawkins appeared with four well-armed ships in the bay of Puerto Plata, laden with slaves and looking for a port in which to careen two of the ships. The Spanish officials of Puerto Plata "in order to get rid of them sent them to the port of La Isabela, which is twelve leagues from there . . . in the unpopulated regions which lie between the settlements of Monte Christi and Puerto de Plata." Hawkins's ships left for La Isabela, where they anchored offshore (apparently to the north of the Bajabonico), and the men came on land for meat, water, and wood. Learning of this, the officials in Santo Domingo commanded one Lorenzo

Bernáldez, a lawyer of the court of appeals, to ride to La Isabela, raising a force along the way, and arrest the Englishmen. Bernáldez managed to raise a contingent of "120 horsemen on the pretense that they were wanted to go against Negroes in rebellion," but when they arrived at La Isabela they found that they were greatly outnumbered by the English. The Spanish force managed to capture two of the Englishmen, and Hawkins agreed to ransom them for 140 slaves, on condition that he be allowed legally to sell thirty-five of them to Spanish residents of the area. Bernáldez issued an illegal license to sell the slaves, and Hawkins did so. This was the first official case of English trade in Hispaniola, and the illicit exchange — *rescate* — accelerated during the subsequent years of the century.

Twenty years later Sir Richard Grenville's 1585 voyage to Virginia brought him first to the north coast of Hispaniola. He anchored in June at La Isabela, then in the jurisdiction of Puerto Plata, where he waited for the "Governour" of "Isabella" and the "Captaine" of "the Port de Plata." It was understood that these authorities were well disposed toward the (illicit) English, and that they would undoubtedly soon visit them. An expedition member provided the following account:

> The 5. day the aforesayd Governour accompanied with a lusty Fryer, and twenty other Spaniards, with their servants, and Negroes, came downe to the Sea side, where our ships road at anker, who being seene, our Generall manned immediately the most part of his boates with the chiefe men of our Fleete, every man appointed, and furnished in the best sort. . . . In the meane time while our English Generall and the Spanish Governour discuoursed betwixt them of divers matters, as of the state of the Countrey, the multitude of the Townes and people, and the commodities of the Iland, our men providing two banquetting houses covered with green boughes, and a sumptuous banquet was brought in served by us all in plate, with the sound of trumpets, and consort of musicke, wherewith the Spaniards were more than delighted. Which banquet being ended, the Spaniardes in recompense of our courtesie, caused a great heard of white buls, and kyne to be brought together from the mountaines, and appointed for every gentleman and captaine that would ride, a horse ready sadled, and then singled out three of the best of them to bee hunted by horsemen after their maner, so that the pastime grewe very pleasant for the space of

three houres. wherein all three of the beasts were killed, whereof one tooke the Sea, and there was slaine with a musket.

After this sport, many rare presents and gifts were given and bestowed on both parts, and the next day wee played the Marchants in bargaining with them by way of trucke and exchange of divers of their commodities, as horses, mares, kine, buls, goates, swine, sheepe, bullhides, sugar, ginger, pearle, tabacco, and such like commodities of the Island.[7]

La Isabela's role as a remote locale for illicit trade between Spaniards and foreigners was undoubtedly diminished after the *devastaciones* of 1605, during which the towns of Puerto Plata, Monte Christi, Bayahá, and La Yaguana (the Banda del Norte) were forcibly depopulated and destroyed by the governing officials in order to stop illicit trade. The then governor, Osorio, using 150 soldiers of the Puerto Rican garrison, who had been sent by the Crown, proceeded to destroy the settlers' bohíos—huts—ranches, churches, planted fields, and everything else they needed to devastate in order to discourage the settlers from wanting to remain in these places.[8] There was understandably vociferous and often violent resistance to these measures, and it is likely that some of the inhabitants of northern Hispaniola may have fled to the countryside to live independently.

Much of the livestock was necessarily left behind in the abandoned districts because many of the animals were feral, and they provided the base for the development of buccaneerism. Adventurers of several nationalities, but predominantly French, began to establish hunting camps on the north coast of Hispaniola, killing the cattle, keeping their hides, and drying the meat on racks over open fires known as *boucans*, inspiring the term *boucanier*. These new camps became a political and social fact after 1616, and La Isabela was undoubtedly affected.[9] A few remnants of early seventeenth-century spirit bottles, pipes, and stoneware pottery discovered on the rocky promontory may have found their way to La Isabela through buccaneer visits.

Very little is known specifically about La Isabela between the devastaciones of 1605 and the nineteenth century. For Spanish Hispaniola nearly the entire seventeenth century was a period of declining economic capacity and population, poverty and ruralization, characterized by historian Frank Moya Pons as "an atmosphere of scarcity," in which "each sought the most convenient way to survive. Soldiers were forced to hire themselves out as dayworkers. Convents dedicated themselves to presenting bullfights and requesting alms with which to maintain their devotions. . . . The city's population had little incentive to work as there was no assurance that what they produced would find a market either within the island or abroad. Thus, while the urban population lived an unpromising life in ruined and decaying buildings, the inhabitants of the interior lived almost completely isolated, practicing subsistence farming and cattle herding, and holding daily cockfights to kill boredom."[10]

Hispaniola also suffered from natural disasters during this period. Severe earthquakes struck the country in 1562, 1666, and 1751. The 1562 quake destroyed the cities of Santiago and La Vega in the Cibao and undoubtedly affected the ruins of La Isabela.[11]

The northern towns of Puerto Plata and Monte Christi were not repopulated until the middle of the eighteenth century, when families of Canary Islanders were established there to help stabilize the frontier. By the end of the eighteenth century, the Bay of La Isabela was known as a port in the coastal trade of mahogany and lignum vitae, and it continued in this capacity throughout the nineteenth century.[12]

The site of La Isabela itself was apparently unoccupied during the nineteenth century, and the closest inhabitants appear to have lived about one and one-half miles from the "well-situated rock" on a bluff above the Bajabonico, about eight hundred meters inland from the bay. Casimir N. de Moya's atlas of the island based on data gathered during the late 1880s, for example, shows no contemporary occupation at the site of La Isabela, but it does erroneously identify the "Ruinas de Concepción" there. A settlement identified with the symbol for a *Lugareño* [hamlet] *o Casas diseminadas* and labeled "La Isabela" is shown near the coast on the south side of the Bahabonico, in the vicinity of Las Coles, close to the area known today as El Tablazo. This was no doubt the small hamlet later described by U.S. Navy lieutenant G. P. Colvocoresses and explorer Frederick Ober in 1891.[13]

Several eyewitness descriptions of La Isabela were published by North American visitors to the site in the nineteenth century, particularly as the four-hundredth anniversary of Columbus's voyages approached and interest in Columbus was revived. All of them described La Isabela as densely vegetated and uninhabited, and all noted that remnants of the stone buildings were still visible. One of the earliest of these visitors was William Gibbs, who was trying to gather evidence during the early 1840s that Columbus's original landfall was at Grand Turk Island. He went to La Isabela to examine a stone monument at the site and compare it to monuments in Grand Turk and Sand Key that he believed were of Columbian origin.[14] Gibbs saw and described many of the site's stone ruins, which at the time were still quite visible above ground. He recorded the church with its stone pillars, measuring some 100 by 50 feet, as well as "the remains of the storehouse of the king and the residence of Columbus and of a small fortaleza as well as a small tower with battlements." He also described a tall stone pillar or obelisk with a marble inscription, which formed a conspicuous landmark that projected above the cliff at the north end of the site and was visible from some distance at sea.[14] Fifty years later the obelisk was gone, allegedly blown up and destroyed by treasure hunters who were looking for gold.

Another description of the ruins was given a few years later in a letter written to Washington Irving in 1857 by Stanley Heneken, resident of the Dominican Republic: "Isabella is quite overgrown with forest, in the midst of which are still to be seen, partly standing , the pillars of the church, some remains of the King's storehouses and part of the residence of Columbus, all built of hewn stone. The small fortress is also a prominent ruin, and a little north of it is a circular pillar about ten feet high and as much in diameter, of solid masonry nearly entire; which appears to have had a wooden gallery of battlement around the top for convenience of a room, and in the center of which was placed the flagstaff. Having discovered the remains of an iron clamp imbedded in the stone, which served to secure the flagstaff, I tore it out, and now consign to you this curious relic of the first foothold of civilization in the New World, after it has been exposed to the elements nearly 350 years."[15]

The looting of the site of La Isabela proudly described by Heneken accelerated over the next fifty years as the interest of the United States in Columbus increased and as Puerto Plata grew. Robert Schomburgk, British consul in the Dominican Republic, reported in 1853 that "there are still to be seen some remnants of the fortress and of some houses. The avarice of the inhabitants did not respect these venerable remainders; the walls have been broken and the materials brought to Puerto Plata and other sites to build houses thereof."[16] By 1908, Frederick Ober, who had been a special commissioner to the United States Columbian

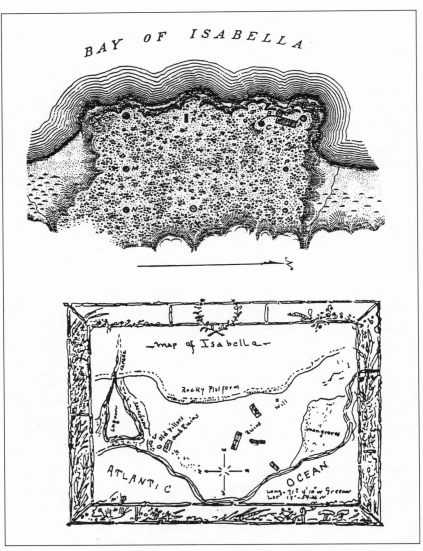

5.1. Maps of La Isabela in 1891. *Top*, by Lt. Colvocoresses (in Thatcher 1903). *Bottom*, by Frederick Ober (in Ober 1893). Key to Colvocoresses map: *A–C:* "Small Martello towers." *D, F, G:* "Remnants of walls, nearly 40 feet long, which connect to a fourth wall marked 'H,' that runs parallel to the first." *K:* "A rectangular structure, 40 feet by 20 feet." *L:* "A structure enclosed on the east by a circular wall." *M–P:* "Circular towers." *S:* A pit of some 20 feet in diameter and 15 feet in depth; it is said that it was excavated by treasure hunters."

Exposition in Chicago, observed of La Isabela with no trace of irony that "very little of it remains in situ, since its ruins have mostly crumbled, and the last of the rocks composing the walls were sent to the Columbian Exposition of 1893."[17]

Two important descriptions of La Isabela were made by North American expeditions gathering information and relics in 1891 for the Columbian Exposition. Both accounts not only describe the deteriorated state of the ruins by that time but also decry the extent of looting (although this did not deter either expedition from removing elements of the site themselves).

In May 1891, a group of officers from the U.S. Navy ship *Enterprise* carried out investigations at La Isabela, producing a report and a detailed map of the site (figure 5.1).[18] The report is invaluable for archaeological interpretations both of the site remains and of the alterations to the site over the past century. The navy team noted that the site was heavily vegetated and matted with roots, and that by 1891 the stones of the ruins were barely visible.

Lt. Colvocoresses recounted that "the application of pick and spade revealed nothing of particular interest" but did enable him to follow the traces of walls in some instances. These are shown in figure 5.1, and they include not only the still-visible remnants of the alhóndiga but also the remains of several earthen bastions around the periphery of the site.

A second North American research expedition to La Isabela was made just a week later by Frederick Ober, who traveled throughout the Caribbean looking for relics to display at the Columbian Exposition. He spent nearly a week exploring La Isabela, and he also prepared a map (figure 5.1).[19] His description concurs with that of the Colvocoresses expedition, although Ober collected fragments of crucibles near the Columbus house and wrote that "I have had in my hands a fragment of chain armor, and a stone ball, which were found here, and I possess pieces of the tiles that covered the houses erected by the Spaniards, and of the crucibles in which the first gold was smelted." Ober also noted when writing of the deterioration of La Isabela that "the hand of the vandal has been more destructive than the tooth of time."[20]

During the following year, 1892, the Dominican Junta para la Celebración del Centenario was established in Puerto Plata, and in June it inaugurated an archaeological investigation at La Isabela.[21] The junta members excavated around and sketched the largest structure at the site, which they interpreted to have been the church (but since identified as the alhóndiga). The two-day excavation recovered chain mail, a stone lombard shot, glazed tiles, and both Spanish and Indian pottery (the chain mail and shot were those loaned to the Columbian Exposition through Ober). They furthermore recommended that the materials from La Isabela should be in a national museum. Although the conclusions of the junta's report were misinformed by the dominant desire to commemorate the first Catholic church in the Americas, it is useful as a description of the alhóndiga's condition at the end of the nineteenth century.[22]

As a consequence of the junta's activities and the growing recognition of La Isabela's historical importance, measures to protect the site were initiated by the Dominican government in 1892. The then governor of the maritime district of Puerto Plata, Miguel Peralta, gave orders to the authorities at La Isabela prohibiting any kind of excavation at all in the ruins, stating that any excavation there had to be permitted by and coordinated with the Junta para la Celebración del Centenario. The attention garnered by La Isabela during the years of the quadricentenary seems to have died out rather quickly. A proposal was made in 1892 to create a separate maritime district at La Isabela and to people it with "Dominican families chosen for their hard work and morality, with government assistance."[23] Neither this plan nor one to place a commemorative Columbus lighthouse at La Isabela was implemented, although the lighthouse project was discussed and planned for more than a century after, culminating finally in 1992 with the construction of the Faro de Colón in Santo Domingo.

In 1903, the provincial governor of Puerto Plata designated one Silvano Reynoso, "a serious man of the place," to be responsible for guarding the ruins from "contemporary pirates" and looters. A few years later, Ober reported that the owner of La Isabela was "Mr. Passalaigue, who generally resides there [and] is cultured and hospitable."[24] The Passalaigue residence was located on the high bluff on the north side of the Bajabonico known in the late nineteenth century as El Tablazo, about a kilometer inland from the bay (see chapter 4, figure 4.2).

Little activity related to the ruins of La Isabela is documented during the first three decades of the twentieth century. On the *Día de la Raza* (Columbus Day, 12 October) of 1932, the organization Amantes de la Luz from Santiago erected a monument to mark the ruins of La Isabela. Part of the alhóndiga wall still existing at the time was removed

5.2. La Isabela, ca. 1938. Central part of La Isabela, facing west. The man near the center is standing in front of a large excavation, referred to at the time as the "algibe," or cistern (perhaps the large pit noted by Colvocoresses in 1891). On the right side of the photo a wooden rancho is located in the approximate vicinity of the alhóndiga. The town of El Castillo is not yet in evidence. (Photo: Emile Boyrie de Moya, in Demorizi 1980:180–83.)

so that the monument could be placed over the threshold of the original entrance on the west side of the alhóndiga (see figure 5.3).

In 1936, surveyors Máximo Arzeno and Rafael Pla Vásquez of the Escuela Normal de Puerto Plata made a survey and map of the site, indicating several features that have been lost since then. Among these was a circular *fortín*, or bastion, at the southern end of the site and an *aljibe*— a well or cistern—near the southeastern corner of the rocky plateau. That aljibe was in evidence in 1938 when the site was visited and photographed by Dominican researcher Emile Boyrie de Moya (figure 5.3).[25]

Neither the settlement of El Castillo nor the road that exists today at the site was shown on either the 1936 map or its key or in Marino Incháustegui's 1939 geography of the country. This was also confirmed by Emile Boyrie de Moya's visit in 1938 (figure 5.2).[26] In his photos the rocky promontory appears to have been cleared for grazing, but the rest of the site to the east was still densely forested at that date, and no road or settlement was present. There was a small *rancho* complex of three palm-thatch structures in the vicinity of the alhóndiga, apparently related to the flock of sheep shown grazing on the site. On the beach at the north end of the site there was another palm-thatch structure, used as a lumber depot, probably for the storage of wood for transport by sea (figure 5.3). A thatched building, possibly a storehouse, was located approximately where the dock is located today.

La Isabela Ravished: 1945–1965

In May 1945, the Patronato Interamericano pro Restauración de la Isabela was established in Santo Domingo, comprised not only of members of the Dominican archaeological and political communities but also of representatives from Cuba, Mexico, Colombia, and the United States. Later that month there was an official visit to the site by members of the patronato accompanied by local dignitaries.[27] Local tradition recounts that in preparation for this distinguished international delegation, the government of General Trujillo ordered local authorities to "clean up" the site. This included, disastrously, the leveling and partial grading with heavy equipment of the area containing the remnants of structures.[28]

The patronato sponsored three days of excavation to correspond with the site visit, and it was noted that no above-ground remnants of the buildings remained. The excavations consisted of opening a long trench parallel to the east wall of the church structure (figure 5.3).[29] Indian pottery, "lead" rings, and glass beads (thought to be trade goods) were found, leading the expedition to conclude that this was an area of Indian habitation. The team members also began a test pit in the interior of the church, but they were only able to excavate to a depth of twenty-five centimeters in the time available.

On 4 August of the following year, 1946, the region was struck by a severe earthquake and tidal wave that nearly destroyed both Santiago and Cap Haitien, Haiti. According to the elderly residents of the area, the tremors caused the Río Bajabonico, which at that time flowed into the bay via the Río Tablazo, to break out of its canal and reopen a course that discharged where the present mouth of the river is today, adjacent to Las Coles (see chapter 4, figure 4.2). The flood destroyed the Passalaigue residence and wood-shipping business at El Tablazo and undoubtedly had a severe impact on the sites at both El Castillo and Las Coles.

Archaeological interest in the site continued intermittently through the 1950s, largely at the instigation of Emile Boyrie de Moya. Boyrie and John Goggin of the University of Florida made surface collections at the site in 1952 with the intention of studying the aboriginal and European ceramics there. Even after the earlier grading of the site, they collected 1,091 sherds of unglazed European earthenware and *melado* glazed earthenware, and 102 sherds of Spanish majolica. Goggin noted that "at the present time [1952] a few houses occupy the southern part of the site."[30] Visits to the site and surface collections were also made with Boyrie by José Cruxent and Luis Chanlatte during the 1950s. It was during this visit that Cruxent recognized the unique nature of the unglazed Spanish ceramics from the site and postulated that they were probably locally produced there.[31]

The years from the early 1950s to the late 1960s were a period of great political turmoil for the region and brought another hiatus in archaeological activity at La Isabela. In 1949 anti-Trujillo forces made up of Dominican exiles had invaded the nearby town of Luperón in an attempt to overthrown the dictator. Although the invasion did not succeed, it provoked a general military reinforcement of the region, including the construction of a military parade ground on the site of the La Isabela ruins.

During the years of the Cuban Revolution, but before the invasion of 1959, military officials of the Trujillo government brought two H-16 Alice Chalmers tractors to the site in order to level, grade, and "clean" the rocky promontory and create a flat field. One of the tractor operators was interviewed by Cruxent in 1990, and he verified that he leveled several mounds of earth and stone rubble, using some of the soil to fill in holes and low spots on the site and pushing the rest over the cliff into the sea.[32] In some areas nearly a meter of soil was removed, and La Isabela's archaeological record indicates that only between five and thirty centimeters of the 1945 ground surface at the site was left intact. At that time the roads were reported to have been seasonably impassable, even for an all-terrain vehicle.

A second anti-Trujillo invasion took place in 1959, with exiles entering the country by sea at Maimón and Estero Hondo. By this time La Isabela—located between the two invasion points—was a reconnoitering spot for government patrol boats based in Puerto Plata.[33] In 1960, the dock at El Castillo (which remained in use until it was remodeled in 1991) was constructed by a private cotton company owned by Rafael Leonidas Trujillo and Galadas María. Abraham Peña, one of the men

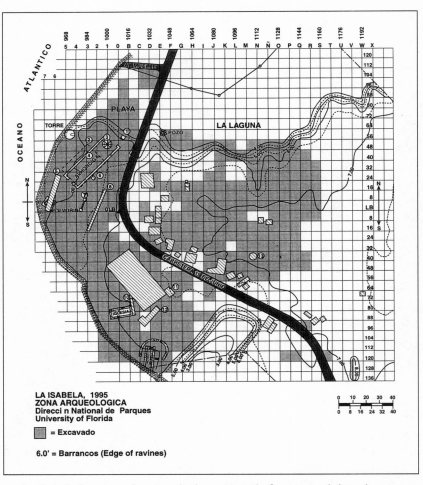

LA ISABELA, 1995
ZONA ARQUEOLOGICA
Direcci n National de Parques
University of Florida

■ = Excavado

6.0' = Barrancos (Edge of ravines)

5.3. La Isabela basemap showing the human-made features and disturbances to the site during the nineteenth and twentieth centuries.

who worked on the construction of the dock, was interviewed by Cruxent in November of 1992. The dock took five months to construct, and rock was brought by truck to the site, deposited with heavy equipment and cranes, and leveled by men with shovels and wheelbarrows. By this time a road was doubtless in place at El Castillo, as trucks came there not only to construct the dock but also to bring in loads of cotton for shipment by sea. The first shipment, made on the steamship *Antares* in 1960, carried eighteen thousand sacks of cotton.

A few years later, in 1963 or 1964, yet another grading episode took

1. Monument.
2. Location of excavations by the Junta para la Celebración del Centenario (1892) and also by Lt. Colvocorresses (1891).
3. Roofed, circular cement *palapa* constructed in 1987 as a field lab (1987).
4. Monument placed in the west wall of the alhóndiga by the Amantes de la Luz (1932).
5. "Trinchera construída por los Dominicanos cuando La Restauración"—an "entrenchment built by the Dominicans during the War of Restoration" (1863–1865). Noted by Pla and Arzeno during their survey of the site in 1936.
6. *Rancho* and animal grazing area, 1930s.
7. Monument and flagpoles erected in 1965.
8. Earthen dais prepared for the visit of the king of Spain in 1965.
9. Cement drying platform for corn and other crops (1964–1987).
10. Excavations by the Patronato Interamericano Pro Restauración de La Isabela (1945).
11. Excavations by the Museo del Hombre Dominicano (1983).
12. Excavations by the Museo del Hombre Dominicano and the University of Florence (1985–1986).
13. Large pit thought to have been excavated by treasure hunters (early twentieth century).

Shaded geometric areas are earth-fast wood and thatch structures with associated privies and outbuildings, mapped in 1989.

place at the site, when a tractor prepared the ground for a concrete *secadero*, or drying platform, used by the residents of the area for cacao and peanuts. It consisted of a concrete slab platform measuring 40.9 by 21.5 meters and was located about 15 meters north of the church structure (see figure 5.3). The secadero was in use until 1987. By the early 1960s the hamlet of El Castillo was apparently already established on the site of La Isabela.[34]

By 1965, the site of La Isabela had been extensively looted by relic hunters, excavated three times by projects for which no reports or arti-

5.4. El Castillo in 1990.

fact collections have been found (in 1891, 1892, and 1945), surface collected several times, subjected to three major earthquakes, and been graded and "cleaned" by heavy equipment three times (1945, 1959, and 1964). It had a road through its center and contained some forty earth-fast wooden buildings and their associated gardens (figure 5.4).

Archaeology and Political Vicissitudes: 1965–1985

By the late 1960s a variety of international organizations, including the Organization of American States, UNESCO, the Congreso Interamericano de Cooperación Intermunicipal, and the Congreso Hispano-Luzo-Americano-Filipino began to take an active interest in the preservation of La Isabela.[35] In the context of this renewed interest, the Universidad Católica Madre y Maestre of Santiago in the Dominican Republic conducted an investigation at La Isabela in 1966, under the direction of historian Carlos Dobal and engineer Juan Dobal Román. Dobal and his students measured the site, studied and mapped the remaining stones, and collected ceramics that were subsequently analyzed by Elpidio Ortega.[36]

On 24 August 1967, the Dominican president Joaquín Balaguer issued presidential decree number 1804, which established a commission charged with securing funds from UNESCO to protect and stabilize the site of La Isabela. In response to this, the Comité Regional pro Embellecimiento y Restauración de la Isabela was formed in 1971 at the instigation of Rafael Cantisano, a physician and long-time advocate of La Isabela's protection. Working with officials from Puerto Plata, Santiago, and Luperón, they garnered the support of the Dominican government and particularly the Oficina del Patrimonio Cultural in the study and restoration of the site. As a consequence, the regional government of Puerto Plata constructed a fence to isolate the part of the site that contained the stone foundations. This work was monitored by archaeologist Luis Chanlatte Baik, who also supervised an excavation in the southeastern corner of the alhóndiga during the two-day project on 19 and 20 September 1971. On the following day, 21 September 1971, La Isabela was declared in law number 197 of the Dominican Government to be El Solar de las Américas, and the Oficina del Patrimonio Cultural was charged with excavation, preservation, and touristic development of the site.[37]

Relatively little study or conservation was done at La Isabela during the 1970s, although the site received intermittent international attention, such as the visits by the king of Spain in 1975 and Don Cristóbal Colón, Duke of Veragua, in 1972. Disturbance to the site continued during this period, however, including the construction of an earthen dais to the east of the alhóndiga in preparation for the king of Spain's visit. This platform, still in evidence in 1983, was undoubtedly built of displaced archaeological deposits.[38]

The first modern extensive excavations at La Isabela were carried out in 1983 by Elpidio Ortega, Fernando Luna Calderón, and José Guerrero of the Museo del Hombre Dominicano, funded by the Organization of American States. They excavated in the vicinity of the Columbus house and the church foundations, and located part of the cemetery of La Isabela as well as an area of previous Taíno occupation.[39] The skeletal remains of some seventeen individuals were excavated, and a wooden structure was erected to protect the exposed burials (which have since been removed to the Museo del Hombre Dominicano for study).

During the same year, the first systematic underwater archaeological survey of the Bay of La Isabela was made by the Institute of Nautical Archaeology of Texas A and M University.[40] The team located several underwater anomalies, established permanent datum references on land, and mapped the site and its remains.

In April 1984, the 1971 decree that had established the site of La Isabela as El Solar de las Américas was modified to create the Comisión para la Revalorización y Desarrollo de la Isabela, presided over by Rafael Cantisano. The commission was charged with the development of a plan for the scientific study, public interpretation, and touristic development of the site, as well as with seeking international funding to implement it. The Museo del Hombre Dominicano was responsible for archaeological excavations at the site, working in collaboration with the Office of Cultural Patrimony, which was responsible for the consolidation and preservation of the site's remains.

In July of the following year, the Museo del Hombre Dominicano entered into a cooperative agreement with the University of Florence in Italy, for a collaborative project to both excavate and interpret the site of La Isabela. The first field phase of this *convenio* took place in December 1986 and January 1987, during which a number of additional burials were excavated and the site was once again mapped.[41]

Meanwhile, however, the government had changed after the election in May 1986 that returned Joaquín Balaguer to power. Among many of the changes in administration that took place during the first year of the new regime was the transfer of responsibility for La Isabela from the Museo del Hombre Dominicano and the Office of Cultural Patrimony to the Dirección Nacional de Parques (the National Park Service), or DNP.

In 1987 the DNP initiated a long-term program of archaeological research at La Isabela intended to lead to the salvage and interpretation of the site as part of the country's observation of Columbus's quincentenary. José Cruxent was invited to direct the excavations on behalf of the park service, and the project on which this book is based was formally inaugurated on 7 May 1987 by President Balaguer.

At that time La Isabela had been physically subjected to nearly five hundred years of natural and cultural alteration, nearly all of it destructive. Dense vegetation covered the site for centuries, undoubtedly causing root damage and considerable soil disturbance. The cliff at the western side of the site had been eroding, particularly at the southern end where the remaining portions of the Columbus house are located. Hurricanes and earthquakes had also taken their toll, contributing to erosion of rock, soil, and structures.

Damage from human intervention, however, has far outweighed that from natural causes. Looting of the site for relics and building materials continued unabated from the early years of the sixteenth century until 1892, when the Dominican government gave the first official recognition of the site's importance. Despite government efforts, a brisk trade in artifacts for sale to tourists has taken place since then, and has accelerated along with the pace of tourism.

La Isabela has also been subjected to a number of archaeological excavations for which no detailed stratigraphic reports or curated collections can be found. These include projects done in 1891, 1892, 1945, 1971, 1983, and 1986. The site was also surface collected several times. In addition, it was subjected during the twentieth century to a series of constructions and nonarchaeological uses that had an impact on the archaeological record of the site, including rancho occupation, animal grazing, military activities, the construction of a cement grain-drying platform, construction of an earthen dias, the grading of the road between El Castillo and Luperón (which runs through the center of the site), and once the site had been placed under government protection, daily sweeping by maintenance workers. This practice, continuing over several years, removed a considerable amount of site deposit from the surface by sweeping it into the sea. By far the most destructive impact on La Isabela, however, were the grading activities of the late 1950s, which removed a considerable portion of the site to the west of the present roadway and pushed it into the sea.

Given the short duration—four years—of the site's colonial occupation and the alarming amount of disturbance during the subsequent five centuries, it is remarkable that anything at all of the archaeological record survived. When Cruxent arrived in 1987 to begin the study of La Isabela, he was faced with the task of reconstructing and interpreting life at the Columbian town through excavation of a severely ravaged and altered site.

The Archaeological Present

Two things seemed evident to Cruxent when he recognized both the extent of past disturbance to the site and the potential for continuing disturbance by development and the tourist antiquities market. First, he realized that the project had to be especially attentive to the local community, both to involve residents in long-term protection and interpretation of the site and to integrate the existing community with the intended development of the site for tourism.

El Castillo was settled gradually during the 1950s and 1960s. When the current archaeological program began there were no homes within the boundaries of the Solar de las Américas national park. There were, however, some twenty domestic structures with associated outbuildings on privately owned lands that were once part of fifteenth-century La Isabela but were not included within the national park boundaries in 1987 (figures 5.3 and 5.4). From the very beginning of the project it was acknowledged that those properties should be purchased by the government in order to provide protection for the archaeological resource.

This concern was inextricably tied to the urgent need for infrastructural improvements in basic life services. El Castillo in 1987 had neither running water nor any local source of fresh water, which had instead to be trucked in or brought to the town on burros. It was very difficult to reach El Castillo by vehicle because of the wretchedly bad condition of the unpaved roads, not to mention flooding during the rainy seasons. The town lacked electricity, running water, postal service, telephone service, public transportation, and law-enforcement and medical services. A large portion of the residents were unemployed. The principal means of subsistence were farming, fishing, and manual labor in surrounding communities when it was available. It was hoped that a concentrated international effort to rehabilitate and develop the site of La Isabela for public interpretation could at the same time bring basic infrastructural improvements in housing, sanitation, health, communications, employment, and transportation to the community.[42]

The residents of El Castillo have been central to the long-term success of conservation and protection efforts at the site, as the local stewards of the area's cultural and natural resources. They are also the primary source of a work force for archaeological excavation and laboratory analyses, construction work, site and museum maintenance and protection, visitor guides, local craft production, food and beverage services, and so forth.

Cruxent took up residence in El Castillo and began programs to train local residents in field and laboratory methods, as tourist guides, and in site maintenance. Given the high unemployment and low wages in the rural Dominican Republic, coupled with the consequent economic temptation to loot and sell artifacts, he found it necessary to become an advocate for social and economic welfare in the town. This included negotiations between the Park Service and the residents of El Castillo who owned property and resided within the confines of the fifteenth-century town but beyond the park boundaries. These continued until 1992, when a new, planned town was built outside the site boundaries, and the residents moved there from their former homes on the site.

Cruxent's second realization provoked by the massive past disturbances and the probable future developments at La Isabela was that only a broad-scale approach, emphasizing the opening of large areas, could recover information that would permit the interpretation of how life was lived in fifteenth-century La Isabela. The very short occupation of the site, coupled with the severe disturbances to the soil deposits after abandonment rendered most traditional approaches to archeological recovery inadequate. The kind of recovery that most archaeologists strive to capture—discrete events, associated deposits, or individual household units—was essentially destroyed and impossible to achieve within the original area of the national park. That did not, however, preclude the possibility of useful and appropriate recovery and analysis on a different and larger scale, in much the same way as variations of scale in North American sites have been cogently assessed by James Deetz.[43]

Very small units of either horizontal or vertical control were unlikely to yield any reliable distinctions in vertical or spatial organization of the site, and they would furthermore impede the efforts at broad areal excavation coverage. Cruxent believed strongly that extensive excavation approaching a total recovery was the only scale of recovery that would permit inference from the severely disturbed deposits and, at the same time, record and recover materials before they were destroyed by development or looting.

With these concerns in mind, Cruxent established a horizontal grid across the site, and a survey team prepared a topographic map. The site was divided into units of eight by eight meters, referred to as *calas*, which were further subdivided into subunits of two by two meters, designated *cuadros*. Excavations in the area of the Solar de las Americas proceeded in arbitrary vertical increments of twenty-five centimeters (apart from encountered features or intrusions), as virtually all traces of the natural stratigraphy had been obliterated. The severe disturbance to the soil deposits also obliterated most evidence for features other than those constructed of stone, such as building foundations. Documentation of the excavation protocols, controls, and methods, as well as a detailed consideration of the site stratigraphy and its problems, can be found in chapter 4 of our *Archaeology* volume.

As we saw earlier, when the project began in 1987 the area of the site

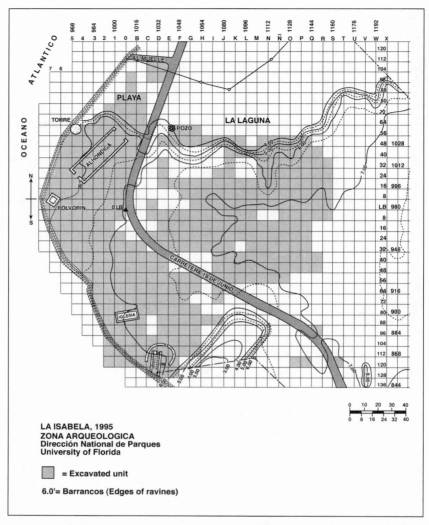

5.5. Archaeological basemap showing locations of excavated areas at La Isabela.

located outside the national park boundaries (that is, the land on the east side of the Carretera 19 de Junio referred to as the Poblado) was occupied by the wood and palm-thatch structures of the town of El Castillo (figures 5.3 and 5.4). This part of the site, although quite disturbed from gardening and construction activities, had apparently not been subjected to the same degree of leveling and grading by heavy equipment as had the area to the west of the Carretera, inside the park boundaries.

The Poblado was first investigated in 1989, when Cruxent and the Dirección Nacional de Parques invited the University of Florida to collaborate in the study of La Isabela. As Cruxent continued his work in the Solar area, the University of Florida team began a systematic subsurface survey of El Castillo in order to define more precisely the limits of the fifteenth-century town, and also to assess the condition and integrity of the deposits. Excavations using five-centimeter excavation increments were subsequently carried out in the Poblado in 1990 and 1991.[44]

Between 1988 and 1994, 434 units of eight by eight meters were excavated at La Isabela (figure 5.5). Nearly one million objects (including noncultural items) were recovered from these units, and all of them were catalogued and analyzed by 1996.[45] The information recovered from the excavations and study of the recovered materials forms the basis for our understanding of life in fifteenth-century La Isabela, which we describe in the chapters ahead.

Chapter 6

The Medieval Enclave:
Landscape, Town, and Buildings

Before embarking on a rescue archaeology program within the park, José Cruxent took steps to define the larger cultural landscape of the settlement. He knew from earlier research trips to the site that that the area occupied and used by the Spaniards was not restricted to El Castillo.

During the 1950s, Cruxent, together with engineer Emile Boyrie de Moya and archaeologist Luis Chanlatte, collected bricks, roof tiles, and pottery at the El Castillo site. They strongly suspected that these had been produced locally, but they were unable to locate any ceramic kilns in the area at the time.

Thirty years later, Cruxent was still interested in learning about the pottery kilns, as they may have produced the tiles and bricks used in the construction of La Isabela's buildings at El Castillo and would therefore have been among the first things established by Columbus. While collecting oral histories from the residents of El Castillo, Cruxent was told by Celestino Torres ("Papalo"), a long-time resident of the area and a park guide then in his sixties, that his mother, already dead for

6.1. Excavations at Tamarindo.

many years, said that there used to be an old "bakery" across the bay at the place known as Las Coles ("the cabbages," presumably because it was a rich agricultural zone).

Cruxent immediately associated the bakery with furnaces (kilns), and he set out to explore Las Coles (see chapter 4, figure 4.2). This area is located about seventeen hundred meters by boat from the site at El Castillo and is a flat plain on the south bank of the Bajabonico River (Río La Isabela). Surface collections and limited tests near the river in an area known today as El Tamarindo revealed quantities of European-style ceramic and tile sherds identical to those known from the Solar de las Américas at El Castillo (figure 6.1). Even more suggestively, he found large sections of clay adobes—clay walls—with a heat-altered, silici-fied interior surface almost certainly associated with firing activities.

During this search, a resident of Las Coles known as Negro Dulce recognized what Cruxent was searching for and showed him another concentration of European materials, some two hundred meters from El Tamarindo. This area is known today as La Breña, and it contained fifteenth-century Spanish domestic ceramics, including some majolica, although the density of materials was much sparser than at El Tama-rindo.

There seemed little doubt that some kind of European settlement from the late fifteenth century was located at Las Coles, contemporary with the site at El Castillo. This settlement was completely unknown to historians or archaeologists before 1989, and it significantly alters our assessments of Columbus's colonizing strategy for La Isabela. As we saw in chapter 4, the settlement(s) at Las Coles may explain the confusion engendered over the past five centuries by Dr. Chanca's comment that "nearby there is one main river, and another of reasonable size, not far off, with very remarkable water. On the bank of one a city, Marta, is being built." It has long been assumed that Chanca was confused or mistaken, but it now appears possible that he was in fact speaking of the settlement at Las Coles.

The Las Coles site (Ciudad Marta?) is ideally situated for access to the Bajabonico River and to alluvial clays and fuel. It is also in an area of rich agricultural soils. Cruxent contends that this was the original point of disembarkation for the seventeen ships in Columbus's fleet, and the first installation at La Isabela. It potentially had a protective shelter for the ships a short distance in from the mouth of the Bajabonico, where there is also convenient access to the banks of the river for easy unloading of livestock and goods. Cruxent reasons that the immediate access to fresh water provided by the site (which was not available at the "well-situated rock") would have been essential to the exhausted members of the expedition. It is alternatively possible that the Las Coles settlement served either as the initial campsite while the fortified city was being constructed or as a service settlement for artisanal, industrial, and agricultural activities in support of the fortified center at El Castillo.

Subsequent excavations at Las Coles recovered Spanish materials from both El Tamarindo and La Breña, although identification of archaeological features was almost impossible because of the tunnels made by the enormous population of burrowing land crabs in the area, exacerbated by holes made subsequently by the *cangrejeros* who gather the crabs for food.[1] At El Tamarindo, however, excavations uncovered the remains of a fifteenth-century pottery kiln, the first European craft installation in the Americas (figure 6.2).[2] There is also both archaeological and documentary evidence that Columbus established water wheels in the vicinity of Las Coles (figure 6.3). These could have provided energy for a variety of industrial tasks, such as grinding, milling, crushing minerals, or driving bellows.

The remains from Las Coles may indeed solve the mystery of Ciu-

6.2. Excavation of the kiln at Las Coles.

dad Marta, although the archaeological materials do not support the notion of a large settlement. Much sparser than those from El Castillo, they reflect a more limited range of activities, related primarily to craft and agricultural activities, and a small area of domestic occupation.

Another important physical component of the La Isabela colony was the stone quarry. This was a large outcropping of limestone, located about two hundred meters south along the coastline from the El Castillo site, where the masonry buildings were constructed (figure 6.4; see also figure 4.2). Dressed blocks and saw marks are still evident in parts of the quarry. Its location near a small estuary of the Bajabonico suggests that the stones may have been transported to the town site by water, particularly given the virtual absence of draft animals in the early days of the town, mentioned in chapter 4.

The discoveries made during the surveys around the Bay of La Isabela revealed the true extent of Columbus's conception of colony, which recognized and incorporated the natural resources and geographic configurations of the entire bay. Columbus's settlement strategy incorporated not only the fortified site on the "well-situated rock" (already known to modern researchers) but also a second, satellite community in the river drainage area to take advantage of clays, water, and fuel. Water engines were also located in this area to exploit the river as

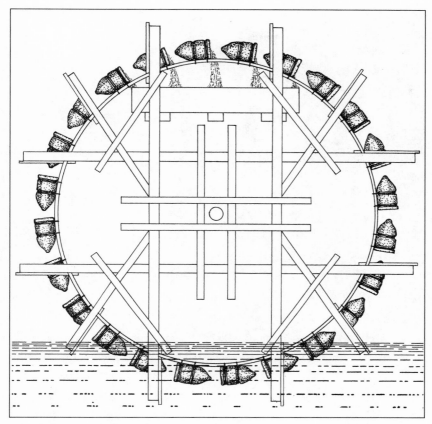

6.3. Noria de Vuelo, the Islamic-style waterwheel with ceramic cups known as arcaduzes or canjelones. This example is probably similar to the waterwheels used at Las Coles. (After Lister and Lister 1987:22. Courtesy of the University of Arizona Press.)

a source of energy. The stone quarry located between the two settlements provided building materials and a source of lime, and the river could be used to transport stone to the fortified town.

This new information considerably alters the traditional view (based only on the site at El Castillo) that Columbus made a misguided and poorly informed choice of site that led ultimately to the colony's demise. We suggest instead that Columbus recognized the riverine and soil resources of the region and decided to create a colony comprised of multiple locations that together met the needs no single site provided.

With this context established, archaeological attention was concentrated on the site at El Castillo, which was not only Columbus's prin-

6.4. Stone quarry near La Isabela.

cipal settlement but also the intended focus for development. Columbus planned to establish a town that would become the capital of Spain's (and his) American colony, and this was clearly expressed in the ways the Spaniards organized their physical landscape and living space. No contemporary maps or drawings of the site have survived (if they were ever made), and the eyewitness descriptions of the town and its buildings are contradictory and vague. Thus, the fundamental spatial organization of Spanish life at La Isabela has been recovered almost exclusively through archaeology.

As the first European "urban" enclave in America, El Castillo–La Isabela has been profoundly interesting to European and American scholars of Ibero-American urban planning. Apart from the important insights into Columbus's settlement strategy that the physical organization of La Isabela reveals, the town also provides new information about the imposition of the urban rectilinear grid plan on the American landscape.

La Isabela was founded at a time of great innovation and change in European urban planning, attributed by scholars both to emerging Renaissance sensibilities of the late fifteenth century, and to dramatic changes in the organization of defense provoked by the increasing dominance of firearms and artillery.[3] Established medieval cities in Europe (including those of Spain and Italy) are generally characterized as serving the needs of the community as an organic whole. Many of these cities were originally established as Roman colonial towns laid out in a grid pattern, but after the Roman period they grew informally and unself-consciously in response to community—usually commercial—needs. The plans of such cities reflected concern with the corporate everyday life of the parish, and they were organized around communal entities, such as churches, guilds, and markets. Lewis Mumford cast the medieval city as having "small numbers, small structures, intimate relationships," and "a short-range view, with its walking distances, its closed vistas, its patchwork spaces."[4]

During the fifteenth century, however (and particularly in Italy), the intimate, organic medieval perspective of Europe's cities began to give way to a new Renaissance order based on the "long-range world of baroque politics with its wheeled vehicle and its increasing desire to conquer and make itself felt at the other side of the world." Principles of order, symmetry, formality, and humanism came to dominate the physical and social organization of life, and many researchers have characterized the grid plan found so widely in Spanish-American towns as a very visible extension of these Renaissance principles to the Americas.[6] Various other authors have attributed the precedents and origins of the American grid-plan town to classical Roman and Greek influence in general and the Roman *castrum* in particular, to the requirements of military encampments in general, to the grid-plan towns of Puerto Real and Santa Fe de Granada established in Spain by Ferdinand and Isabella, and occasionally to the influence of pre-Hispanic Native-American urban planning.[7]

We should note, however, that not all medieval towns in Europe were spontaneous and organic in their form. Nor were all Renaissance towns established on a grid plan. From the twelfth century onward, the rulers of Spain, France, England, Germany, and Italy established new towns on their frontiers that served to occupy and secure new territories and provide a seat for agricultural production. A town of this kind is generally termed a *bastide* or, in Italy, a *terranuova*.[8] Although they varied in their sizes and purposes, all of these towns shared three characteristics: they were new urban foundations established with a predetermined form; they were laid out using a rectilinear gridiron plan; and the main inducement to settle in them was the grant of a house plot within the town and farmland outside the town. The bastides were essentially frontier towns intentionally settled with specific economic and defensive purposes, not unlike the towns of Spanish America. Mumford in fact points to these planned frontier settlements of the Middle Ages as the model for Spanish-American town plans, arguing (in contrast to nearly all other students of the question) that in the New World "the medieval order renewed itself, as it were, by colonization."[9]

Although the grid-plan town became the standard for sixteenth-century Spanish-American colonization, it was not the only Renaissance model available in Europe. During the second half of the fifteenth century, a number of Italian architects, such as Francesco di Giorgio Martini, León Battista Alberti, and Antonio Filarete, developed and wrote theoretical treatises on the "ideal city," addressing both city plans and architecture. This work was deeply influenced by the rediscovery of Vitruvius's *De architectura* in the early years of the fifteenth century, in which Vitruvius emphasized symmetry and proportion and conceptualized the city as a self-conscious stage for human action. He also proposed arranging a city's streets in a radial fashion according to the eight dominant winds, which offered the added military advantage of providing direct lines of communication from the periphery to the center. Italian architectural treatises and city plans implemented during the late fifteenth century drew on these ideas to combine elements of the radial city with elements of the grid plan.[10]

Francesco di Giorgio Martini (after whose designs Martinian military architecture is named) was particularly influential in Italy during the second half of the fifteenth century. His *Trattati* were written and published shortly before 1474, and he is known as one of the first Renaissance architects "who became the practical executors of Renaissance rulers' political aspirations through the construction of cities and fortresses. . . . The main piazza was the city's articulating element and is surrounded by the cathedral, civic buildings and public facilities. Provision is made for commerce and industry while the main fortress provides the base from which the duke or prince can rule—a place of safety for the ruler and the focus of control for the town."[11] This was done by Martini with a practical eye to terrain and specific attention to site, asserting that each geographical configuration required distinctive planning solutions for economy and defense.

Martini and his contemporaries developed and implemented the first town plans consciously to combine symbols of authority with defensive fortifications that could ensure both external protection and internal control. In fifteenth-century Italy, these precepts provided the design and structure necessary for securing the early modern capitalist state. In fifteenth-century America, they could potentially provide a design and structure for securing the first New World colony.

There is good reason to believe that Columbus was familiar with these ideas. Although self-educated, he was well read in geography, philosophy, and history. He devoted much of the period between 1485 and 1492 to reading and study, writing that "in this time I devoted myself to the study of books of cosmography, history, chronicle, philosophy, and other sciences."[12] Columbus owned a number of volumes (today held in the Biblioteca Colombina in Seville), and he is thought to have been a bookseller himself in 1487 and 1488. Most of these books were imported from Italy or Germany, as few books were being printed in Spain at that time and the Spanish Crown offered lucrative tax incentives to encourage the import of books and manuscripts.

By the time La Isabela was founded, Columbus was undoubtedly familiar with both grid-plan and radial forms of settlement design, as well as with the communal, organic, and self-regulated medieval plan. It has been argued by some scholars that Columbus's stay at Santa Fe de Granada in 1492 and 1493 during the time it was being laid out as a grid-plan town probably influenced him to establish La Isabela on the same rectilineal plan.[13] The fragments of La Isabela's organization revealed on the ground by archaeology, however, share more features with the precepts of the Italian Martini school than they do with any of the other contemporary possibilities (particularly in its attention to site topography and defense), and they suggest that Columbus may indeed have been influenced by that new school of thought.

Many of the factors that motivated European town planning in the late fifteenth century obviously did not pertain at La Isabela. The primary enclave was laid out on a landscape that had not experienced major and permanent physical alteration through human construction, other, perhaps, than the cleared fields and conucos of the Taíno farmers. There were therefore no pre-existing urban features to constrain the town plan. Furthermore, La Isabela was the only European town in the hemisphere, with no roads to or from it and separated from the nearest similar settlement by thousands of miles of water. It was dedicated to the very specific activities of the trading factoría, military occupation, and, to some extent, religious conversion. The settlers were salaried employees of the Crown, and thus no internal market or guild organization was anticipated. The town's defenses were designed to repel enemies who had no firearms or metal weapons.

Fifteenth-century descriptions of La Isabela tend to suggest that the town was, in fact, formally laid out on a regular plan. Guillermo Coma records that "they have done the houses, and are constructing the protective walls, which adorn the city and give secure refuge to its inhabitants. A wide street like a straight cord divides the city in two parts, this street is cut transversally by many other streets to the coast [cortada . . . por otras muchas costaneras]. At the beach a magnificent castillo is being raised, with a high defense [elevada fortaleza]." Las Casas reports that Columbus "hastened to proceed to the building of a fort to guard their provisions and ammunition, of a church, a hospital and a sturdy house for himself; he distributed land plots, traced a common square and streets; the important people grouped together in a section of the planned township and everyone was told to start building his own house. Public buildings were made of stone, individuals used wood and straw for theirs."[14]

These descriptions have led most researchers to conclude that the town was the first example of the classic Hispano-American grid town.[15] The archaeological evidence disputes this. There is no indication in the shape of the town, the alignment of structures, or the distribution of remains that a regular rectilinear pattern was imposed. On the contrary, the orientations of the principal buildings suggest that few if any of the town's elements shared even the same cardinal declinations (figure 6.5). The unifying element in the layout of the town is instead a conformance to the geographical features of ravines and sea. The town itself, as indicated by the distribution of archaeological remains, is in the form of an irregular parallelogram bounded by these geographical features (figure 6.6). It extended some 150 meters east to west and between 190 meters (along the west shoreline) and 105 meters (along the eastern end) north to south, encompassing approximately 15,025 square meters (1.5 hectares).

The attention to geographic features as a defining factor in the layout of La Isabela was undoubtedly related to defensive considerations. Columbus's own accounts make it clear that one of his first concerns was to construct a defense wall around the town. With the memory of

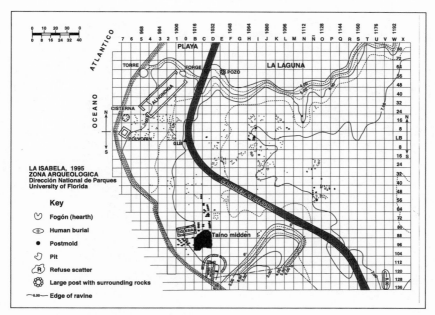

6.5. Archaeological basemap showing major features and excavated units at La Isabela.

La Navidad still fresh, he was concerned that "one Indian with a burning faggot could bring about [the loss of people and supplies], setting fire to the huts." He wrote in February 1493 that "with those few healthy that remain here, every day is employed in enclosing the settlement and putting it in some posture of defense and the supplies in a secure position. This will be done in a few days, as there need be nothing but dry walls."[16] Guillermo Coma characteristically embellished Columbus's account, writing that "they have done the houses, and are constructing the protective walls, which adorn the city and give secure refuge to its inhabitants."[17]

Both documentary accounts and the archaeological evidence show that the town walls were not of stone but of packed earth, or *tapia*. No remnants of the wall itself survived into the twentieth century, owing both to the very perishable nature of earthen construction under tropical conditions and to the many modern disturbances to La Isabela discussed in chapter 5. We can nevertheless suggest with some confidence where the defense wall was probably located, by correlating surviving archaeological features with the map made by Colvocoresses during his 1891 visit. The horizontal distribution of buried fifteenth-century arti-

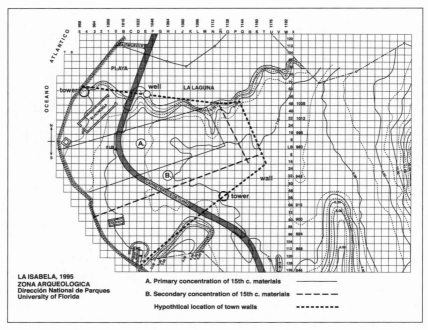

6.6. Hypothesized boundaries of the town and major concentrations of remains.

facts also corresponds quite closely to the suggested position for the wall.[18]

Like the town walls, La Isabela's principal public buildings also conformed to the immediate topography of the rocky shelf on which the site was located. The alhóndiga—the customhouse and storehouse—for example, was oriented to command both the cliff on the west and the beach access to the north at the northwest corner of the rocky promontory. The *polvorín*—munitions magazine—slightly to the south was constructed with its long walls roughly parallel to the cliff. At the southwest corner of the site the Casa de Colón was situated to command the cliff and bay to the west and the mouth of the Bajabonico to the southwest. The only structure that was not oriented according to topography was the church, which has an alignment running approximately east to west, consistent with Catholic liturgical precepts of both the medieval and the early modern periods.[19]

The area enclosed and defended by the town walls defined the space in which most of La Isabela's public and private life was played out. The internal organization of La Isabela is more difficult to reconstruct, as no remnants of roads or paths were found during excavation, and only a few above-ground elements remain to indicate where various kinds of community activities took place. We can, however, suggest possible locations for areas of general activity within the town by correlating the distribution of buried remains with documentary accounts.

Guillermo Coma (who was prone to enthusiastic exaggeration) asserted that "a wide street like a straight cord divides the city in two parts, this street is cut transversally by many other coastward streets [*cortada . . . por otras muchas costaneras*].[20] If this can be believed, we might speculate that the wide street divided the town into eastern and western sections in much the way that the site is divided today by the Carretera 19 de Junio, with the public and elite sector to the west (along the shore) and the residential zone (the Poblado) to the east. If streets extended from east to west from the residential Poblado to the seafront, the town would have had the form of a wedge, or section of a radial plan.

As usual, the best clues to where more specific community functions and activities took place come from the distribution of buried remains, particularly when they are correlated with documentary accounts, topographic features, and historical information about spatial patterns in fifteenth-century Spanish towns. Figure 6.6 shows the suggested sectors of fifteenth-century La Isabela as inferred from these sources.[21]

All of the available documentary and archaeological evidence suggests overwhelmingly that perceived notions of social status conditioned the spatial organization of daily life in the town, just as it conditioned nearly all kinds of social and material experience there. Public, military, and domestic spaces were separate and distinct from each other, and the residential domestic areas were apparently segregated according to the status of their occupants—hidalgos and caballeros versus commoners. As in most Spanish towns of the period, high-status residences were located closer to the center of town as defined by the church, plaza, and public buildings. In the case of La Isabela, these were along the center of the rocky promontory. The church, with its cemetery to the east and the plaza on the north side, was clearly a focal point for community life. The fortified house of Columbus marked the southern end of the town, some twenty-five meters to the south of the church, and there may have been an open area between the church and the admiral's house. The principal plaza itself (indicated by a marked absence of either features or subsurface artifacts) was immediately to the north of the church, and it appears to have been about thirty meters

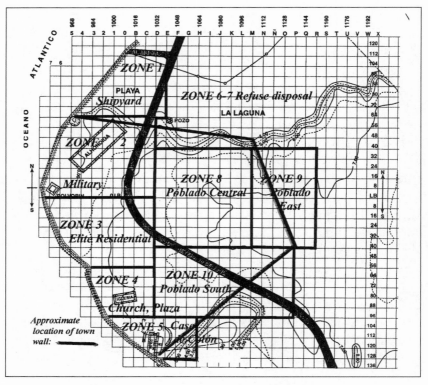

6.7. Functional or spatial zones assigned within La Isabela.

wide from north to south. The plaza was bordered on its north side by a dense concentration of artifacts normally associated with elite residences, and we infer that this area was the residential sector for elite members of the colony. The military sector and the storehouse dominated the north end of the site along the waterfront, and the shipyard seems to have been in the estuarine ravine that formed the northern boundary of the town.

The entire area to the east of these public and elite areas appears to have been devoted to domestic occupation in bohíos, and this is probably where most of the expedition members lived. Within this general arrangement, we have somewhat arbitrarily designated nine spatial subzones within the town in order to develop an analytical framework for assessing the ways in which both public and domestic life at La Isabela were organized—and varied—spatially. These subzones are shown in figure 6.7, and they are discussed in more detail in chapter 5 of our *Archaeology* volume.

La Isabela's Buildings

We recall Las Casas saying that Columbus "hastened to proceed to the building of a fort to guard their provisions and ammunition, of a church, a hospital and a sturdy house for himself; public buildings were made of stone, individuals used wood and straw for theirs."[22] Columbus, having spent most of his life at sea, was not a builder of houses. He did, however, bring with him to La Isabela masons, carpenters, and others in the building trades. The structures they built there reflect the traditions and techniques with which they were familiar. These derived largely from fifteenth-century Andalusia, with its blend of Roman, Iberian, and Muslim influences, but were obviously influenced by local materials.

La Isabela's buildings are the only surviving remnants of fifteenth-century European architecture in the Americas. Outlines remain only for the five masonry structures at the site, which include the alhóndiga (customhouse and storehouse), the *iglesia* (church), the Casa de Colón (the house of Columbus), the polvorín (powderhouse), and a *torre* (watchtower). Of these, the house of Columbus is the best preserved and most informative.

Except for the metal hardware and fasteners used for construction, the Spaniards at La Isabela used locally available materials in their buildings. Limestone, earth, clay, tropical woods, and palm leaves were worked with European tools and techniques into forms familiar to the colonists. The presence of stone was one of the principal advantages of the site of La Isabela in Columbus's opinion; "at fifty paces [*pasos*] there is a mountain of quarrying stone [*cantería*], better than that of which the church of Santa María in Seville is built." This was not simply fortuitous. Las Casas reports that Columbus was mindful of the availability of stone during his first voyage to this area, recording the stone outcrops at Monte Christi: "He saw there many colored stones of various shades, or a quarry of such stones, naturally shaped, very lovely, he says, for church buildings or for other royal works."[23] Stonemasons were specifically included in the second expedition, and Columbus clearly intended to build substantial permanent stone buildings in his first town.

Various statements by Columbus and other chroniclers led to the conventional assumption that La Isabela's principal buildings were in fact built entirely of stone. Excavation of these buildings, however, has shown that their longitudinal walls were instead made of reinforced rammed

6.8. Segment of a massive wall built of tapia and faced with brick at El Alcazar, Seville.

earth (tapia), with the foundations and short walls made of stone. Remnants of the tapia walls have only survived in one of the buildings—the Casa de Colón—and there only because the tractor drivers did not grade that corner of the site, which was eroding into the sea.

Tapia is made from rammed earth shaped by forms, a technique known as *pisé* in French-influenced areas, tapia in the Spanish-speaking world, *tabya* in Islamic countries, and *cobwork* in English. Tapia was used widely in the vernacular housing of medieval France, Spain, and North Africa, and earth was said to have been the most common building material in fifteenth-century Córdoba and Seville. It was also the standard construction method in many Muslim countries after A.D. 1200, particularly for military structures. The city walls of Carmona, near Seville, were built of tapia to a height of between ten and twelve meters, and an example of monumental tapia construction in Seville is shown in figure 6.8.[24]

The facades of La Isabela's tapia buildings appear to have been constructed of cut stone, quarried nearby and brought to the site by water.

6.9. Tejas from the Columbus house excavations.

With the exception of the stone portal in the Casa de Colón, none of the dressed stone has been found in situ, although numerous examples of skillfully worked stones have been recovered from the vicinity of the Casa de Colón and elsewhere on the site, reflecting the work of the masons who accompanied Columbus.[25]

At least three of the principal buildings were roofed with *tejas*, the curved roof tiles ubiquitous throughout Andalusia (also known in English as barrel tile). Hundreds of thousands of fragments from these tejas were excavated at the site (figure 6.9), and a large proportion of the tejas, if not all of them, were produced at the kiln(s) of Las Coles.

The Spanish tile makers at Las Coles probably also produced the flat rectangular bricks known as *ladrillos*, which are widespread throughout Spain and were the most common method of Spanish construction in stone-poor areas of sixteenth-century Hispaniola. They are relatively uncommon at La Isabela, however, and are thought to have been used as finishing and trim elements, rather than in wall or floor construction.

Masonry work in both stone and tapia requires the use of mortar and plaster. The region immediately around La Isabela abounds in raw materials for making lime from both limestone and marine shell, and the Spanish builders took advantage of this. The surviving tapia wall remnants were plastered inside and out, and both the Casa de Colón and the iglesia may have had floors made of lime mortar with aggregate.

6.10. Hand-wrought fasteners from La Isabela.

Although no lime kilns or lime-burning pits have been located in the vicinity of the site, there was clearly an abundant supply of reduced lime at La Isabela, no doubt produced nearby.

The only architectural elements either imported from Spain or produced at La Isabela from imported materials were construction fasteners and hardware (figure 6.10). More than four thousand nail and spike fragments were excavated at La Isabela, along with more than 150 whole fasteners. These were used to fasten framing elements and wooden walls in buildings, as well as in a variety of finishing and casing tasks.[26]

Casa de Colón

Guillermo Coma wrote from La Isabela to his friend Nicolò Syllacio that "the Admiral's residence is called the royal palace, for, at some future time if God . . . wills it, the sovereigns may set out from Cádiz to visit this well favored land . . . won for them so far from home."[27]

Despite the fact that its western end has eroded into the bay, the best-preserved building at La Isabela, and the only one with intact remnants of above-ground walls is the Casa de Colón. The foundations are identified as the Columbus house because they conform to documentary de-

6.11. The Columbus house foundations and wall remnants.

scription of that structure and by process of elimination could not be any of the other masonry buildings known to have been at the site.

The house built by Columbus for his own residence was referred to variously by the chroniclers as a *palacio*, a *casa fuerte*, and a *castillo*. These terms all describe a category of fortified structure found commonly in fifteenth-century Spanish cities that served as symbols of authority and control, functioned to defend the city or lord, and also housed noble personages. Similar structures were incorporated into the early Renaissance Italian town plans discussed in the preceding chapter as a place of safety for the ruler and the focus of control and defense of the town.[28] The Casa de Colón was clearly intended to perform these functions.

The house was sited with great skill, providing spectacular views of the bay, Las Coles, and the Bajabonico River, as well as strong, fresh breezes at virtually all hours of the day. Columbus's house is still well-known in the community today as the coolest respite from the tropical heat. It was a simple rectangular structure designed to command the bay and its traffic, and it apparently also served as the southwestern corner anchor of the overall town defenses (figure 6.11). The corners of the house and the tower met at angles slightly offset from 90 degrees, giving it a somewhat irregular shape. Its principal room was 5.5 meters wide and somewhat more than twelve meters long, and it was floored with a cementlike plaster. The possibility of another separate room is suggested at the southwest corner of the house where it erodes into the bay.

6.12. Ceramic gozne (door pivot) being uncovered at the west end of the Columbus house south wall.

A small watchtower was located at the northeast corner of the house, represented archaeologically by a stone rubble and tapia foundation. Its small dimensions—2.9 by 1.25 meters—implies that it was a solid structure of tapia with the top serving as a watchtower platform, rather than a tower with interior rooms. There was no archaeological evidence for steps or stairs near the tower, suggesting that the top was reached by ladder or wooden steps.

The Columbus house has three surviving doorways, including the main entrance with its stone portal in situ in the east facade, and smaller accesses on the north and south sides of the building. A fourth doorway is indicated by a ceramic door pivot, or *gozne*, in the southwest corner of the building at the point where the south wall erodes into the sea (figure 6.12). All of the doors gave access to a patio or courtyard enclosed by a surrounding defense wall.

This roughly circular defensive wall enclosed the house and tower on its north, south, and east sides, describing an area of some eighteen meters in diameter. There is only one opening in the wall foundation, positioned directly opposite the main entrance to the Columbus house, and it is thought to have been the gate. The gate had a wooden door, indicated by two ceramic goznes found near the break in the wall.[29]

6.13. Conjectural reconstruction of the Columbus house. (Painting by Arthur Shilstone. Courtesy of *National Geographic* magazine.)

The house-tower-wall complex could be used as a citadel and retreat from attack, as it was during the Roldán rebellion of 1497, when Diego Colón and his few loyal men retreated into the house and remained there while Roldán had the run of the town.[30] This feature was integral to the plans for early Renaissance towns, as embodied by di Giorgio Martini and others.[31]

Although small for a palace, the single remaining room of some seventy-two square meters is quite large for a house of the period. In fifteenth-century Granada and Córdoba, for example, houses of less than fifty square meters were the most common size. Houses at the Portuguese-occupied town of Qsar es-Seghir in Morocco of the same period as La Isabela averaged from three to six rooms, and occupied some sixty square meters.[32]

While the Columbus house was a protected, elite structure set off from the rest of the town, the church was central to the life of the community. Church construction was an urgent priority in the founding of La Isabela, not only because of the deep religiousness of Columbus and many of the expedition members but also no doubt at the urg-

6.14. Church foundations, La Isabela.

ing of the often ill-tempered Father Buil. It is perhaps owing to this haste that the church of La Isabela is the least prepossessing of all the masonry structures in the town. As Peter Martyr D'Anghiera noted, "Once he had raised in a brief period, according to what the pressures of time allowed, some houses and a chapel, the holy mass was sung by three priests together, on the day on which we celebrate the feast of the three Kings according to our custom, as much as it could be done in another world, so far and so alien to all culture and religion."[33]

The iglesia did not escape the tractor blades of either the 1940s or the 1960s, which removed any remaining wall remnants and interior deposits above the floor level and apparently created disturbances that extended in places below the floor level. The stone foundations, however, survived largely intact (figure 6.14).

The church was quite small even by frontier standards, measuring fifteen by six meters, with about ninety square meters of interior space. The church at Puerto Real, Hispaniola, built in about 1504, in contrast, had 189 square meters of interior space (although only 140 square meters were thought to be the church proper), while the wood-and-thatch frontier mission churches of Spanish Florida averaged two hundred square meters of interior space.[34] The church at La Isabela was furthermore the only masonry building in the town that did not have a tiled roof, possibly because it was built in haste before the tile kilns at Las

Coles were in operation. The roof was instead made of thatch or wood, or possibly of plaster.[35] More substantial construction and adornment may have been planned, but the circumstances that developed at La Isabela undoubtedly dampened any enthusiasm for improvement or embellishment of the town's buildings.

Its form is that of a simple, single-naved, monastic-style church with a bell tower, *campanario*, on one side, a pattern that was to become standard throughout the Spanish frontier mission territories of the sixteenth century.[36] Prior to the edicts of the Council of Trent (1545–1563), these churches were oriented from east to west, with the altar and sanctuary at the east end and the principal door and choir loft, or *coro*, at the west.[37] The church at La Isabela conforms to this pattern. It differs from contemporary Spanish churches in the absence of graves inside the church, possibly because of insufficient soil depth—less than a meter—over the underlying bedrock at La Isabela. Graves were instead placed to the east and south of the church.

The iglesia's short east and west facades were apparently constructed of cut stone, which may have wrapped slightly around the church corners. The long walls, like those of the other buildings at the site, were made of tapia. The principal entry was located in the western wall opposite the sacristy, and a secondary doorway is thought to have been located in both the north and south walls. The stone foundation for what is interpreted as the bell tower was located near the center of the north wall. Its small size and traces of tapia among the stones of the foundation indicate that, like the watchtower of the Casa de Colón, this was a solid tapia structure.

The inside of the church was floored with a thick layer of lime mortar, which only survived in badly broken fragments. No fragments, however, were found in the eastern three meters of the structure, suggesting that this may have been the area of the altar and sacristy. The sacristy, in keeping with liturgical tradition, may have been raised and floored with some other material, such as brick, wood, or stone, that has not survived.

No examples of ornamental tiles or stone sculpture were found in direct association with the church, but it is nearly unthinkable that the deep religiousness of the Spaniards would have permitted a complete neglect of ornamentation for their place of worship. A single fragment of molded and painted plaster from the church excavation may provide a clue to its interior decoration (figure 6.15).

6.15. Carved and painted plaster from the church site. Blue and green paint, 4.7 by 2.5 centimeters; thickness: 11 millimeters.

To the extent that the beleaguered masons at La Isabela were able to create ornamental stonework, it seems most likely to have been in the church (Columbus, we recall, had identified the most attractive stone he saw during the first voyage as particularly appropriate for church buildings). Although none of the dressed stones from the church's east and west facades has survived in situ, a stone taken from the iglesia by Bartolomé de Las Casas in 1526 is preserved in Puerto Plata.[38] The original provenience of other stones thought to be from La Isabela (including a slender column base and the keystone of an arch) is not known, but they represent elements that could have been incorporated into the church.

A badly weathered and crudely anthropomorphic limestone figure, eroded but clearly sculptural, was recovered in the vicinity of the iglesia and tentatively identified by Cruxent as a gargoyle. The figure is quite similar to a gargoyle recovered at the sixteenth-century site of Nueva Cádiz in Venezuela.[39]

Local tradition asserts that the bell from the church at La Isabela— a gift to the town from Queen Isabela, brought to the colony by Columbus—was taken to Concepción de la Vega (the second town established by Columbus, in 1495 and 1496) when La Isabela was abandoned. It hung there in the cathedral tower until Concepción was destroyed by an earthquake in 1562, and the bell remained encased in the ruins until the

6.16. Bell thought to have been taken from La Isabela to Concepción de la Vega during the late fifteenth century. (From Ober 1893:327.)

nineteenth century. It was revealed again (miraculously, in local opinion) by the growth of a tree, "which had entered the belfry, and emerged with the long-hidden bell in its ligneous arms, bringing it to the light of day after a lapse of at least three centuries."[40] The bell was taken to Santo Domingo, and in 1891 it was loaned to the United States Columbian World Exposition. It returned to the Dominican Republic after the exposition and resides today in the modern cathedral of La Vega (figure 6.16).

The largest and most impressive building at La Isabela was the king's storehouse, or alhóndiga, a medieval term used to describe a combination of warehouse, grain exchange, and customs building. Ferdinand and Isabela had ordered that "immediately upon arrival, God willing, the said Admiral and Viceroy will provide for the erection of a customs house for the storage of all the merchandise of Their Highnesses, including the merchandise to be sent from here [Spain], and that to be collected for return shipment."[41]

The alhóndiga served as the storage place for both imported supplies and locally produced goods bound for Spain. As such, it was the economic center of the factoría. The building commanded the beach and dock area at the north end of the town. In fifteenth-century Spain the alhóndiga also sometimes served as a meeting place, a market, and a place for the control of weights and measures.[42]

It was the symbol of royal presence and authority at La Isabela, and as such was apparently fortified. Las Casas wrote that Columbus "hastened to proceed to the building of a fort to guard their provisions and ammunition," and Guillermo Coma (as recorded by his friend Syllacio) observed that "high up on the shore stands a mighty fortress with lofty battlements."[43] The alhóndiga's defenses were possibly intended to provide security as much against the discontented Spaniards as against the Indians. We remember that it figured largely in Francisco de Roldán's mutiny against Columbus. Las Casas noted that Roldán "returned to Isabela, going to the granary of the King where the food supplies, weaponry and ammunition were stored and, taking the key by force from a client of Diego Colón who had it, or else by cutting the locks to pieces, he went in with fifty men, shouting 'Viva el Rey,' and took all the weapons he needed for himself and his companions in crime."[44]

Of all La Isabela's buildings, the alhóndiga has suffered the greatest damage over the years. Remnants of its pillars or columns were still standing at the end of the nineteenth century, but by the 1930s any aboveground traces of the structure's walls, floor columns, or stonework were gone. Even the foundation itself has been disturbed, graded, and, in places, partially removed by the activities we outlined in chapter 5.

For many years the alhóndiga remains were identified as those of the church, both because of the columns and the assumption that the largest and most impressive structure would naturally be that dedicated to God. It was with this assumption that the Junta para la Celebración del Centenario sponsored excavations at the alhóndiga in 1892. They recorded that the walls were of "mud," half a foot high, and some two meters thick (undoubtedly slumped and widened tapia). There was a doorway in the west wall, and opposite it the group found four column bases.

Like the Casa de Colón and the iglesia, the alhóndiga is slightly ir-

6.17. Aerial view of the alhóndiga during excavation.

6.18. Alhóndiga foundations after consolidation by the Agencia Española de Cooperación Internacional in 1993. The square structures in the center surround the stone pillar bases that supported the alhóndiga roof.

6.19. Base of an alhóndiga pillar.

regular in its dimensions. The long walls on the east and west are somewhat more than forty-eight meters long, and the short north and south
walls somewhat more than thirteen meters (figures 6.17 and 6.18). The
long walls of the alhóndiga, like those of the Casa de Colón and the
iglesia, were constructed of tapia. The alhóndiga's huge size and the
consequent weight of its roof, however, required wall foundations considerably deeper than those of any of the other buildings at the site, as
well as interior supports. The interior of the immense building contained the bases for sixteen stone pillars or columns, each about seventy
centimeters square (figure 6.19). These were arranged in two rows, four
meters apart, along the north-south length of the alhóndiga. The
columns divided the interior space into three north-south "corridors,"
each four meters wide, and the configuration of walls and pillars divided the interior of the alhóndiga into twenty-four square units of approximately four by four meters each.

Entrances to the building appear to have been located in the western
(seaward) and southern walls. The north end of the structure may have
been partially open and supported by arches, opening onto an area
where metallurgical activities and a forge were located.[45]

The deep disturbances to the alhóndiga structure left no remnants of
either floor or wall fabric, and we can therefore only speculate about the
interior surfaces. It is possible that the same lime-mortar surfacing

6.20. The tower foundation.

found in the other masonry structures was used here as well, but it is more likely that the alhóndiga had a wooden floor. This is suggested by the fact that 65 percent of all the headless and L-shaped nails from the site—those most likely to have been used in flooring—came from the alhóndiga. Headless and L-shaped nails were the majority of nails in the alhondiga, in dramatically higher proportion than anywhere else on the site.[46] A wooden floor would also have insulated the expedition's supplies against moisture from the ground.

The alhóndiga's roof is less open to speculation. The densest concentration of tejas at La Isabela occurred in the vicinity of the storehouse, and there is no doubt that it was roofed with these tiles. The interior pillars were no doubt needed to help support the roof, which would have covered some eight hundred square meters. More than twenty thousand tejas would have been required to cover the roof, and these would have weighed somewhat more than forty-seven thousand kilograms (105,000 pounds, or 52.5 tons).

The stone base of a circular tower is located slightly northwest of the alhóndiga and may have been related to a tower shown in that position on the Colvocoresses map (figure 6.20; see also chapter 5, figure 5.1). We believe that this tower may have been the only structure at La Isabela constructed entirely of stone masonry, and it is certainly the only remnant of the town's encircling defenses. The tower was described

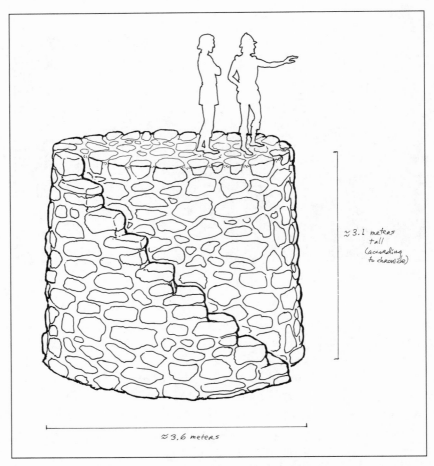

Annotations on the drawing:
≈ 3.1 meters tall (according to chronicle)

≈ 3.6 meters

6.21. Conjectural reconstruction of the La Isabela watchtower. (Drawing: Merald Clark.)

by William Gibbs when he visited the site in 1846 as "a small tower with battlements." Stanley Heneken provided additional detail the following year: "The small fortress [the alhóndiga] is also a prominent ruin, and a little north of it is a circular pillar about ten feet high and as much in diameter, of solid masonry nearly entire; which appears to have had a wooden gallery of battlement around the top for convenience of a room."[47]

The diameter of the tower foundation is approximately four meters, and about forty-seven centimeters of its base remain above the level of the bedrock. It is made of dry-laid stones in a stepped spiral configu-

6.22. The foundations of the polvorín (powder house).

ration, suggesting the possibility of an exterior stone stairway or ramp. If the nineteenth-century descriptions are accurate, it was made of solid masonry, with a battlemented room on the top. Figure 6.21 shows a conjectural reconstruction of the tower.

Several other features, including a powderhouse (polvorín), a cistern and drain, and what may have been a raised walkway *(calzado)*, were also part of the military complex at the north end of the town. The stone foundations of the small structure (roughly five by seven meters) thought to have been the polvorín is located about twenty-four meters south of the alhóndiga (figure 6.22). It appears to have been connected to the alhóndiga by a delimited concentration of small uncut rocks describing the base of a curving pathway or wall (also seen in figure 6.22). This latter feature was interpreted by Cruxent during his excavation to have been a calzado that provided a well-drained walkway between the two buildings.

The polvorín consisted of a single, thick-walled room with a doorway on the north wall opening onto the calzado. Instead of having a wall-foundation width of sixty centimeters that was standard in La Isabela's other masonry buildings, the walls of the polvorín were eighty centimeters wide. Thick, sturdy walls are in keeping with the requirements of a munitions magazine. There are no remnants in situ of the walls themselves, which could have been either of stone or tapia.

To the west of the calzado, between the polvorín and alhóndiga, a

6.23. The pit cistern during the wet season, with standing water. (The drain has been reconstructed.)

large pit had been dug into the bedrock (figure 6.23). The pit measures some four meters in diameter and is three meters deep, and it appears to have been used for water storage. It may have served to capture not only rain but also runoff from the area to the east of the calzado and south of the alhóndiga, which would have had shed a great deal of water from its roof during the rainy season.

These public buildings along the waterfront were apparently the only substantial stone structures at La Isabela. The houses for the majority of the people were those described by Michel de Cuneo as "200 houses, which are small, like the cabins [*cabañas*] we use for hunting, and they are covered with grass."[48]

Very little archaeological or documentary information has survived about these houses, or bohíos, but it is clear from documentary accounts that the colonists' huts were built by the Spaniards (under considerable protest) rather than by the Indians. They were constructed hastily by weak and often sick men, and were probably intended at first to provide only the minimum shelter necessary. Any plans or enthusiasm for expanding and enhancing domestic structures later, however, were probably attenuated by the miserable conditions that seem to have quickly developed and persisted in the colony, discussed in chapter 4.

6.24. Excavation of a Spanish post structure at La Isabela.

Under the best of circumstances, wood and thatch buildings are highly perishable in tropical settings, and the severe earth-disturbing activities at La Isabela in the mid-twentieth century rendered even the surviving evidence for such structures tentative. Because most of the soil-zone deposits were disturbed or removed, it is often difficult to distinguish fifteenth-century posts from those of the twentieth century.

Nevertheless, excavations in the residential area—Poblado—to the east of the modern roadway, where twentieth-century grading activities were less destructive, uncovered clusters of post molds—stains left in the ground by rotting or removed posts—that are thought to date to the Spanish occupation of La Isabela (figures 6.5, 6.24, and 6.25). Only a few of them, however, provided enough information from which to extrapolate the size and layout of houses. Many household activities apparently (and understandably) took place outside the bohíos, where hearths or fire pits and trash deposits have been located. Along with postmold patterns, hearths—or *fogones*—are among the best archaeological indices of La Isabela's residential areas (figures 6.1 and 6.26).

Two of the more complete postmold complexes in the Poblado indicate that roughly rectangular wood or thatch buildings were constructed with considerable informality and little attention to durabil-

6.25. Postmolds for a fifteenth-century Spanish structure, cut into the underlying bedrock.

6.26. Profile of a fifteenth-century hearth (fogón), later filled in as a trash deposit.

6.27. Detail from *Hunting on the Lagoon*, showing Italian hunting cabins of ca. 1490–1495. (Vittore Carpaccio, 1495. J. Paul Getty Museum 79.PB.72.)

ity.[49] They incorporated between forty and sixty square meters of floor space (or slightly more), which is quite consistent with modest housing in late fifteenth-century Spain. As we mentioned earlier, houses in Córdoba averaged about fifty square meters, while those at Portuguese Qsar es-Seghir were about sixty square meters, with individual rooms ranging from six to twenty square meters. The bohíos at La Isabela are also somewhat larger than the typical houses at Bealí in eastern Spain, which averaged just 11.2 square meters in floorspace during the fourteenth and fifteenth centuries (rising to twenty square meters in the region during the seventeenth century).[50]

We recall that Cuneo described the huts of the colonists as "small, like the cabins [*cabañas*] we use for hunting, and they are covered with grass." Such houses were also common throughout rural Iberia in the fifteenth and sixteenth centuries, and one visitor to the Portuguese countryside of the sixteenth century noted that "there is no house with roofing tiles, but all of thatch, and all had dirt floors."[51] Although few depictions of such humble structures in Europe are available, figure 6.27 shows wood-and-thatch Italian hunting cabins painted between 1490 and 1496. These bear a similarity to the Taíno structures depicted by Oviedo in his *Historia natural* (shown in chapter 3, figure 3.5), and both the American and European structures may provide clues to the appearance of the La Isabela huts.

The public buildings at La Isabela were consistent with the architectural traditions found in the Mediterranean region during late medieval times. The materials used to build them were both typical of Andalusia with its Moorish heritage and in keeping with the resources available at La Isabela. Although simple in their outlines, a certain standardization of construction is suggested by the wall materials, wall-foundation widths, post mold diameters, and roof-tile dimensions. An emphasis on solidity and substance in these public structures seems to have been intended from the beginning, suggested not only by their size but also by the immediate establishment of production centers for ceramic architectural elements.

The construction of residential structures, in contrast to the more formal traditions employed in public buildings, was apparently haphazard, casual, and done with minimal investment. This is not surprising, given Las Casas's comment that as soon as the town was founded, "everyone was told to start building his own house." The houses, however, seem to have been consistent in size, shape, and materials to contemporary rural houses throughout southern Iberia, with the exception that the hearths appear to have been outside rather than inside—a logical response to the tropics.

It was in and around these bohíos that much of the colony's day-to-day activities took place, and we shall chronicle them archaeologically in the following chapters.

Chapter 7

A Spartan Domesticity: Household Life in La Isabela's Bohíos

After the first euphoric months of settlement, La Isabela's chroniclers wrote of virtually nothing about life in the town other than the starvation, sickness, and misery of its residents. While their focus is understandable, it ignored most of what was happening on a daily basis in the town, and it is the material world of La Isabela that reveals the cultural practices and texture of daily life there in the late fifteenth century.

La Isabela was clearly different from other fifteenth-century towns in its virtually all-male population and its utterly isolated frontier position. It was nevertheless a community of people with many of the concerns common to households and communities everywhere: cooking and eating, household organization, health and sanitation, religious life, personal appearance, social hierarchy, leisure activities, and personal economy. What little we know about how the people at La Isabela dealt with these issues comes from the archaeological record.

While the absence of women undoubtedly shaped domestic life in a dramatic way, the men who formed the households of the town still had to provide food, clothing, lighting, sanitation, and other domestic necessities. Social class predicted the ways in which these needs were met, and there was a marked difference between the households of the elite and those of the non-elite in La Isabela. This is brought into sharp focus when we compare the needs of Columbus's household with those of "the people," as reflected in the requests for supplies (tables 7.1 and 7.2).

Starvation in Paradise

The Spaniards at La Isabela were obsessed with food—particularly with the lack of it. This is one of the most puzzling aspects of the Isabeline project, particularly in light of the colonists' exuberant accounts of the land's richness during the first months of settlement and the evident bounty of resources that had sustained the region's much larger Taíno population for centuries. As Dr. Chanca noted, "The land is very rich for all purposes." Even today, after five centuries of increasingly intensive use, the area is known for its agricultural fertility and abundant marine life.

Nevertheless, within three months of their arrival, the Spaniards began to complain increasingly of the lack of food and the hunger they suffered, as we saw in chapter 4. The supplies they brought were intended to sustain them until the first crops could be planted and harvested, but shortages and spoilage took their toll, and administrative attention turned to military construction and the search for gold rather than to establishing a stable subsistence base. As Michel de Cuneo observed in 1494, "They have not yet found the way nor the time to sow, the reason being that nobody wants to live permanently in these countries."[1] Even with attention thus diverted, however, it is difficult to understand the colonists' apparent preference for starvation over a shift in food resources from Spanish staples to locally available crops and seafood.

It has also been suggested that the Spaniards' incessant demands for food from the Taínos in the region around La Isabela could not be sustained, given that the Taínos grew their crops yearly and did not accumulate large surpluses.[2] Although this may have been true of crops in the immediate vicinity of the town, it does not help to explain the absence of fish, manatee, rodent, and turtle bones in the archaeological deposits of the town. Furthermore, the Spaniards seem to have quickly established mechanisms for acquiring manioc from other parts of the island (discussed below and in chapter 4).

All of La Isabela's chroniclers, especially the eyewitnesses, extolled the abundant plant and animal resources of the area, clearly recognizing them as acceptable food items. Nicoló Syllacio reports that "close by the city is an admirable harbor abounding in fish of the most delicate flavor, which doctors, after tests, have prescribed as food that helps restore the sick to good health. Huge fish as large as cattle are caught here; they are eaten avidly (after their legs have been removed) and have the taste of veal [manatees?]. Once you have tasted these you will give up eating any other kind."[3]

Ferdinand Colón had this to say of the land: "So fertile was it that they ate fruit from the trees in November, at which time they flowered again, indicating that they bear fruit twice a year. Plants and seeds continually bear fruit and flower. All seasons they found in the trees birds' nests containing eggs and young."[4]

One of the most detailed discussions of praiseworthy local food resources was given by Michel de Cuneo. He described the many fruits used by the Taínos and the Spaniards at La Isabela, including papayas, mameys, passion fruit, guavas, pineapples, plums, and more than forty others. Animals eaten by Cuneo (presumably at La Isabela) and pronounced as delicious included several kinds of birds, iguanas, and " fish, in which these islands abound. There are squid, crayfish, seals, mussels, clams, shrimps, tunny, codfish and dolphins, and some other sea pigs not known to us. Others are long and very big, weighing from twenty-five to thirty *libre*, excellent to eat, somewhat like sturgeon. Still other fish are of unusual shapes and very good. There is a kind of fish very much like the sea urchin, and an infinite number of small sharks that are good to eat. There are also many very big turtles, weighing from two to fifteen *cántara*, that are excellent to eat."[5]

In addition to the abundance and delectability of the plant and animal resources in the vicinity of La Isabela, the fertility of the land for agriculture was consistently lauded. Dr. Chanca, for example, noted that "they have sown many vegetables, and it is certain that they grow more in eight days than they do in twenty in Spain."[6] Ferdinand Colón also emphasized the rapid growth of Spanish agricultural products, recounting (although probably with some embellishment) the progress after about two months of effort:

On Saturday, March 29th, he arrived at La Isabela [from the Cibao], where the melons were ripe enough to eat, though they had been planted less than two months before; cucumbers had come up in twenty days, and a native wild grapevine had already produced large fine grapes while they were still cultivating it. . . . Next day, March 30, a laborer harvested spikes of wheat which had been planted at the end of January; they also picked chickpeas larger than those they had planted. All the seeds they had sown sprouted in three days and were ready to eat by the twenty-fifth day. Fruit stones planted in the ground sprouted in seven days; vine shoots sent out leaves at the end of the same period and by the twenty-fifth day green grapes were ready to be picked. Sugar canes germinated in seven days.[7]

Cuneo's description is somewhat more balanced, but it still reflects the fertility of the land: "We brought with us from Spain all sorts of seeds, and tried those that would do well and those that could not. Those that do well are the following: spring melon and cucumber, squashes and radishes: the others, like onions, lettuce, other salad plants, and scallions do badly and grow very small except for parsley, which grows very well. Wheat, chickpeas and beans grow nine inches in ten days at the most; then all at once they wilt and die. Although the soil is very black and good, they have not yet found the way nor the time to sow, the reason being that nobody wants to live permanently in these countries."[8]

Domestic animals seem to have done equally well at first in the colony. Columbus himself noted that when pigs were given time to breed before they were killed for food, they reproduced at a remarkable rate. Cuneo reiterated this, remarking that "we found that pigs, chickens, dogs and cats reproduce there very quickly, especially pigs, because of the huge abundance of . . . fruits."[9]

The Spaniards also initially appreciated Taíno agricultural products and apparently relied on them to a considerable extent. Chanca records that "there come here constantly many Indians. . . . All come laden with *ages* [manioc or patata] which are like turnips, very excellent for food; of these we make here many kinds of foodstuffs in various ways. It is so sustaining to eat that it comforts us greatly."[10]

The Spaniards at La Isabela learned to prepare cassava bread, and apparently made it with some regularity. Ferdinand Colón, when recounting Columbus's journey from Española to Spain in 1496, wrote that "being familiar with the Indian method of making bread, they [Columbus's crew] took their [the Indians of Guadalupe's] cassava dough and made enough bread to satisfy their needs . . . after having made enough bread to last them 20 days, and having an equal amount already on board the ships [from La Isabela] the Admiral prepared to continue his voyage to Castile."[11]

Other Taíno agricultural products that were undoubtedly known to the Spaniards and eaten at La Isabela included corn, sweet potatoes, beans, peppers, and peanuts (as we mentioned in chapter 3).

The potential food resources of Hispaniola were well known to Columbus from his first voyage, during which he commented often on the bounty of fish, birds, root crops, and fruit.[12] The second expedition nevertheless brought large amounts of Spanish food staples that were intended to sustain the colony while it established sources of familiar crops and livestock. The supply lists for the expedition itself have not been found, but Las Casas notes that the fleet carried biscuit, wine, wheat, flour oil, vinegar, cheeses, all kinds of seeds, tools, mares, several stallions, fowl, and "many other things that could reproduce in the Indies and be of benefit to those who were there."[13] Much of this did not survive the voyage, however, and Columbus requested more supplies within a month. The request for supplies that Columbus sent to the Crown with Antonio de Torres in 1494 not only provides insight into the Spanish items that were brought to La Isabela but also reveals the vast differences between the diet of Columbus's household and that of the rest of the expedition members (tables 7.1 and 7.2).

While the staples of the men were biscuit, wine, beans, bacon, cheese, salted fish, and salted beef supplemented with small amounts of oil, garlic, and onions, those of Columbus included such delicacies as candied citron, "all types" of conserves, dates, olives, white and rose-colored sugar, saffron, rice, ham, fresh pig's lard, scented waters, good honey, and fine oil (table 7.1).

In response to complaints of short rations and hunger by those returning to Spain from La Isabela, in 1495 the Crown reiterated the minimum monthly rations for each man at La Isabela.[14] These included:

10 celemines of wheat [equal to ten fanegas, or 15 bushels, or 480
    pounds per year; or 1.3 pounds per day)
1 arroba of full-strength wine [1 pint per day]
8 pounds of bacon or 2 pounds of cheese [4.1 oz. or 1 oz. per day]

1 azumbre of vinegar [2 liters or 4.2 pints per month;
  or 2.2 oz. per day]
1 pint of oil [.5 oz. per day]
2 pints of beans [.13 cup per day]
3 pounds of dried fish (from Spain) for fish days [1.6 oz. per day]
½ quintal of biscuit [1.6 pounds per day]

The emphasis on wheat and wheat products in this ration list is consistent with lower-class European diets of the period, which typically included up to two hundred kilograms of bread a day. Although heavily weighted toward carbohydrates, the rations theoretically allotted to the settlers at La Isabela potentially provided some 4,200 calories per day, which is more than sufficient to maintain the weight of a 175-pound male between the ages of 18 and 35 doing strenuous activity.[15]

Documentary accounts make it clear, however, that these rations were not in fact provided. Las Casas recorded that the rations consisted instead of "one *escudilla* of wheat [about a cup], that they had to grind in a hand mill [*atahona a mano*] (and many ate it cooked) and one chunk of rancid bacon or of rotten cheese [*queso podrido*] and I don't know how few haba or garbanzo beans; of wine, it was as though there was none in the world."[16] Complaints of illness and starvation were constant and vociferous, and from documentary accounts alone it would appear that the settlers did not think of supplementing the inadequate rations with the fish, manatees, turtles, fruits, cassava, and other crops of the region.

Disappointingly, the archaeological evidence for the Spanish diet at La Isabela does little to clarify this puzzling situation. The many disturbances to the site we chronicled in chapter 5 severely compromised the reliability of the floral and faunal remains recovered during excavation, which are in any case extremely scarce. Very few intact, undisturbed fifteenth-century soil deposits survived at the site, making our reconstructions of the fifteenth-century Spanish diet at La Isabela both difficult and unreliable. Even though twentieth-century and fifteenth-century artifacts can be easily distinguished from each other (even in very disturbed contexts), this is not true of the bones from animals of the fifteenth century, which are generally morphologically indistinguishable from those of the twentieth century.

Perhaps the most puzzling aspect of studying the food habits of La Isabela, however, has been the virtual absence of animal bone (including fish bone) or plant remains in any excavated contexts, even from the

TABLE 7.1 Food and Food Supplies Requested for La Isabela, 1494

"For the people"

Wheat, 600 cahices
   (cahice = about *17.5* bushels)
Barley, 100 cahices
Biscuit, 600 quintales
   (quintal = about *100* pounds)
Wine, 12,000 arrobas
   (arroba = about *4* gallons liquid, *25*
   pounds dry)
Vinegar, 2,000 arrobas (in casks)
Oil, 410 arrobas (in jars)
Beans, chickpeas, and lentils, 70 cahices
Bacon, 500 sides
Beef, 100 carcasses (in casks)
Raisins and figs, 200 quintales
Unshelled almonds, hazelnuts, and walnuts,
   30 quintales
Salted fish, 300 barrels
Onions, 4,000 bunches
Garlic, 5,000 strings
Sugar, 50 arrobas
Mustard, 6 flasks
Honey, 9 arrobas
Molasses, 10 jars
Other seeds and vegetables
Sheep and goats
Calves, 20
Chickens, 400
Anujos (?) for wine, 20
Wine flasks of 2, 3 or 4 azumbres
   (azumbre = about *4* pints)
Water casks, 500 dozen
Strainers and ajonarlos (?), 10 dozen
Seives and sifters, 10 dozen

"For the Admiral and his household"

Candied citron, 20 pounds
Sweets without pine kernels, 50 pounds
All types of conserves, 12 jars
Dates, 4 arrobas
Quince preserve, 12 boxes
Rose-colored sugar, 12 jars
White sugar, 4 arrobas
Water scented with orange blossoms, 1 arroba
Water scented with roses, 1 arroba
Saffron, 1 pound
Rice, 1 quintal
Raisins from Almunecar, 2 quintales
Almonds, 12 fanegas
Good honey, 4 arrobas
Fine oil, 8 arrobas
Olives, 2 jars
Fresh pig's lard, 3 arrobas
Ham, 4 arrobas
Chickens, 50 pairs
Roosters, 6
Tablecloths, 5 yards each, 4 pairs
Small cloths, 6 dozen
Towels, 6
Tablecloths for cupboards and for his men
   when they eat, 6 pairs of 6 yards each
A pewter cutlery
Silver cups, 2
Jugs (silver?), 2
Salt cellar (silver?)
Spoons (silver?), 12
Brass candlesticks, 2 pairs
Copper pitchers, 6
Large pots, 2
Small pots, 2
A large cauldron
A small cauldron
Large frying pans, 2
Small frying pans, 2
Stewing pans, 2
A large copper pot with lid
A small copper pot with lid
A brass mortar
Iron spoons, 2
Graters, 1 pair
A grill to roast fish
Forks, 2
A colander
Kichen towels of thick linen cloth, 12 yards
A large basin for cleaning
Large tapers, 12
Candles, 30 pounds

volumes of soil separated by flotation techniques (which involve agitation of soil in moving water so that heavy soil particles fall to the bottom, while lighter seeds and bone and charcoal float to the top and are skimmed off).[17] This scarcity may in part be owing to the nature of the official food ration, of which only the wheat and beans (and then only if carbonized), and possibly the bones of salted meat, would have survived archaeologically. Only ten seeds were recovered from the flotation samples, and a mere three of those were definitely of archaeological origin (that is, carbonized).[18]

The absence of faunal bone and archaeological plant remains at La Isabela is mysterious. The site soils are quite basic, with a pH of between 7.5 and 7.7, and should not contribute to deterioration of bone from acidity. Furthermore, human bone is relatively well preserved in the town cemetery, and animal bone is quite abundant in the Taíno midden underlying the southern part of the site. The short occupation of La Isabela by the Spaniards and the subsequent disturbances to the site are certainly factors in the paucity of subsistence remains, but they do not adequately explain it, particularly given the great abundance of fifteenth-century artifacts recovered at the site.

It is more likely that cultural or behavioral factors played a major role in this radical departure from the subsistence patterns found at other Spanish colonial sites in Hispaniola. These factors might include rigorous disposal of organic refuse into the sea, which would seem to be a sensible practice for people with a seafood diet in the tropics. Certainly the greatest density of faunal bone was in the ravine at the north end of the town that was used for trash disposal both by La Isabela's fifteenth-century residents and by El Castillo's twentieth-century residents. The bone refuse from the ravine, nevertheless, was recovered in relatively small amounts compared to either Taíno sites or sixteenth-century Spanish sites, and clearly included modern as well as fifteenth-century bones. Furthermore, if the Spanish residents did in fact dispose of food bone in the sea, they must have carefully separated it from the rest of their garbage (including shells), which remained in the soil throughout the town site.

Systematic disposal of refuse in an as yet undiscovered location or composting of organic remains for use in gardens and fledgling agricultural fields might be other possible factors in the scarcity of remains. The simplest explanation, however, is that the residents at La Isabela were telling the truth—they had nothing to eat, or thought that they

7.1. Spanish food consumption items typical of La Isabela's households. (Photo: James Quine.)

had nothing to eat. If indeed they depended entirely upon the provisions brought from Spain, it was inevitable that hunger would be the consequence. A diet of manioc bread would leave few archaeological traces (particularly if it was already prepared when acquired), and it may not have been psychologically satisfying. It is difficult to imagine that hungry Spaniards would not have taken advantage of the abundant seafood (which they recognized as good to eat) immediately at hand, yet both documentary and archaeological records suggest that this may in fact have been the case.

Another important source of information about the diet and cuisine at La Isabela are the items used to procure, prepare, and consume food. In contrast to the food remains themselves, artifacts related to the consumption of food are extremely abundant at La Isabela, which either casts doubt on the scarcity of food or indicates that the Spaniards were optimists in the face of starvation.

The colonists were unrelenting in their adherence to typical and traditional Spanish cooking and eating utensils. The kinds and proportions of food-related items from La Isabela do not differ significantly from those that might have been found in the kitchens and dining rooms of late fifteenth-century Seville (figure 7.1). In both late medieval

7.2. Spanish cooking pot known as a puchero, produced at Las Coles. (Photo: James Quine.)

Spain and La Isabela, most of the food technology items were ceramic vessels. The pottery from La Isabela, both in its forms and in the relative proportions of cooking and eating vessels, is remarkably similar to that documented in Seville and Carmona in Spain, at Qsar es-Seghir in Morocco, and throughout late fifteenth-century Andalusia in general. At all of these sites and at La Isabela, the ceramic vessels included a mixture of Islamic and Christian forms and decorative techniques.[19]

Unlike the inhabitants of nearly all other Spanish colonial sites in the Americas where locally made American Indian pottery was used for cooking, the residents of La Isabela clearly felt that the production and availability of familiar Spanish cooking and eating dishes was a high priority.[20] Fragments of at least 2,651 European pottery vessels were recorded during analysis, and more than 70 percent of these were apparently made locally in the kilns of Las Coles.

The most common cooking vessels at La Isabela were forms known as *pucheros* and *ollas* (figure 7.2), and these are still found today throughout Spain. Used over an open flame from a stove, or *anafre*, they were ideal for the preparation of the liquid-based stews, pottages, and por-

7.3. Unglazed mortar and escudilla, made at Las Coles and used at El Castillo. (Photo: George Avery.)

ridges that dominated late medieval Spanish cuisine.[21] These *potajes, guisados,* and *gachas* typically consisted of combinations of vegetables, beans, grains, meat or fish, and seasonings, much like the *paellas* and *asopaos* found throughout the Spanish-speaking world today. These, together with bread, made up the diet for most of non-elite Spain, and the ceramic evidence from La Isabela suggests that the same was probably true for the Spaniards who lived there.

The basis for many of the potajes prepared at La Isabela was probably wheat, which at the time was the dietary staple for most Europeans. Wheat was a major part of the colonists' rations, and each person laboriously (and apparently reluctantly, according to Las Casas) grind his or her wheat in hand mortars [*atahona a mano*]. These may well have been the ceramic mortars found abundantly at the site (figure 7.3). These mortars are much more common at La Isabela than they are at early sixteenth-century sites in Spain, possibly because the residents of sixteenth-century Seville had access to already ground wheat.[22] Two hundred and forty strainers, sieves, and sifters were requested for the town in 1494 (see table 7.1), and these were probably used to bolt, or sieve, the ground grain, a necessary task to produce flour of various consistencies. Occasionally the grain was simply cooked like gruel and eaten.[23]

Although there is no compelling archaeological evidence that the Spaniards at La Isabela adopted Indian pots for cooking, there is some indication that they did learn to make cassava bread using Taíno technology. Ferdinand Colón's accounts of Columbus's return voyage to Spain in 1496 makes it clear that the fleet members were familiar with the preparation of cassava bread, and that they in fact stole sufficient cassava dough from the Indians of Guadalupe to make twenty days worth of bread before continuing the voyage.[24] Making cassava bread may also have been the norm at La Isabela, although it is documented that already prepared cassava was accepted as tribute and brought fairly regularly to the town (see chapter 4).

The most recognizable archaeological evidence for cassava preparation is the round, flat Taíno burén, or griddle, which is usually ceramic but occasionally made of stone (see chapter 3, figure 3.8). Burenes at La Isabela are most densely concentrated in the Spanish elite residential zone, perhaps suggesting that the Spaniards did in fact adopt this aspect of Taíno technology into their kitchens.

The colonists at La Isabela, however, clearly perceived their greatest pottery need to be for vessels used to serve and eat food, with an emphasis on bowls and plates for individual use. More than half of all the Spanish pottery at La Isabela occurs in forms used for serving and eating by individuals, most commonly *escudillas*—small carinated bowls (figures 7.3 and 7.4)—*platos*—deep, saucerlike plates—and Islamic-style bowls known as *fuentes* (figure 7.4). All of these were appropriate for the serving and eating of liquid-based dishes. Small handleless cups, or *tazas*, and narrow-necked small jars, *jarritas*, were typically used for drinking; liquids were dispensed from pitchers (*picheles* or *jarros*), large narrow-necked jars, shown in figure 7.5. Three fragments of stemmed ceramic drinking vessels (goblets) were also found. The majority of these drinking vessels were glazed, which is obviously an advantage for vessels containing liquid, but the great majority of the plates and bowls were unglazed and locally made. Approximately 15 percent of the vessels used at table were majolica or lead-glazed dishes imported from Spain (see, for example, figure 7.7).[25]

Food was eaten with spoons, knives, and fingers. Portions of two copper-alloy spoons were excavated (one of which is seen in figure 7.1), with pear-shaped bowls and long, slender handles characteristic of spoons used throughout Europe at the end of the fifteenth century.[26] Forks were

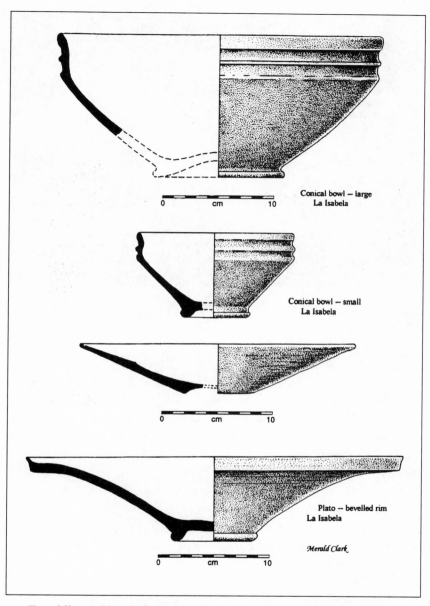

Conical bowl — large
La Isabela

Conical bowl — small
La Isabela

Plato — bevelled rim
La Isabela

Merald Clark

7.4. Escudillas and bowls from La Isabela. (Drawing: Merald Clark.)

7.5. Locally made small jar or jug of unglazed earthenware. (Photo: James Quine.)

rarely used at table during this period, and the forks listed as requirements for the admiral's household were probably large kitchen forks.[27]

All the various sources of evidence bearing upon the Spanish diet at La Isabela—documentary accounts, plant and animal remains, and material culture—tend to indicate that the colonists clung to traditional Spanish food practices at their own expense, with only very limited concessions to American resources and cuisine, such as cassava bread. The evidence, however, is unsatisfyingly inconsistent and often contradictory. It leaves two of the most interesting questions about Spanish subsistence largely speculative. What did the colonists eat? And to what extent did they come to incorporate native foods and food technology into their daily lives?

Historical accounts at La Isabela began with delighted descriptions of the succulent fish, abundant fruits, and nourishing Taíno bread and potatoes, but they quickly turned to desperate complaints that there was no food and the colonists were starving. And if the accounts are to be accepted, many people did indeed die from hunger. The provisions from Spain were apparently not able to sustain the colony for very long, and both documents and the faunal record suggest that rather than turning to local resources, the Spaniards chose to starve. It is also pos-

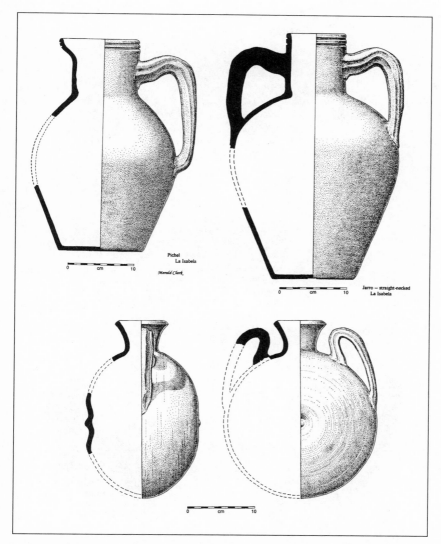

7.6. Liquid containers and serving vessels: *Top left,* cántaro; *top right,* pichel; *bottom,* cantimplora. (Drawing: Merald Clark.)

sible that they did in fact turn to local resources but perceived themselves to be starving for want of familiar foods.[28]

The typically most important direct evidence for past diets—the remains of plants and animals that had been eaten—was peculiarly absent at La Isabela. We have invoked preservation factors, disturbances to the archaeological record, and past behavioral factors as potential rea-

7.7. Isabela Polychrome majolica plate designs. (Photo: James Quine.)

sons for the very low incidence of archaeobiological remains at the site. But we cannot reject the possibility that the colonists simply did not have foods that were potentially preservable in the archaeological record, supporting their contention that they were starving.

A conclusion that the settlers of La Isabela had nothing to eat, however, is not supported by the technology of food preparation and con-

sumption. Apart from being abundant (particularly given the short occupation of the town), the food-related artifacts at La Isabela closely
parallel those found in contemporary Spanish sites, and they were locally produced in the kilns of Las Coles, presumably in response to
local need and demand. Looking only at the assemblage of artifacts
from La Isabela, one could easily interpret the Spanish occupation as
having been intensely dedicated to cooking and eating in a very Spanish
tradition.

Life in the Bohíos

Household furnishings appear with equal scarcity in both the documentary and archaeological accounts of La Isabela, and the dirt-floored
bohíos of the settlers were undoubtedly primitive. Most were probably
furnished only with bedrolls, trunks, or coffers and possibly tables or
benches made locally. Copper tacks that may have been used to attach
fabric or leather to chairs or trunks, and a single ornamental furniture
clavo, or nail, are among the few surviving remnants of such furniture.

The relative absence of furniture is consistent with conditions in late
medieval Spain and throughout Europe before the eighteenth century.
Inventories of households in late fifteenth-century Córdoba indicate
that neither poor nor well-to-do households had much furniture. A
bed, some trunks, and sometimes chairs and a table constituted the furnishings of most households. Even the interiors of Spanish palaces
were simple, and very little furniture was used before the sixteenth century.[29] In this context, the households of La Isabela do not appear to
have differed dramatically from the European norm.

Some form of lighting was needed by all households, and La Isabela's settlers provided this in several ways. They brought with them
tallow and wax, at least some of which was undoubtedly used to make
candles. No metal candle holders have been found at La Isabela, but
several tube-shaped ceramic fragments may have been parts of ceramic
candlesticks. More common are ceramic lamp fragments, probably used
to burn oil or tallow (figure 7.8). These lamps were commonly produced by medieval Muslim potters in Seville, who continued the Roman
tradition of making and using ceramic oil lamps. In Spain, however, the
lamps seem to have been gradually replaced by candles as lighting
equipment by the end of the fifteenth century.[30]

Three dozen glass lamps were among the supplies sent to La Isabela,

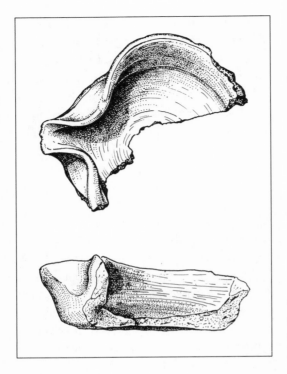

7.8. Oil lamp fragment, approximately 7.5 centimeters in diameter. (Drawing: Merald Clark.)

but no recognizable evidence for any of these was found archaeologically. Two varieties of late medieval Spanish glass lamps using oil or candles have been identified by glass scholars, and those brought to La Isabela may have been similar.[31]

Hygiene in general was not a major preoccupation of fifteenth century Europeans. As Fernand Braudel observed, "Bodily cleanliness left much to be desired at all periods and for everyone." It has been suggested, however, that personal hygiene in southern Spain and Portugal may have been somewhat better than in the rest of Europe because of the Moslem influence in those areas.[32] Columbus did in fact request that a thousand pounds of soap (roughly the equivalent of 3,200 five-ounce bath-size bars) be shipped to the colony in the first year. This request, coupled with the the relative abundance and wide distribution of *lebrillos*—large basins—at the site of La Isabela, may suggest that the colony's organizers were more attentive (at least initially) to cleanliness in general than were many of their European contemporaries.

Household sanitation needs were met in large measure by ceramic *bacines*, or chamber pots, and lebrillos (figure 7.9). Of the seventy-one

7.9. Household utility ceramics: *Top,* bacines; *bottom,* lebrillo. (Drawing: Merald Clark.)

fragmentary bacines found at the site, only nine were glazed. These were imported from Spain and may have been among the sixty chamber pots that were brought with the expedition supplies (table 7.2). The rest were probably made locally. Compared to vessels for food preparation and consumption, chamber pots are relatively uncommon at La Isabela and appear to have been an elite accessory. They are five times more common in the elite residential areas than in all of the Poblado areas combined.[33] Common settlers undoubtedly took advantage of vegetation and the sea in the absence of chamber pots and privies.

The lebrillo was the quintessential Andalusian washbasin, for washing clothing as well as the body.[34] It is a large shallow basin form with a flat bottom and outward-sloping sides ending in a characteristic folded rim. They are the largest vessels in the ceramic assemblage, measuring up to seventy-two centimeters in diameter at the rim.

Lebrillos are both more numerous and more often glazed than bacines at La Isabela, and their distribution in the town is the opposite of that for bacines; lebrillos are some seven times more plentiful in the Poblado than in the elite residential zone. They are clearly domestic in function and non-elite in status. It is possible that hidalgos and elite residents of La Isabela did not themselves perform many of the domestic chores that required lebrillos such as laundering clothes, but rather had them done by subalterns in other parts of the town.

Concern for both household sanitation and community health would have been complicated by the difficulties of obtaining fresh water at the El Castillo site. Columbus often mentioned plans to bring water into the town via canals, and his son, Ferdinand, wrote that this was in fact accomplished by "digging a wide channel to the river, for which purpose he had a dam built that should also provide power for a grist-mill. This he did because the town lay about a cannon shot from the river, and without that channel the people would have had great difficulty in supplying themselves with water, particularly as most of them were weak and ill with certain diseases caused by the thinness of the air."[35]

There is no direct archaeological evidence that a canal system was ever achieved at the walled town (although canals may have been dug at the settlement of Las Coles). Nor was any evidence recovered for water wells within the town, other than the brackish water well near the edge of the lagoon at the base of the ravine. The only documentable water-capture system was the rustic cistern discussed in chapter 6. During the rainy seasons, collection of fresh water would not have been especially problematic, but during the hot, dry summers, supplying water for drinking, washing, bathing, or animals would have been a major occupation, relegated no doubt to the non-elite members of the community.

Water resources, sanitation, and waste disposal are all closely related to health, and sickness was second only to starvation in the litany of complaints from La Isabela's settlers (detailed in chapter 4). According to Columbus most of the men fell sick within a few days of their arrival, and although many died, he pointed out that "the country tries them for some space of time and after that they recover" and that "the cause of the illness, so general among all, is the change of water and air, for we see that it spreads to all one after another, and few are in danger."[36] Las Casas also noted that "the Spaniards became adapted to the land, recovering from the illnesses that inevitably tested them not because they were infirm, but because the air here is softer, the water thinner, the food of different qualities and our own food so far away."[37]

These initial bouts of illness must surely have been exacerbated, if not caused, by malnutrition and the crowded, unsanitary conditions suffered during two months at sea, as well as new kinds of American parasites and baccilli. As we noted in chapter 4, other scholars have suggested that the early illness at La Isabela may have been influenza spread by pigs and horses, Reiter's syndrome (a dysenteric affliction with long-lasting effects), and intestinal dysentery.[38]

This initial reaction to the Americas was by no means exclusive to the settlers of La Isabela. The 2,500 colonists who arrived at Santo Domingo with Ovando in 1502 immediately fell prey to a similar bout of illness and seem to have been even less fortunate than the men of La Isabela. According to Las Casas, within a few months more than a thousand of the newcomers had died and some five hundred more remained desperately ill.[39]

Despite the recovery of many of the Isabela expedition members from their initial maladies, sickness and general ill health persisted at La Isabela, perhaps related to weakness and susceptibility to illness provoked by overwork, malnutrition, and inadequate sanitation. As the months and years passed, syphilis was probably also a contributing factor. When in 1496 the adelantado Bartolomé Colón returned to La Isabela after his visit to Behechio in Xaraguá, he "found about 300 men had been stricken by various diseases, this caused great labor for Don Bartolomé, and supplies were increasingly scarce, and no ships came from Castile; he determined to divide and send all the sick and weak to the fortalezas and the pueblos of Indians that were near them, for at least they would have, if not doctors and medicines, food that the Indians were not lacking and that they would give them [the Spaniards] and thus they would have only to fight against sickness, not that together with hunger."[40]

Physicians accompanied the expedition on the second voyage, and a hospital was one of the first structures to be built in the town. Chanca was overworked and undersupplied, and Columbus asked the sovereigns in March 1494 to authorize a pay supplement for the doctor, as "despite all this he still shows the greatest diligence and charity in all that concerns his duty."[41] Apparently it was the custom for physicians accompanying military expeditions to receive as a supplement a day's pay each year from each expedition member, although Columbus asked that a flat-rate supplement be paid instead to Chanca.

A shortage of medicine occurred almost immediately because of the unexpectedly high rate of illness, and medicines were among the most urgently requested items solicited by Columbus. Other items requested as necessary for the sick included rice, raisins, sugar, almonds, molasses, and honey.[42]

Packaging for the medicines brought to La Isabela included both the ceramic jars known as *albarelos* and, less frequently, glass vials of a distinctly medieval form (figures 7.10 and 7.11). These pharmaceutical containers may have held salves, oils, ointments, and plant infusions. The albarelo form derives from the early Spanish Muslim pharmaceutical ceramics of the ninth and tenth centuries, and it is thought to have been modeled on the bamboo-tube sections in which Asian medicines were shipped to the Arab world.[43] Fragments of one hundred albarelos were found at La Isabela, and unlike most other ceramic forms, almost all of them are glazed. They were apparently not produced locally, in keeping with their function as containers for specialized medical items coming from Spain.

Both albarelos and glass vials were found most commonly in the Poblado residential zone, with only a single fragment found in the elite residential area. This perhaps suggests that the town's medical facility was located in the Poblado (away from the public and elite spaces) or that medicine was distributed among the settlers and administered in households rather than in a central location.

Death from illness and other causes was undoubtedly all too familiar to the residents of La Isabela. It is perhaps surprising then, that fewer than a hundred burials have been located by the various physical anthropologists and archaeologists working at the site, given the apparent high mortality from illness over the town's four years of occupation. Nearly all of the area encompassed by the town walls has now been excavated, with no evidence for any cemetery other than the one located adjacent to the church. It is quite likely that after 1494 many deaths and burials probably occurred away from La Isabela.

The human remains excavated between 1985 and 1990 are currently being studied at the Museo del Hombre Dominicano. Neither the archaeological nor the bioanthropological analyses of these remains have been completed or reported, and so the demographic characterization of the burial population—gender, race, age, and pathology—is not yet known. These studies will undoubtedly reveal much about the health profile of La Isabela's colonists.

For those who survived at La Isabela, clothing was of greatest con-

7.10. Albarelo medicine container of the type used at La Isabela. Caparra Blue; height: 16.8 centimeters; Caparra, Puerto Rico. (Instituto Nacional de Cultura Puertorriqueña collections. Photo: James Quine.)

7.11. Glass vial. (Photo: James Quine.)

TABLE 7. 2 Domestic Items Imported to La Isabela
(Excluding Kitchen Items)

"For the maintenance of people"	"For the Admiral's household"
Medicines (60,000 maravedís worth)	Clothing and footwear for himself
Shoes and sandals	A bed made of 6 mattresses of fine Brittany
Other items of clothing and footwear	linen
Glass lamps, 3 dozen	Pillows of cambric, 4
Chamber pots in 6 straw boxes, 5 dozen	Bedsheets of half cambric, 3 pairs
Coarse cloth (jerga), 1,000 yards	A light quilt
Coarse canvas, 1,000 yards	Green and brownish serge silk cloth
Measures for bread, wine, and oil,	A cushion (alhambra)
plus other glasses	Cloth tapestries depicting trees
Lenteduas (?), 5 dozen	Door hangings of the same, 2
Tallow, 59 quintales	Coverings with his coat of arms, 4
(quintal = about 100 pounds)	Decorated coffers, a couple
Soap, 10 quintales	Perfumes
Wax, 2 quintales	Paper, 10 quires
	Ordinary mattresses, 12
	Thick bedsheets, 12 pairs
	Ordinary blankets, 12
	Green and brownish cloth, 80 yards
	Shirts, 80
	Leggings and jackets, 4
	Vitre (coarse canvas), 100 yards
	Ordinary shoes, 120 pairs
	Black thread, 6 pounds
	Black twisted silk, 3 ounces.

cern after food and shelter. This was not only because of the need for body cover and protection but also because of the immense social importance of clothing and personal adornment in late fifteenth-century Spain for those who were, or wished to be, hidalgos.[44] Spanish-style clothing, footwear, and fabric could only be acquired from Europe, and the items brought initially with the expedition were soon depleted. Given the infrequency of supply ships, the Spaniards in Hispaniola were soon reduced to rags, and European clothing became an extremely valuable commodity. By 1502, when the contingent of 2,500 new Spaniards arrived, even the wealthiest of the original colonists in terms of land and slaves were "going around *desnudos*" and barefoot. The newcomers who came with clothing were able to sustain themselves by selling it to the people already in Hispaniola.[45]

Clothing, like food, reflected the sharp distinctions that were made along social lines in the life of La Isabela. The contrast is strikingly evident between the items of clothing imported for "the people" (sandals, shoes, coarse cloth, and "other articles of clothing") with those provided for Columbus's household, which included silk fabric, silk thread, green and brownish cloth, shirts, leggings, jackets and shoes (see table 7.2). The social importance of clothing was underscored in Las Casas's scornful comments about men he considered common who were exploiting the Indians: "It was laughable to see the presumptuous and haughty manner of these men who did not have a Castilian linen shirt, nor a cloak, coat or shoes to their name, but only a cotton shirt worn above another from Castile if they could afford it, or if not, the cotton shirt alone with their legs sticking out of it, and sandals and leggings instead of shoes or boots."[46]

The men of La Isabela represented a diverse spectrum of Spain's social classes, from peasant and farmer to hidalgo and prelate, and clothing in the town must have been similarly diverse. Figure 7.12 illustrates some of the typical modes of Spanish dress of the time. As at most archaeological sites, very few material remnants of either elite or common clothing were recovered at La Isabela, and nearly all of these were fragments of metal clothing fasteners, including buckles, strap tips, grommets, pins, hook eyes, and lace tips (aglets, or *agujetas*; figure 7.13). Lacing was the most common method of fastening clothing in the Spanish colonies until the second half of the seventeenth century—for breeches and doublet closures, attachment of hose to doublets, fastening hose, and the like—and no buttons were found at La Isabela.[47]

Buckles and strap tips were the most common apparel-related items found at La Isabela (figures 7.14 and 7.15). Many of these were probably used with brigantine plate armor, which is widespread at the site, and the strap tips and buckles from La Isabela could have functioned either as armor or as clothing fasteners.

It is somewhat unusual that no thimbles were recovered from the site, as they are quite common sewing accessories in other early Spanish colonial sites. Coupled with the small number of pins, their absence suggests that tailoring and sewing were not prominent activities in the life of the predominantly (if not exclusively) male community at La Isabela.

Jewelry, like clothing, carried great weight as a social signifier in late fifteenth-century Spain. It was worn by both men and women, and in its popular forms by nearly all social classes, and a number of popular jewelry items were recovered at La Isabela.[48]

Elite classes during the late fifteenth century wore wide, elaborate

7.12. Modes of Spanish dress at the time La Isabela was established. (From *Espejo de la vida humana*, 1491, Biblioteca Nacional, Madrid.)

collars of enameled and bejeweled links, square-cut stones set in elaborate foliagelike settings, and a variety of precious religious jewels. Some of the gifts Columbus gave to Taíno leaders hint at the nature of elite jewelry at La Isabela. During the first voyage he gave a young Taíno cacique "some very nice pieces of amber I was wearing around my

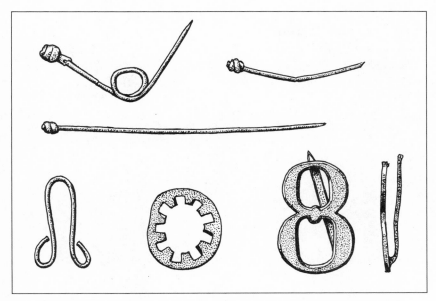

7.13. Clothing-related artifacts. Copper-alloy straight pins, grommet, hook, and "figure 8" (*cifra moresca*) clothing ornament. (Drawing: Merald Clark.)

7.14. Copper-alloy buckles. (Photo: James Quine.)

7.15. Copper-alloy strap tips. (Photo: James Quine.)

neck," along with some red shoes, a wall hanging, and a flask of orange water. Columbus later took from his own neck and gave to Guacanagarí "a collar of good bloodstones [*alaqueques*] and very beautiful beads of very pretty colors." He also gave the Taíno cacique a large silver finger ring, because he learned that Guacanagarí had seen a sailor wearing such a ring and desired it greatly.[49] Two pale-orange, lozenge-shaped carnelian beads were excavated at La Isabela, and they may have been part of necklaces like those worn by Columbus. Curiously, given their importance as trade items in the Americas, no glass beads were found at La Isabela.

Items of fine jewelry were undoubtedly very well cared for accessories of many hidalgos who came to La Isabela, but only remnants of humbler forms of adornment have been recovered archaeologically. Most of the pieces from the site could have been used by either men or women, and all were made from nonprecious substances. It is quite possible that some of these items could have been intended for trade with the Taínos rather than as personal adornment for Spaniards. Columbus himself listed many of the European trade items found to be popular on the first voyage, which included glass beads, brass rings, hawks' bells (small

7.16. Finger rings excavated at La Isabela.

7.17. Ornamental items. *Left,* part of a reliquary pendant; *center,* filigree cap, possibly to a cassolet; *right,* pendant element, possibly from a rosary. (Photo: James Quine.)

closed brass bells attached to birds' feet in falconry), lace ends, broken glass and crockery, strap ends, and broken barrel hoops. Above all, "they wish for nothing so much as for hawk's bells . . . for they almost go crazy for them."[50]

The most abundant items of jewelry at La Isabela are finger rings. Thirteen rings have been found, including simple copper bands, signet rings, stirrup rings, and rings with settings for stones (figure 7.16). Some of these were probably trade items. Several other ornamental items from La Isabela are Islamic in style or origin, including earwires, pins,

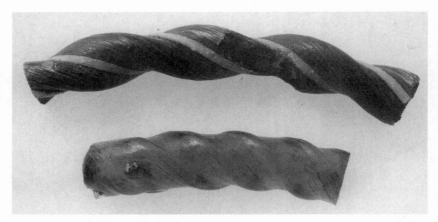

7.18. Glass bracelet fragments. Length of bottom fragment: 2 centimeters; diameter of bottom fragment: 4 millimeters. (Photo: James Quine.)

and filigree work, all of which are consistent with jewelry known to have been in use in fifteenth-century Spain (figure 7.17).[51]

Among the most unusual items of adornment for an American site are fragments of thin, ring-shaped glass bracelets of a variety long known in the Muslim world (figure 7.18). At least twelve were lost or discarded at La Isabela. Glass bangle bracelets have a long tradition dating from the medieval era to the present in the Islamic world and in India.[52] There is some indication that this kind of bracelet may have been associated with young or adolescent girls, as they were found on the wrists of adolescent girls buried in the Christian cemetery at late fifteenth-century Portuguese Qsar es-Seghir in Morocco. Bracelets, or *manillas*, of glass are also known to have been ordered by Queen Isabela for her daughter, the infanta.[53] They are one of the few categories of material culture associated with women at La Isabela, although they may also have been brought to America as trade items.

Given the desolation with which life at La Isabela was portrayed by its chroniclers, it is hard to imagine that leisure, entertainment, or cultural pursuits were significant aspects of life in the town. A number of the expedition members, including hidalgos and those in holy orders, however, were literate and probably not unfamiliar with such cultured activities as reading and music. Music and troubadours were certainly important elements in late medieval entertainment, particularly among the elite.[54] It is not known if musicians were actually present at La Isabela, but it seems as though they were at least a perceived need. In mid-

1497, as Columbus was preparing to return to Hispaniola on his third voyage, Ferdinand and Isabela commanded him to include in his contingent "some musicians and instruments for the entertainment of the people there."[55]

There were undoubtedly also some books at La Isabela, even though printing with movable type was still a relatively new phenomenon and books were not common before 1500. Columbus himself collected books probably brought some to La Isabela, while Bibles and other theological works may have been among the belongings of the priests and other hidalgos. Books of the late fifteenth century were carefully and sturdily bound in leather, often with ornate metal hardware used to close the book and to decorate the cover.[56] Some of the numerous copper-alloy ornamental inlay fragments excavated at La Isabela (and discussed in chapter 8 of our *Archaeology* volume) could have adorned books as well as furniture, and a single, once gilded and enameled hinge found in the ravine refuse dump may have been a segment of book hardware.

Once the town was established and built, there must have been some idle hours, at least for the hidalgos. The traditional leisure preoccupations for the elite class—jousting, tournaments, and hunting—would have been difficult at La Isabela, not only because of the absence of audiences and game but also because of the need to conserve scarce horses and weapons.[57] More democratic forms of entertainment in late medieval Spain included dice, board games, and gambling, to which people from all social classes had a passionate attachment despite official sanctions and prohibitions against them.[58] The men of La Isabela had money and, as Columbus noted, they were eager to spend it. It is inevitable under these circumstances that the combination of ready money, nothing to buy, and little entertainment would have encouraged gambling. Although no dice were recovered from the site, four small discs (three ceramic and one of shell) may have been gaming markers, used in board games of medieval origin, such as *tablas reales* (backgammon), *damas* (draughts), or *fallas* (fayles). Gambling may in fact have been an important factor in the development of an internal economy at La Isabela, a supposition that we examine further in chapter 9.

Elite Misery and Subaltern Endurance

The domestic lives of the majority of La Isabela's colonists, while dominated by problems of food, health, gender imbalance, and disillusionment, were not dramatically different in a material sense to those of their contemporaries in Spain. Clothing, household furnishings, and domestic organization at La Isabela were quite typical of those in lower- and middle-class Iberian households of the late fifteenth century.

This characterization, however, applies primarily to the non-elite residents of the town, who were in the majority. For the hidalgo group, the conditions of life at La Isabela were dramatically different from those in Spain. There they had enjoyed a degree of luxury and ease that was not possible in La Isabela. The distinctions in social class that governed much of the social life of the town apparently could not be fully sustained in the material aspects of domestic life, as there appears to be little significant difference between the elite residential areas (near the plaza and the Casa de Colon) and the non-elite areas (the Poblado) in patterns of food or household items and organization. The possible exceptions to this are the inverse proportions we mentioned of bacines and lebrillos between the elite and non-elite areas, which may reflect greater access to both personal sanitation equipment and to servants by those living in the elite area.

In any case, the shock of the difficult conditions at La Isabela may have been more dramatic to the hidalgos, who had greater expectations, and who were able to write chronicles. It is possible that the profound hardships that have come historically to represent life at La Isabela may have been to some extent an elite misery.

Chapter 8

God and Glory

Much of what happened at La Isabela was conditioned by the inextricably connected concerns of religion, defense, and personal honor. These were not only important elite cultural ideals held in common with late fifteenth-century Spain but for the community of La Isabela also defined (along with wealth through gold) the purpose and justification of the expedition. Religion and defensive concerns were among the most important elements shaping the cultural practices and social organization at La Isabela.

Much has been written about the deep religiousness of Columbus himself, which must have influenced the role of religious activity at La Isabela. Archaeological and architectural evidence suggests, for example, that the church was one of the first and most hastily constructed public buildings in the town, probably owing to the perceived urgency of having a sanctuary in which to hold Mass (chapter 6). Nearly all of La Isabela's chroniclers made note of the first Mass in America, but little is mentioned after that about religious observances in the town. Presumably the daily, weekly, and annual rounds of Catholic Mass, Holy Communion, confession, and prayers were maintained, at least initially.

Although very few items directly identifiable as religious in origin have been excavated at La Isabela, this is probably not an accurate reflection of the fervent Catholicism and religiosity of late fifteenth-century Spaniards. Indeed, one cannot overemphasize the profound influence of the Catholic Church in shaping both daily life and public policy in Spain and the Spanish Americas. Church, state, and people were inextricably interconnected through the *Patronato Real*, by which the pope granted the kings of Spain papal authority in the administration of church and ecclesiastical affairs in Spain. This included the right to establish churches and monasteries and to receive and administer such ecclesiastical benefices as tithes and endowments. At the request of Ferdinand and Isabela, the Patronato Real was extended to the Spanish Americas in papal decrees between 1493 and 1508, which recast it as an agreement between the Crown and the pope that ecclesiastical control of the Americas would remain in the hands of the Crown so long as the monarchs fulfilled their obligation to convert the American natives and see that church precepts were properly administered. Rules of social conduct were largely set forth and enforced by the church (backed by the state), and social activities were scheduled and organized by the annual round of religious feasts and observations. Mass was a daily ritual.[1]

These religious activities would have been led by members of the sizable contingent of friars and priests who came to La Isabela in 1493. News of Columbus's discovery inspired missionary fervor, particularly among the Franciscans, and the friars who took part in the establishment of La Isabela came both to tend to the spiritual welfare of the Spaniards and to convert the Taínos.[2]

As we saw in chapter 2, the group was headed by Fray Bernardo Buil, a member of the Franciscan Minor Order from the monastery of Monserrat, who was appointed by Isabela and served as the papal nuncio. Other religious representatives are thought to have included the Franciscan friars Juan de la Duela, Juan de Tisín, Juan Pérez, Rodrigo Pérez, and Antonio de Marchena, also from the monastery of Monserrat; Mercederians Juan Infante and Juan Solórsano; the Hieronymite father Ramón Pané, and four secular priests who were not members of orders, including Pedro de Arenas and Angel de Neyra. Several of these priests left in disillusionment within a year, some with Antonio de Torres in April 1494 and others, including Fray Buil, with Torres in 1495 (as we saw in chapter 4). It is unclear how many remained to perform the necessary religious offices after 1495, or to what extent the round of religious observances continued in La Isabela, as circumstances deteriorated and Columbus was increasingly absent.

Material items of religious significance are less likely to have entered La Isabela's archaeological record than many other categories of goods. Church furnishings were undoubtedly removed to Santo Domingo or Concepción de la Vega when La Isabela was abandoned, and personal possessions with religious significance were probably more carefully looked after than other more mundane categories of goods. Some items, such as the various finger rings bearing religious motifs we discussed in chapter 7, undoubtedly carried multiple meanings associated with economy, personal adornment, and social identity as well as with religion. The same is true of the carnelian beads from the site, which could have been used in either rosaries or jewelry (although no beads attributable exclusively to rosaries were found). If rosary or devotional beads were lost at the site, they were probably of wood or bone and did not survive. Only one artifact from La Isabela was of unequivocally religious affiliation: a crucifix with a corpus excavated in the Poblado area, shown in figure 8.1.

Although not one was found at La Isabela, it is known that veneras—small devotional images—to the Virgin Mary came to the Americas on Columbus's first voyage, and probably with the second expedition as well. Las Casas recounts that Columbus obliged a member of the *Santa María*'s crew to wear a silver image of the Virgin Mary around his neck, because the sailor had said "some mischievous and derogatory things against our Holy Faith."[3] Upon his return to La Navidad in 1493, Columbus also convinced the Taíno cacique Guacanagarí to wear a silver image of Mary around his neck.[4] Many of the conquistadors were devotees of Mary and carried images of her constantly, attributing many of their victories—such as the one over the Taíno forces in the Cibao in 1495—to her intervention.[5]

Burial of the Spanish dead was probably one of the more frequent, if unhappy, religious rituals performed at La Isabela. Nearly one hundred human burials were encountered in the cemetery, all of them outside the church itself.[6] As we mentioned earlier, the analysis of these remains is not yet complete, but the investigators report that among the burials excavated in 1983 they found an American-Indian woman with a newborn infant. They also identified a European man buried face down and suggested that he may have been one of the mutineers hanged by Columbus. In a group of four skeletons buried in the Christian fashion,

8.1. Crucifix from La Isabela. Copper alloy and white metal. Height: 4.5 centimeters. (Drawing: Pauline Kulstad and Patricia D. Farrior.)

a male and a female skeleton were thought to been buried together in the same grave.[7]

Some general observations can be made about mortuary patterns at La Isabela. Although priests, hidalgos, and those who could afford substantial contributions to the church were ideally buried inside the church in late medieval Spain, there were no graves inside the church at La Isabela.[8] This was no doubt because of the shallow soil deposit in that area and the limestone bedrock underlying it. Burials were instead densely concentrated to the east of the church in an area of about forty by twenty meters, where earlier Taíno burials were also found (figure 8.2). At least eighty-five Christian burials (or portions of burials) were located in this area. José Cruxent located at least fifteen additional burials on the south side of the church, but these were disarticulated, deeper, in the Taíno midden and were therefore of uncertain origin. They were left unexcavated.

The Christian skeletons are extended and oriented facing east—

8.2. La Isabela cemetery. (Photo: J. M. Cruxent.)

heads at the west end and feet at the east end—with their arms crossed on their chests. None was in a coffin and they all appear to have been buried unclothed or wrapped in shrouds. The graves are very shallow, starting between twelve and thirty centimeters below the present ground surface (which could have been as much as eighty centimeters to one meter below the original ground surface). Although information about burial stratigraphy, sequences, clothing, and accompaniments awaits the report on the skeletal excavation and analysis, it appears from preliminary observations that mortuary practice at La Isabela was consistent with traditional late medieval Catholic precepts.[9]

The heritage of the reconquista as a holy war deeply connected religion, military prowess, and status, and even though La Isabela was not organized primarily as a military expedition, these elements were still very much interconnected during the lifetime of the colony. Many of the elite military participants in the expedition, for example, were members of religious brotherhoods, such as Mosen Pedro Margarit, who wore the habit of the Order of Santiago, and the military contingent of the Lanzas de Jinetas, who were members of the Santa Hermandad brotherhood.[10]

Public defense at La Isabela was reflected in both the architecture and the material culture of the community. The town walls, the wall surrounding Columbus's fortified house, and the massively constructed al-hóndiga not only served as protection but also expressed the strength and God-given invincibility of the Spaniards. The community—at least after the earliest months—also boasted a full complement of the military technology available at the end of the fifteenth century, including firearms, artillery, crossbows, edged weapons, armor, pole arms, and horses.

Columbus had left his men at La Navidad in 1492 believing that the Taínos constituted no threat at all to the Spaniards. "They are the most timorous people that there are in the world, so that the men that I have left there alone would suffice to destroy all that land, and the island is without danger for their persons."[11] At least partly because of this view, military strength and defensive might were not overriding concerns in planning what Columbus hoped would be a mining and mercantile center in the Americas.

Despite this complacent assessment, however, the heritage of the reconquista and the large number of hidalgos and soldiers of fortune accompanying the expedition gave it a distinctly military flavor, and most of the men bore arms. Arms, armor, and horses were not only essential for defense and aggression but were also imbued with social meaning in medieval Spain. While knives and pole arms, for example, were used by all social classes at the end of the fifteenth century, swords and horses were symbols of status and authority, as they had been throughout the medieval period.[12]

Las Casas recorded that most of the expedition members, whether soldiers, farmers, or trademen, "took arms with them for fighting if the need arose." In addition to these personal arms, the Crown also provided one hundred crossbows, one hundred cuirasses, or breastplates, and one hundred *espingardas*, or firearms.[13] But with the myth of Taíno docility dispelled, the arms apparently seemed inadequate. In his letter to Ferdinand and Isabela written in February 1494, Columbus asked for more and better arms. "Inasmuch as yesterday, in the inspection which was held, the people were found to be very deficient in arms, which I think resulted in some degree from the exchange which was made there in Seville . . . it seems that it would be well that 200 cuirasses [*coracas*] and a hundred espingardas and a hundred crossbows should be ordered to be sent, for it is material of which we have much need, and from all these arms, those who are unarmed could be supplied."[14]

It is not known if Columbus's request was honored, but the archae-

8.3. Crossbow bolt heads.

ological record suggests that the settlement was well supplied with a range of arms, armor, and ammunition.[15] Although most of the aggressive and defensive use of these weapons took place in other parts of the island (see chapter 4), enough of them were present at La Isabela in the storehouse or as personal arms to illustrate the range of European military items brought to America in the fifteenth century.

The late fifteenth century was a time of rapid change in weapons technology, and the weaponry items from the site provide an unparalleled material expression of late fifteenth-century defensive technology. Innovative developments in construction and ignition systems enhanced the use of firearms as personal weapons and permitted them to make inroads into the dominant role held up until then by crossbows.[16] Archaeological evidence for both crossbows and firearms has been recovered at La Isabela, including iron crossbow bolt heads (figure 8.3) and fragments of what may have been bronze crossbow triggers.

At least three categories of guns were present, including the espingarda and/or *hacabuche* shoulder arms that shoot lead balls of between ten and seventeen millimeters in diameter; light *verso*-type mounted swivel guns using balls of between about twenty and thirty millimeters; and larger, carriage-mounted *falconeta*-type artillery that shot metal and stone balls of about sixty-five millimeters (figures 8.4 to 8.6).[17]

Artifacts relating to guns were heavily concentrated in the vicinity of

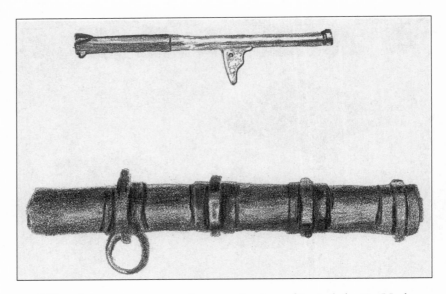

8.4. Fifteenth-century gun types in use at the time of La Isabela. *Top,* Hacken-buschen/hackbut/espingarda variety of hand-held gun; *bottom,* cañón de bom-bardete/culverin-type field gun. (Drawing: Peter Pilot.)

8.5. Ammunition from La Isabela. (Photo: James Quine.)

8.6. Stone shot mold and iron ball, 45 millimeter diameter. (Photo: James Quine.)

the alhóndiga, suggesting that their allocation and use were closely controlled. The only exception to this is the distribution of lead sprue—presumably resulting from shot making—which, although densest in the alhóndiga, is also present in fairly large quantities in the residential sections of the town. The making of ammunition may to some extent have been an individual undertaking.

The remains of swords (figure 8.7) and pole arms are concentrated in the military zone, whereas crossbow bolt heads and tips are distributed relatively evenly across the site. Crossbows, knives, and daggers may have been standard weapons used by most of the men at La Isabela, while firearms and swords were more typically used by the military elite. A similar distinction can be made for types of armor, with brigandine plate found commonly in all areas of the site and chain mail restricted more typically to the elite residential areas (as we shall see further in a moment).

Mounted soldiers were a minority at La Isabela, yet they nevertheless figured prominently not only in the military makeup of the second expedition but also in the disciplinary problems that confronted Colum-

8.7. Copper-alloy scabbard tips. (Photo: James Quine.)

bus in his governance of La Isabela. The right to be mounted on a horse was in itself a distinction, implying privileged status and personal honor. In the thirteenth-century *Partidas* of King Alfonso X we read: "In Spain they are called *caballería*, not for the reason that they go mounted on a horse, but more because those who go by horse go more honorably (that is to say, with more honor). Thus, those who are chosen as caballeros are more honored or have more honor than all other defenders." Priests, commoners, and women rode mules or asses.[18]

By the end of the fifteenth century, however, service on horseback was no longer restricted exclusively to those of high social class. During the reconquest of Granada, two kinds of mounted soldiers were distinguished—the *caballero armado*, who was formally knighted by the king in a ritual ceremony, and the *jinete*, or escudero, who, although serving on horseback, had not been formally recognized by the king. These escuderos constituted a cavalry force essentially of commoners, and they played an important role in the final stages of the reconquista. By the time La Isabela was established, they had developed a kind of light-cavalry style, with a stripped-down set of arms consisting of a short lance (jinete), an oval shield (*adarga*), and a dagger. The stirrups on the escuderos' saddles were very high (*a la jineta*), allowing greater mobility of movement. The caballeros armados, on the other hand, wore their stirrups low *(a la brida)* and carried a relatively cumbersome set of accoutrements, including sword, mace, lance, heavy set of body armor, and a mounted page.[19] The horse equipage from La Isabela indicates that the jineta style of riding and tack used by the escuderos was considerably more common than the a la brida style used more typically by knights.

The twenty escuderos and their horses—the *Lanzas de Jinetas*—were arguably the most organized and formidable military component of the second voyage. Ferdinand and Isabela ordered that this contingent should accompany Columbus's expedition in part because of a perceived threat that the king of Portugal was assembling an armada to send to the Indies, and probably also in part out of royal interest in law and order. The monarchs' secretary, Fernando de Zafra, was told to organize the royal detachment from "among the people of the *Hermandad* (brotherhood) who are in the kingdom of Granada . . . the said twenty lanzas, who would be safe and trustworthy men, and who go with goodwill, and five of them should bring extra mounts, and the extra mounts that they bring should be mares."[20] They were to be paid in advance by the treasury of the Hermandad.

The Santa Hermandad was a kind of national militia or vigilante group organized by Isabela in the early years of her reign to combat roadside banditry and violence. Each town contributed its quota of men from its citizenry, and they were given broad powers of arrest, trial, and punishment. Over the years their savage but successful methods of repressing criminals came to be greatly feared.[21] The Lanzas' primary loyalties at La Isabela were to the Crown and the Hermandad rather than to Columbus, and not unexpectedly, the admiral's heavy-handed insistence on their obedience very quickly engendered their hostility, along with that of a great many other expedition members (which we discussed in chapter 4).

A number of other men who were socially eligible to be caballeros, and perhaps caballeros armados, came to La Isabela without horses. Las Casas noted that at least twenty of the gentlemen on the expedition came as foot soldiers, "although most were hidalgos or others who, if they could afford them, would have been able to serve on horseback."[22]

The twenty horses of the Lanzas de Jinetas that survived the journey to La Isabela were of course valued greatly both as symbols of status and for work and transport. These horses occasioned one of Columbus's first disciplinary crises at La Isabela, when the escuderos denied

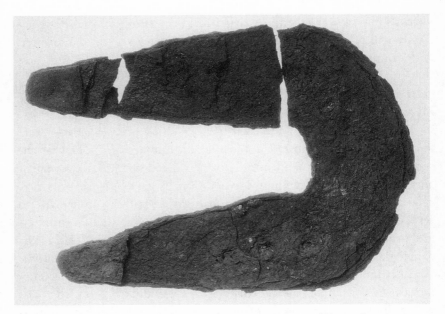

8.8. Horseshoe from La Isabela. Length: 11.2 centimeters. (Photo: James Quine.)

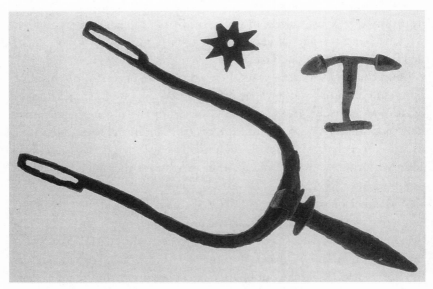

8.9. Spur varieties from La Isabela. *Left*, Moorish-style iron prick spur, total length: 22.5 centimeters; *center*, eight-pointed iron spur rowel, diameter: 3 centimeters. The clasp on the right could have been used in either horse harness or clothing. (Courtesy of Rafael Cantisano; photo: James Quine.)

him the use of their horses to help build the town and till the fields. They claimed that only they could use the horses, and that furthermore they should not be required to do anything that was not done on horseback. When Columbus complained to the sovereigns about the Lanzas' insubordination and suggested that the Crown buy the horses, he was rebuked by the king and queen and told to control the Lanzas and order them to make the horses available. Ultimately the horses did remain in La Isabela, and the Lanzas left.[23]

Horse equipage, unlike weaponry, was concentrated not in the military zone of the alhóndiga but in the elite residential zone and most notably in the house of Columbus. More than half of the horseshoes excavated at the site came from the Casa de Colón (which was the smallest excavated area), suggesting that Columbus himself closely controlled the horses and guarded the horse equipment in his own house rather than in the alhóndiga with the other supplies. Chroniclers made note of a horse ranch apart from La Isabela (perhaps at Las Coles) by the end of the town's occupation, and this may have been another measure to try to control use of the highly valued horses.

Horseshoes were made by the blacksmiths at La Isabela, and Las Casas recounts that as soon as Columbus returned to Spain in 1495 Roldán, who was the supervisor of the workers, "began to assemble large quantities of horseshoes and nails, more than had ever been needed before, though at the time less was needed than previously, or so it seemed." The rebels later raided the royal horse farm and took the horses they needed.[24]

The horseshoes are U-shaped, and they are quite consistent in size and shape (figure 8.8). Other horse-related artifacts include spurs and spur holders, bit fragments, and bridle hardware, although no evidence for horse armor has been recovered.[25] The most intact pieces of horse equipage believed to have been used at La Isabela were not excavated during the current project and are at present in the private collection of Rafael Cantisano. They include stirrups and spurs, all with forms of Moorish origin (figures 8.9 and 8.10). The intact iron spur was an Arabic, or "prick," spur with a single point. Three bronze stirrups, loaned by the Cantisano family to the museum at La Isabela, are of the a la jineta form, associated with Arab horsemen of the fifteenth century. These are characterized by their boxlike form, with a broad footplate enclosed on two sides by wide sideplates (figure 8.10). These stirrups were especially useful with the jineta style of riding, with a high saddle

8.10. Box stirrup used in the jineta style of riding. (Courtesy of Rafael Cantisano; photo: James Quine.)

and short stirrup leathers. The broad footplate permitted a surer footing, allowing greater control for the rider, whose knees would have been high and bent.

Horsemen, foot soldiers, and hidalgos all wore some form of armor in late fifteenth-century La Isabela (figure 8.11). Both chain mail and brigandine plate armor were found throughout the site, but there is no evidence for full body armor (or for the cuirasses known to have been brought to the town). Brigandine plate was by far the most frequently found type of protection and was well represented in all parts of the site except the church, plaza, and Casa de Colón. The brigandine plates were rectangles of iron measuring about 2.5 centimeters wide and about five centimeters long (figure 8.12). They were fastened by copper rivets to a cotton or leather jerkin in an overlapping pattern.[26]

Chain mail was considerably less common than brigandine armor at La Isabela, and it was probably used in a much more limited manner, where flexibility was needed. There is also some indication that it was more frequently used by elite members of the community, as mail con-

8.11. Spanish foot soldier of the late fifteenth and early sixteenth centuries. (Drawing: Merald Clark.)

8.12. Brigandine plates and chain-mail links. (Photo: James Quine.)

stituted 21 percent of the armor fragments in the elite residential area, 80 percent in the Casa de Colón, and just 8 percent in the Poblado.

All the major categories of armor used at the end of the fifteenth century—brigandine plate armor, chain mail, and, to a much lesser extent, body plate armor—used small buckles and straps to fasten sections of the armor together, employing from five to ten or more buckles and straps per set of armor. Some of these are shown in chapter 7, figure 7.14.

As the supplies brought with the expedition were depleted or became worn out, most of the material items used for personal protection, symbols of power, and public defense were either made or repaired at La Isabela. Blacksmiths, farriers, metal founders, and soldiers maintained the weapons, armor, ammunition, and horse equipment needed for both protection and honor. Like the other craftsmen and artisans in the town, they often made do with whatever resources they could find in the isolated and dramatically un-European environment and economy of Hispaniola. It was in this material production that we see the first American alterations to the late medieval Spanish ideal represented by Columbus, and it was first brought about in the non-elite working sector of the community.

Chapter 9

Commerce and Craft

The day to day operation of the colony depended much less on the hidalgos, soldiers, and priests—despite their visibility in the historical record—than it did on the farmers and artisans who accompanied the expedition. Documentary accounts are vague about these men, Las Casas noting only that there were "several men for each of the various trades,"[1] and Ferdinand Colón that his father recruited "artisans of all kinds."[2] Regardless of their essential contributions to the functioning and survival of the medieval community (as at La Isabela), artisans were irrevocably relegated to the lower levels of the Spanish social hierarchy. The hidalgo class despised physical work in any form, and those who performed it. Although they demanded the goods and luxuries they considered necessary to their station, hidalgos felt that the handiwork needed to supply those goods was beneath contempt.[3] This attitude must have also pervaded the community at La Isabela, with the result that very little is recorded either about the artisans themselves or about their work.

The archaeological remains from La Isabela therefore provide the best information about the range of crafts and industries practiced in the colony. Stone masonry, lime and charcoal burning, woodworking, blacksmithing, metal smelting and assaying, pottery production, tile making and shipbuilding are evidenced either by the products of these activities or in the raw materials, tools, and implements used in their practice.

Many of these crafts undoubtedly took place primarily at the Las Coles settlement, where raw materials and water were more readily at hand. Pottery making, for example, required ready access to clay sources, water, and fuel, which were plentiful at Las Coles but not available at El Castillo. A number of documentary accounts attest to the fact that Columbus intended to (and quite possibly did) install waterwheels in the vicinity of Las Coles. We read in Las Casas, "Despite the exposure to northwest winds, he [Columbus] decided leave the ships there and go ashore because the riverbanks looked green and fertile, and water could be brought to town by canals, thus making possible the construction of water mills and other commodities."[4] Ferdinand Colón reports, "He had a dam built that should also provide power for a gristmill."[5] Chanca writes that "they have begun to canalize a branch of the river, and the foremen say that they will bring this through the center of the town and that they will place it on mills and water wheels and whatever can be worked with water."[6] And we find Columbus himself recording that "at this river, which here is close to the city, such as Santa María in Seville is toward the river, and within one league to another river, not large like this, I am now making the mills."[7]

A fragment of a ceramic *arcaduz* or *cangilón*—a waterwheel jar—was recovered at Las Coles from the mouth of the Bajabonico River. The arcaduce is of a type commonly used on the vertical waterwheel known as *Noria de Vuelo*, a Moorish innovation found throughout medieval Iberia. Waterwheels were employed in a variety of mechanical production tasks, such as milling grain, grinding cane, crushing minerals, and driving bellows and trip hammers in iron forging.[8] Although only a single arcaduce has been identified, it suggests that this new form of generating energy was also introduced to America at Las Coles.

Much of the energy for industrial and other activities both at Las Coles and at El Castillo was provided by burning wood. The demands on local wood resources to fire pottery, smelt and forge metals, burn lime, make charcoal, build houses and ships, and meet the cooking needs of more than a thousand people must have been dramatic in the first few years of the settlement. The implied exploitation of wood must have quickly placed enormous stress on the forest resources of the region, exceeding the demands imposed by Taíno agricultural practices. It must also have been a major labor investment for the craftsmen and artisans of the community. Dr. Chanca's forest, "so thick that a rabbit could scarcely pass through it, and so green that never at all will fire be able to burn it," may well have been quickly depleted.

Many of the artisans who came to La Isabela were involved in various aspects of building construction. We have already discussed much of the material evidence for stone masonry and building construction in chapter 6. The presence of a stone sculptor is implied by decorative elements associated with the church, and also by a small stone tablet carved with a three-turreted castle, the symbol of Castile (figure 9.1). The function of this object is uncertain, but it may have been intended as a seal or perhaps an ornamental element in a structure.

Clay roof tiles (tejas) and bricks (ladrillos) figured prominently in the architecture of La Isabela, and these were produced by *tejeros*, who in fifteenth-century Spain were distinct from the pottery makers, or *al-fareros*.[9] Hundreds of thousands of tejas were used in La Isabela's public buildings, undoubtedly produced at Las Coles, although the *casas tejar*— the production complexes that included the kilns, storehouses, and workspaces for the tejeros—have not yet been located. Tejeros, nevertheless, were almost certainly included in the expedition.

Masonry implies the use of mortar and plaster, both made from reduced lime. Although no lime kilns have been located at La Isabela, the mortar and plaster recovered from the site's buildings leaves no doubt that they were produced at La Isabela. The two most common sources for reduced lime, marine shell and limestone, are both abundantly present in the vicinity of the town, and it is likely that the noxious task of lime burning took place away from the settlement, near the sources of raw materials.

Tools associated with sawing, building construction, or woodworking are rare at La Isabela, no doubt because of the poor preservation conditions for iron. Ax heads (figure 9.2), as well as chisels, hammer fragments, wedges, and a gouge, were identified among the remains from the site.[10] The best material evidence for woodworking and carpentry (as well as for blacksmithing) are the nails and spikes from La Isabela. (Some of these are shown in chapter 6, figure 6.10). More than five thousand fragments of wrought-iron nails and more than two hundred intact nails and spikes were excavated at the site. They included va-

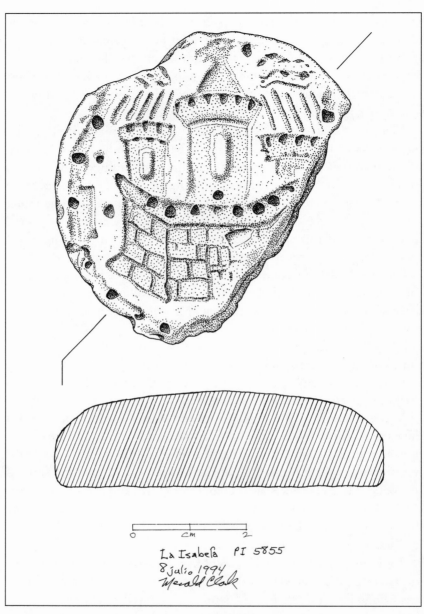

9.1. Carved stone tablet. (Drawing: Merald Clark.)

9.2. Iron ax head. (Photo: James Quine.)

rieties of nails used in carpentry for joining, finishing, and flooring and others with faceted heads that were apparently intended to be visible. About half of the latter group came from the Casa de Colón and iglesia areas, suggesting that they may have served a decorative role on elite doors or gates. Still other nails and spikes are thought to have been used primarily in ship construction. Other products of the blacksmiths at La Isabela are shown in figure 9.3.

Ships were the only lifeline between La Isabela and the rest of the world, and keeping them in good order was of utmost concern. Columbus's first request for supplies included materials needed for ship maintenance, including tar, pintels, and gudgeons for rudders, compasses, mariner's glasses, rigging of all kinds, sails, anchors, oakum, and alcohol for varnish.

Even the most meticulous attention, however, could not prevent hurricane damage. The hurricane of June 1495 sank three of the four ships at anchor in front of La Isabela—probably the *San Juan, Cardera,* and *Gallega.* The shipwrights set about constructing two caravels modeled after the single surviving ship—the *Niña*—using the salvaged remains of those that had sunk. Although this first ship built in the Americas was

9.3. Examples of iron objects probably made by the blacksmiths of La Isabela. *Top left*, doorlock; *bottom left*, fastener; *center*, key; *right*, hinge. (Photo: James Quine.)

named the *Santa Cruz*, it was generally called the *India* by her seamen.[11]

Shipbuilding and repairs at La Isabela were done at the *astillero*—the shipyard—which was almost certainly located in the Playa area of the site (Town Zone 1) immediately to the northwest of the alhóndiga (see chapter 6, figure 6.7). Although filled with sand today as a result of building the road that runs through the center of the site, the Playa was an estuarine lagoon when La Isabela was occupied by the Spaniards. Excavations in the Playa area produced the greatest density of metal items, nails, and tools of any place at La Isabela, and a great many of these were undoubtedly used in ship construction and repair.

Shipbuilding is an extremely complex and highly specialized undertaking. The processes of laying the foundation, framing, reinforcing, planking, and sealing the hull all required special kinds of woodworking techniques, tools, and fasteners.[12] The materials recovered from the nearly contemporary Molasses Reef wreck in the Bahamas and the slightly later Emmanuel Point wreck in Florida illustrate the number and variety of fasteners required in a ship of the period.[13] Analysis of the fasteners from these Spanish shipwrecks suggests that although nails used in carpentry and ship construction had the same nomenclature and size distinctions, those used in carpentry joining had flatter heads than those used to build ships. More than a thousand iron fasteners were excavated at the Molasses Reef site, representing more than a dozen categories ranging from tiny tacks to immense forelock bolts of nearly half a meter in length.

A few of these varieties are present among the materials from the asilledero area of La Isabela, including what may have been forelock bolts, drift pins, and peened head spikes and lead patches.[14] Most of the items excavated from the asilledero, however, are fragmentary and extremely deteriorated after being buried and periodically inundated with salt water over the past five centuries.

Many of the metal objects used by shipbuilders, carpenters, and other craftsmen were undoubtedly made at La Isabela by metal workers, who introduced European metallurgical technology to America. Quantities of "iron", "steel," "lead," and "quicksilver" were included in the 1494 list of supplies to be sent to La Isabela, and the archaeological evidence indicates that they were the raw materials used in a series of other metallurgical activities.[15] These included assaying and smelting of precious metals, ironworking, and the extraction and working of lead. Metalworking at La Isabela took place at the north end of the alhóndiga, where quantities of ore, slag, scrap iron, and lead were concentrated. This location would have been convenient both to the shipyard and to the alhóndiga, providing accessibility to as well as control over the valuable metals and ores.

The primary motive and continual driving force of the colony was the quest for gold, and the materials for gold smelting found at La Isabela are particularly evocative. Most of the gold recovered by the Spaniards (usually via the Taíno Indians) was placer gold, which is gold released from the primary veins by weathering and transported by water to sand or gravel beds where it forms nuggets. Like all unrefined native gold, placer nuggets are actually a natural alloy known in ancient times as *electrum*, which contains between 5 and 50 percent silver.[16] To verify the purity and weight of gold, it was necessary to refine it, often by cupellation (heating the alloy) or by amalgamation with mercury. The crushed electrum ore was mixed with water and mercury and agitated. The mercury-gold amalgam would sink, and other, lighter particles would wash away to be captured for other uses (in a manner not unlike modern archaeological flotation methods). The remaining mercury-gold amalgam would be placed in porous bags of leather or cloth, from which the mercury would be distilled or drip into a container, and the gold dust would remain in the bag.

Liquid mercury (204 grams) was in fact recovered from deposits inside the storehouse, all from a single excavation unit along the center of the alhóndiga's west wall.[17] This area must have been either a storage location for mercury or possibly part of a metallurgical complex where the amalgamation process took place. Columbus clearly perceived a need for miners and metal extractors familiar with mercury, and one of his earliest requests for personnel specified "miners from those who are in Almadén."[18] Extensive deposits of cinnabar—ore for mercury—occur near Almadén, which as a result is the major center for mercury production in Spain. There is no evidence that mercury was distilled from cinnabar at La Isabela. Neither cinnabar nor the iron or ceramic retorts in which it would have been distilled have been recovered.

Mercury was regularly shipped to the Spanish colonies throughout the colonial era, and it has been recovered from Spanish shipwrecks of the sixteenth, seventeenth, and eighteenth centuries.[19] Quicksilver was typically the last thing to be loaded on board, because it rapidly corroded the bags and boxes in which it was packed. This may well have happened to the mercury containers stored at the alhóndiga of La Isabela, allowing the mercury to escape in droplets.

After refining the electrum (or other gold-bearing ore), the resulting gold (or silver) was placed in crucibles and melted in an oven in order to determine its purity. The crucibles recovered at La Isabela are small triangular cupels of extremely hard ceramic, metallic gray in color and measuring from three to five centimeters in height (figure 9.4). They are nearly identical to those commonly used to melt and assay gold during the late medieval era.[20]

Although consistent in form with medieval metal technology in Europe, the crucibles were distributed throughout the site in a somewhat unexpected pattern. Of the forty-six crucibles found, forty-one came from residential areas. None was recovered from either the alhóndiga or the shipbuilding and industrial areas to the north of the alhóndiga, suggesting that the final stage of production may have been done largely by

9.4. Assaying crucible.
Height: 3.2 centimeters.
(Photo: James Quine.)

individuals. At least some of the hearths excavated in the Poblado residential zones were probably used as cupeling hearths (for refining metals
in a crucible in or over a fire). This was unexpected in light of the stern
admonitions by the Crown and by Columbus that no private individuals were to trade for or acquire gold (as we mentioned in chapter 4).

The quantity of gold acquired as nuggets and electrum by the
Spaniards was never great. The archaeological evidence from La Isabela
suggests that Columbus's miners and metallurgists also tried to extract
precious metals from argentiferous lead ore, or galena. This process involved crushing galena, smelting it at a high temperature to combine the
silver and other metals with lead, and separating them from impurities
(which run off as slag). The smelted galena was also a primary source
for lead, which was needed at La Isabela for ammunition and ship fit-
tings. The smelted metal could also be cupelled or heated to a high temperature in a strong current of air. This would separate the lead from
the silver and gold, producing litharge (lead slag).[21]

The base of a furnace was located immediately outside the alhóndiga's north end, and more than eighty-five kilograms of galena
were found in the four excavation units adjacent to the hearth; a mere
two kilograms were recovered from the rest of the site combined. Only
the below-ground portion of the furnace has survived, and so it is not
possible to know what type of construction it featured.[22] Its remains
consist of a large, roughly oval depression in the bedrock, in which the

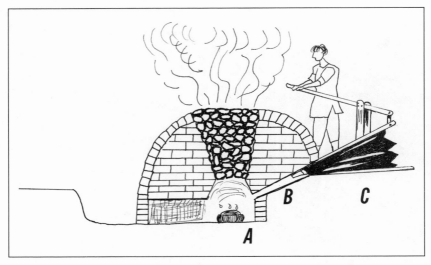

9.5. Simple metallurgy furnace of a type probably used at La Isabela. *A*, ore; *B*, air blast through tuyere and bellows; *C*, soil matrix. (Drawing by Pauline Kulstad after Cotter 1959:12.)

rock lining has been heavily burned and altered by heat, forming slag. At one edge of the pit, a smaller, circular hole had been excavated and lined with rock, creating a sloping, fluelike feature extending from the ground surface into the larger pit. This was probably the entry for bellows or a *tuyere*, a nozzle or pipe that introduces air into the furnace. This configuration is consistent with that of a smelting furnace used to smelt metal from ore (figures 9.5 and 9.6).[23]

The large amounts of lead ore and the relative absence of iron slag or bloom around the furnace suggest that it was used in a process involving lead sulfite, in spite of the potentially noxious and even poisonous fumes that would have been expelled during firing. Because lead was important both for making shot and as sheathing to protect ship hulls from corrosion and terredo worms, the smelting of lead would have been a valuable industrial activity at La Isabela, even if it could not be further refined to capture silver. Figure 9.7 shows a variety of lead objects and by-products recovered from the vicinity of the alhóndiga.

The production and repair of iron objects—nails, horseshoes, tools, armor, weapons, and ship furnishings—was essential in the isolated colony, and blacksmiths must have been critical to the functioning of the community at La Isabela. Ironworking was a highly respected and

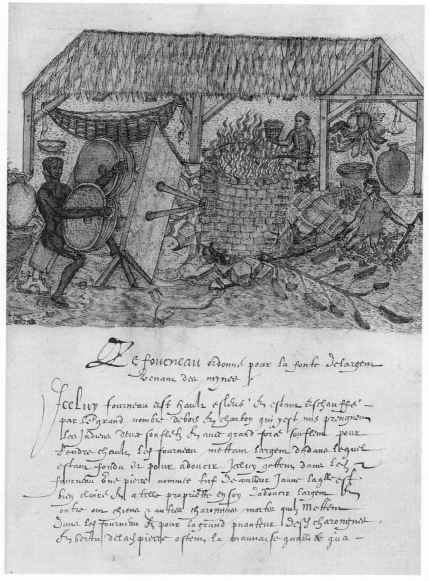

9.6. "The furnace prescribed for the smelting of the silver coming from the mines." An arrangement probably not dissimilar from that of La Isabela's furnace. (Plate 103, *Histoire naturelle des Indes: The Drake Manuscript in the Pierpont Morgan Library*. 1996. Second half of the sixteenth century. Courtesy of the Pierpont Morgan Library.)

9.7. Lead from the alhóndiga in various stages of production and manipulation.

specialized craft in late fifteenth-century Spain, incorporating several distinct *oficios* (trade guilds) based on the objects produced at the forge.[24] Among them were the *herreros* (who produced and repaired general iron implements), the *herredores* (horseshoe makers), the *freneros* (bit and horse harness makers), the *cerrajeros* (who produced locks and keys), *agujeteros* (needle makers), and *armeros*, (arms and armor makers), who were further subdivided into specialized guilds. There is no record of which and how many of these specialized ironworkers were present at La Isabela, but the archaeological record suggests that there were at least several herreros, as well as herredores and armeros working in the colony. The armeros would have been especially important to the defense of the settlement by repairing and possibly making weapons.

Regardless of their guild affiliation, all of these craftsmen worked with iron in a forge. Smelted iron and steel were presumably sent to La Isabela, and fragments of wrought-iron bars were recovered in the alhóndiga. As we indicated earlier, neither iron-bloom fragments nor large quantities of iron slag were recovered from the site, suggesting that wrought iron was brought from Spain. It is possible that human-powered or water-powered forges to smith iron bloom into malleable

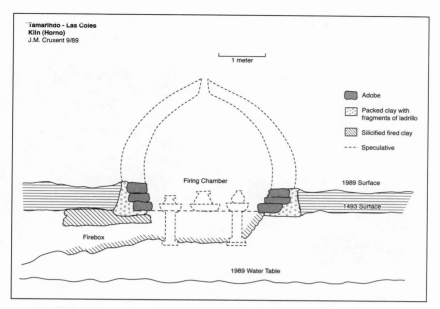

Tamarindo - Las Coles
Kiln (Horno)
J.M. Cruxent 9/89

1 meter

Adobe

Packed clay with
fragments of ladrillo

Silicified fired clay

Speculative

Firing Chamber

1989 Surface

1493 Surface

Firebox

1989 Water Table

9.8. Diagram of the pottery kiln excavated at Las Coles. (Drawing: J. M. Cruxent.)

metal may have been located at an as yet unlocated place near the Las Coles settlement.

Blacksmith forges have not been conclusively located at La Isabela, but at least one was probably at or close to the north end of the al-hóndiga, where a great deal of scrap iron was recovered. Forges and anvils were normally built up to a height convenient for the smith to work at while standing, and the fire to keep the metal hot was above ground.[25] The massive subsurface disturbances in this part of the site would have destroyed any traces of these platforms.

We found no evidence for furnaces or kilns related to ceramic production at El Castillo, and it appears that pottery and roof-tile making were restricted to Las Coles. The discovery of a late fifteenth-century Spanish pottery kiln at Las Coles, along with examples of its products, demonstrated conclusively that the production of wheel-thrown pottery was introduced to America at La Isabela (figure 9.8). The kiln was an oval, two-chambered updraft type, typical of Islamic-style kilns known from medieval Spain and other parts of the Islamic world.[26] Only the lower, subterranean portions of the kiln's foundation have survived, but these show that the walls were forty to fifty centimeters thick and made

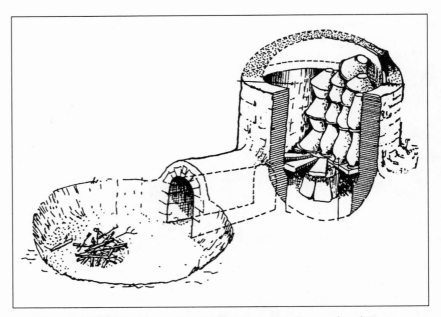

9.9. Moorish-influenced type of updraft kiln used in late medieval Spain, probably similar to the kiln at La Isabela. (After Córdoba de la Llave 1990:330.)

of packed mud. The interior of the firing chamber itself was about 2.1 meters in diameter at its base, with an extension at one side for the fire, and probably had a configuration similar to that shown in figure 9.9. The Tamarindo kiln is at the lower end of size ranges for updraft kilns of the period, which were from about two to five meters in their widest dimension and some three meters tall.[27]

The ceramic products found both inside and around the kiln are all unglazed, wheel-thrown pots of typical late medieval Andalusian shapes. They include products made in late medieval Spain by the *olleros* (makers of table and cooking wares) and the *tinajeros* (who produced the large storage jars known as *tinajas*, as well as other storage vessels).[28] Both categories of potters may have been present at La Isabela.

So far only the kiln itself and adjacent concentrations of wasters— imperfect items—and charcoal have been delineated at Tamarindo, but other features related to pottery production were undoubtedly present. Medieval Spanish and Islamic pottery workshops were designed to organize the many complex tasks involved in making ceramics.[29] The most tedious of these tasks involved preparation of the clay, which had to be excavated, then crushed, sieved, placed in a pit or tank, and soaked. The clay was kneaded while soaking, often with the feet of the workmen, to allow extraneous inclusions to settle. The resulting semiliquid clay was spread out and allowed to dry, after which is was cut into blocks and stored in a cool dark place to increase its plasticity, or ripen. Only then was it ready to throw on the wheel.

Most potter's wheels at the end of the fifteenth century were pit wheels, with the wheel shaft placed in a pit of two to 2.5 feet deep and the wheel itself protruding above the ground. The potter sat on the edge of the pit to work on the pots. Once thrown, the pots were stored in a drying shed for up to several months to remove excess moisture prior to firing. Most of these activities must have taken place at Tamarindo and would have left pitlike archaeological signatures.

Ethnographic and historical studies of pottery production for the kilns of this period suggest that a kiln the size of the one at Las Coles (about two meters in base diameter) had a firing capacity of as many as a thousand pots, with an average of 85 percent of the kiln load surviving the firing in a usable form.[30] If the Tamarindo kiln approached this norm, it could theoretically have produced two thousand pots (ten for each household in the city) in just three firings. Although the productivity was probably not this high, given the demands of securing fuel and clay in the face of illness and hunger, the high potential output helps explain the very large number of unglazed pottery vessels recovered from the site.

There are no clues in either the documentary or material records of La Isabela about the distribution mechanisms for the ceramics made in the kiln(s) of Tamarindo, or for any other domestic consumables produced in the colony, such as charcoal, food, construction materials, or metal items. They could have been sold, bartered, or distributed by Columbus in a spirit of communal production. In the case of Spanish pottery, at least, considerable effort was expended to ensure that abundant supplies of appropriate Spanish plates, bowls, and storage containers were available to all the households in La Isabela.

The differential distribution of goods in the town as well as evidence for a money-based exchange system suggest that an internal (and possibly informal) economy began to develop in La Isabela, despite the salary-based, exclusionary economic policy of the factoría system.

Early in 1494 Columbus suggested to Ferdinand and Isabela that merchants be allowed to send various kinds of goods to the colony for sale to the residents. "All these things the people here would receive with pleasure on account of their pay, and if this supply were brought there by honest agents . . . there would be some economy."[31] Although the sovereigns declined to act on the suggestion, "some economy" appears to have developed nevertheless. The material record of La Isabela suggests that the town had an internal system of exchange based in part on gambling, commodity production, and probably barter, both among the Spaniards and between Spaniards and Indians.

Samuel Morison speculates that "of course there would have been no sense in paying the men off in Hispaniola where there was nothing to spend money on; all of it would have fallen into the hands of the most skillful gamblers."[32] Yet it appears that many of the men were in fact paid salaries in coinage at La Isabela. A number of comments made in correspondence both by Columbus and by the sovereigns indicate that Columbus had a supply of money at La Isabela with which to pay salaries, although not all of the expedition members were paid in the Americas.[33]

Coins are among the most frequently found nonceramic artifacts at La Isabela. One hundred and nine fifteenth-century coins were excavated at the site (figure 9.10), and uncounted others have been recovered and removed illicitly over the years. The coins were found throughout all the residential sectors of the site, but the only concentrations of coins were in the residential zone bordering the plaza, presumed to be an elite living area.

Although many of the coins are fragmentary and eroded, most of them are sufficiently intact to identify, and they have been catalogued by Alan Stahl of the American Numismatic Society.[34] (See table 9.1.) They include coins from throughout Spain, Portugal, Sicily, Genoa, and Alquilea, although the great majority are low-denomination copper-alloy (*billón*) coins known as *blancas* (issued by Henry IV of Spain) and *ceutils* (from Portugal). Only five of the coins were of silver, and only one of these—a half real—was issued by Ferdinand and Isabela.

Stahl notes that "the predominance of coins of Henry IV confirms the early habitation of this site, and the lack of billón of Ferdinand and Isabela demonstrates its abandonment soon after 1497. . . . The finds of La Isabela are of numismatic importance in that they present a detailed view of low denomination Spanish coinage at a particular time, which is unparalleled in Spain itself."[35]

Although coins were found throughout the site of La Isabela, the

9.10. Commonly occurring coins at La Isabela: *top*, Portuguese ceitils of Alfonso V; *bottom*, Spanish blancas of Enrique IV.

other kinds of items related to commerce were concentrated in the southeastern sector of the Poblado area, close to the town wall. These items included two counting tokens, or *jetons*, and two kinds of merchants' weights (figures 9.11 and 9.12).[36] Jetons are round, made of nonprecious metal, and struck with a wide variety of designs that might represent the jeton's maker, its intended user, religious motifs, city coats of arms, rulers, or other themes. Counting tokens were used with a board or cloth with lines designated for various values, such as 5, 10, 50, 100. Counting was done by placing tokens on a line of particular value; for example, two tokens on the 50 line and two on the 10 line would equal 120.

Most examples of counting jetons, including those from La Isabela, were produced in Nuremberg, which was the center for jeton (or *Rechenpfennig*) production from the fifteenth through the seventeenth centuries. The system of calculating with numismatic jetons had been developed in Europe by the end of the twelfth century and was used until the early sixteenth century, by which date it had been largely superseded by arithmetic systems of numeric calculation.

Because the intrinsic value of a colonial-era coin was based on its weight, a means to verify that weight was essential. Coin weights have been used for as long as coins have been minted. Each coin weight was

TABLE 9.1 Coins Excavated at La Isabela

Kingdom	Ruler	Denomination	Mint	Qty.
Castile and Léon	Enrique IV (1454–1474)	One Real		1
Castile and Léon	Enrique IV (1454–1474)	Half Real		2
Castile and Léon	Enrique IV (1454–1474)	Two Blanca		1
Castile and Léon	Enrique IV (1454–1474)	Blanca	Avila	21
Castile and Léon	Enrique IV (1454–1474)	Blanca	Burgos	3
Castile and Léon	Enrique IV (1454–1474)	Blanca	Cuenca	7
Castile and Léon	Enrique IV (1454–1474)	Blanca	Coruña	2
Castile and Léon	Enrique IV (1454–1474)	Blanca	Segovia	8
Castile and Léon	Enrique IV (1454–1474)	Blanca	Seville	23
Castile and Léon	Enrique IV (1454–1474)	Blanca	Toldeo	13
Castile and Léon	Enrique IV (1454–1474)	Blanca	Uncertain	10
Castile and Léon	Ferdinand and Isabela (1474–1504)	Half real		1
Castile and Léon	Anonymous ruler, late third century	Seisén		1
Navarre	Catherine I and John II d'Albret (1483–1512)	Half blanca		1
Portugal	Alfonso V (1432–1481)	Ceitil		6
Portugal	John II (1481–1495	Ceitil		1
Alquilea	Louis II of Teck (1412–1437)	Soldo		1
Genoa	(?) Fifteenth century	Minuto		1
Sicily	Juan of Aragón (1458–1479)	Denaro		1
Sicily	?	Denaro		1
Unidentifiable				4
TOTAL				109

Identified by Alan Stahl

9.11. Merchants' weights from La Isabela: *left*, coin weight, 1.5 cm diameter, 4.5 grams); *right*, cup weight, top diameter: 2 cm, height: 1 cm, weight: 14.2 grams. (Photo: James Quine.)

9.12. A Nuremberg counting token, diameter 2.9 centimeters. (Drawing: Merald Clark.)

made to correspond to the weight of a specific coin, and it was impressed with a design that was easily recognizable as representing that coin (usually including part of the coin's motif or inscription). This design was particularly important during times of widespread illiteracy and correspondingly widespread use of coin weights by merchants. The single coin weight found at La Isabela weighs 4.5 grams and bears a shield with what appear to be two lions rampant.

From the fifteenth century to the present day, brass nested weights (also known as cup weights) were used widely in the Spanish colonies and throughout Europe to weigh a variety of commodities, ranging from gold to grain. Nested weight sets consisted of a series of graduated, cup-shaped weights fittting into one another. The largest (outer) cup usually had a hinged lid that enclosed the nested set in a compact unit. They were made in a wide range of sizes depending on their intended purpose, with sets ranging in weight from sixty-four pounds or more to just a few ounces. The example from La Isabela, shown in figure 9.11, weighs 14.5 grams and is 2.4 centimeters across at its top.

The weights, jetons, and coins support the contention that a certain amount of commercial activity did take place at La Isabela. Although coins are found throughout the site, the concentration of the weights and tokens in the southeastern corner of the community suggests that this may have been an area of trade, gambling, or other kinds of money-based commerce.

From the first days of colonization, Columbus and the Crown attempted to restrict trade with the Taínos to official channels. The instructions for the second voyage given to Columbus by Ferdinand and Isabela repeatedly emphasized that trade with the inhabitants of America was restricted exclusively to the Crown and its representatives: "No person or persons among those who are to sail with the said fleet, of whatever rank or station they may be, may carry or be permitted to carry . . . any merchandise for barter on the said islands and mainland, for none save their Highnesses are to engage in barter" [Item 9], and "all barter is to be carried out by the Admiral or the person he may designate in his place and by the treasurer of Their Highnesses in the Indies, and by no other person" [Item 14].[37]

Such an edict was largely unenforceable in casual encounters between Spaniards and Indians, particularly once the colonists appreciated that the Taínos would "barter the gold and provisions and all they bring for ends of straps, for beads, for pins, for fragments of dishes and plates."[38] Columbus, with little apparent success, had tried during the first voyage to restrain the Spanish sailors' greed by insisting that exchange be reciprocal. Las Casas comments that "the Indians were so liberal and the Spaniards so greedy and unrestrained, it was not enough for them that for a lace end or even for a bit of glass and of earthenware and of other things of no value, the Indians would give them whatever they desired, but without giving anything to them, they wished to have and to take everything. This the Admiral always forbade."[39]

Given the circumstances, it was probably already too late by the second voyage effectively to prohibit trade altogether. The restrictions on barter were undoubtedly even more difficult to enforce as hunger became increasingly prevalent in the colony. Columbus implemented a system of official barter with the Taínos, sending contingents of soldiers to Indian towns to exchange Spanish goods (in the presence of an accountant) for Taíno gold and food (as we mentioned in chapter 4). This scenario of hungry soldiers roaming the countryside to barter must have encouraged frequent abuses, and the increasing hostility between Taínos and Spaniards culminated in the confrontations of 1495 in the Vega Real. After the resulting defeat of the Taíno forces, Columbus ended the barter system and replaced it with systematic tribute, reducing barter to illicit informal exchange. By the time La Isabela was in the process of abandonment, even the tribute system had largely collapsed, and there was relatively little economic exchange (other than tribute in the form of labor) between Taínos and Spaniards.

It is extremely difficult to determine which, if any, of the Taíno artifacts excavated at La Isabela entered the site through Spanish-Taíno exchange. The presence of a dense Taíno midden and cemetery predating the Spanish occupation, coupled with the severe subsequent disturbances to the site, make such an assessment tentative at best.[40] Gold—not likely to be left at La Isabela—and food and cotton—not likely to be preserved archaeologically—were the most common tribute items. A list of goods brought to La Isabela as tribute, however, does include such items as Indian arrows, flint battle axes, Indian hatchets, masks (guaycas) made of cotton and stones, 152 "colored stones," statues, "badges," small pieces of brass, strings of amber, stone necklaces, a copper mirror, and brass spindles.[41] It is possible that some of the carved stone or shell items recovered from the site may have been part of tribute or barter offerings.

Las Casas recorded that among the goods brought to La Isabela on the second voyage were "many coffers of trade goods and merchandise to be given away to the Indians on behalf of the King and Queen, or to be bartered." These goods are unfortunately not listed by the chroniclers, but many casual comments by Las Casas, Columbus, Chanca, and others identify hawk's bells and glass beads as the most common trade items. Others included red caps, tambourine jingles, brass rings, and coins.[42]

Other clues to objects traded between Spaniards and Taínos have come from excavations at Taíno burial sites of the fifteenth century.[43]

These sites contained a variety of metal and ceramic objects that were probably traded, including glazed pottery, finger rings, bells, buckles, clasps, and bits of copper alloy.

Given the importance of beads and bells in the Spaniards' trade with the Taínos, it is curious that so few of them were recovered from excavations at La Isabela. As we pointed out earlier, no glass beads at all were found at the site. Only four crushed fragments of copper-alloy rumbler bells of the type generally called *cascabeles* (hawk's bells) by the Spaniards have been excavated.[44] It is quite possible that most of the bells and glass beads brought to La Isabela were quickly dispersed among Taíno settlements throughout the island.

Some of the finger rings from the site—particularly the brass rings with molded crosses on their bezels—may also have been intended for exchange with the Taínos, and it has been suggested that some of the glass bracelets—manillas—illustrated in chapter 6 may similarly have been intended for trade. Much of the Taíno-Spanish exchange, however, was undoubtedly done informally and illicitly between individuals for whatever items or services were needed or desired.

Significant exchange of material goods between Spaniards and Taínos was probably uncommon after 1497, and, as we related in chapter 4, the decline of economic exchange coincided with the decline and ultimate abandonment of La Isabela as a town. By early 1498, the artisans and traders had been relocated to Santo Domingo, and the kilns, forges, and mills of La Isabela were abandoned. The remains left behind reflected not only the hopeful design for a New Iberia but also the collapse of that design and the expectations upon which it was based.

These remains represent only a portion of what was lost, discarded, or abandoned by the settlers during their brief occupation, but they are nevertheless abundant in comparison to those at slightly later Spanish colonial sites in sixteenth-century Hispaniola (particularly when we consider La Isabela's very brief occupation and terrible physical damage). The archaeological remnants of Columbus's first colony also differ in a number of other ways from the archaeological assemblages of Hispaniola's early sixteenth-century towns, and we shall explore the implications of these differences in the chapters ahead.

Chapter 10

Aftermath

The discovery of gold deposits in the south part of the island in 1496 was the beginning of the end for La Isabela. The decision to build a new town on the south coast, near the San Cristóbal gold deposits, had already been made when Columbus returned to Spain that same year to defend himself at court against his critics' denunciations. It was the rebellion of Roldán and his sacking of La Isabela, however, that most dramatically defined the failure of the Columbian project.

Roldán's rebellion and its consequences also marked a new kind of social sensibility for the Spanish colonists, one that tried to deny class privilege by encouraging even the basest-born Spaniards to claim land and Indian labor in the manner of hidalgos. Roldán and his followers (the *roldanistas*) were predominantly common soldiers, farmers, and artisans, but they rejected demands of obedience from the leaders of the colony and lived as a separate polity in Indian communities with Indian allies. There is little doubt that the roldanistas, collectively and individually, often exploited and abused the Taínos (particularly the women) in many ways.[1] At the same time, they openly embraced a range of American-Indian elements as appropriate to life in the colony, including Indian wives and mestizo families, representing what Anthony Stevens Arroyo has called "pioneers in what became the *criollo* adaptation to life in the Indies."[2] At minimum, the roldanistas established a lifestyle that emphasized accommodation and incorporation of new American elements and circumstances, a pattern that would persist in some form or another throughout the colonial period.

Although Columbus successfully defended himself at court, by 1498 it was clear to everyone that the salary-based, Crown-controlled factoría model was not working. When Columbus embarked on his third voyage to the Americas, he was supplied with instructions quite different from those he had carried to La Isabela in 1493. La Isabela was to be relocated to the south coast, nearer the gold mines, and the number of Spaniards residing in Hispaniola was not to exceed 330. The Crown specified the composition of the group, which ideally was to include 40 squires, 100 foot soldiers, 30 sailors, 30 cabin boys, 20 gold washers, 50 farm workers and gardeners, 20 skilled tradesmen of different types, and 30 women.[3] As at La Isabela, these settlers were to be salaried people, although a limited amount of shipping and open commerce was permitted between Spain and the colony. Columbus was furthermore permitted to make grants of land (repartimientos) to the settlers, who were in turn obliged to establish a household and to work and reside on the land for four years. All precious minerals and brazilwood, regardless of the land on which they were found, belonged solely to the Crown, although licenses to recover these resources could be issued through the government, and the licensees could share in the profits.

After exploring the north coast of South America, Columbus arrived in Santo Domingo on 31 August 1498 and found the new settlement on the east bank of the Ozama well under way. His authority, however, was dangerously threatened by Roldán and his followers, who were living as an independent polity in the western part of the island and were gaining supporters weekly. Faced with Roldán's intransigence and popular support, Columbus was forced to grant the rebels amnesty, land, and rights to Indian vassals in order to secure their allegiance.

This was not the sort of repartimiento intended by the Spanish Crown, which was to be an allocation specifically of land to be used for farming or ranching.[4] Roldán, however, insisted on also receiving the vassalage of the caciques associated with the Spanish land grants, and Columbus acceded. This decision initiated what was to become the Spanish-American institution of encomienda, by which groups of Indians were "commended" to individual Spaniards to whom they owed labor tribute in exchange for presumed instruction in Christianity and civilization.[5] Lands and caciques throughout those parts of the island already vanquished by the Spaniards, principally in the central Cibao area, were allocated to Roldán and his men, who used the caciques to organize their subjects as in Spanish farms, mines, ranches, and households. This naturally provoked demands for labor repartimientos by the other Spaniards on the island who had not supported Roldán, and Columbus was forced to grant these demands in order to prevent mutinies. The already desperate situation for the Taínos was made impossible.[6]

Columbus's recasting of repartimientos to include rights to Indian labor—along with his continuing approval of enslaving Indians—proved to be his downfall. Five ships returned to Spain in October 1498, carrying some three hundred repatriate settlers and five hundred slaves who had been given to the returnees by Columbus. Queen Isabela was outraged: "What right does my Admiral have to give away my Vassals to anyone?"[7] The ships also carried bitter complaints about Columbus's administration and his favoritism in distributing Indians among the Spaniards. At that point, Ferdinand and Isabela determined to end Columbus's governance, and they sent a temporary governor to look into the charges of mismanagement and get things under control. Their choice, Fernando de Bobadilla, arrived in Santo Domingo in August 1499 with two ships and a few settlers salaried by the Crown.

Bobadilla introduced a new kind of social order to Hispaniola. Virtually all the social and economic conditions of life in the colony were in a state of flux when he arrived. There were about three hundred Spaniards living on the island, including the former roldanistas. The principal settlement was the town on the east bank of the Ozama, officially known as Santo Domingo but also referred to as Nueva Isabela.[8] As in the old Isabela, most of the town's buildings were of wood and thatch, and the fort was made of tapia.

Other small Spanish settlements had meanwhile grown up near the interior forts of Concepción, Santiago, and Bonao in the Cibao, and some Spaniards apparently also remained in Xaraguá, where Roldán had been given sizable land grants by Columbus. The discovery of minable gold deposits in the Cibao in 1499 greatly stimulated the growth of the interior settlements, initiating what would become the Hispaniola gold rush and adding insistence to the insatiable Spanish demands for Indian labor in the mines.[9]

Not all Hispaniolan chiefdoms were under Spanish control and repartimiento in 1500. The Higuey region in the southeastern part of the island as well the Guacajarima caciques in the southwestern peninsula were still autonomous. Nor had the northwestern peninsula been subdued. Although parts of the Xaraguá region had been granted to Roldán, an accommodation between him and the leaders of the region had apparently been agreed upon, and the cacica Anacaona was still the ruler of Xaraguá (which included what is today the southern half of Haiti).

New uprisings against Columbus broke out in both the Cibao and Xaraguá in 1500, involving Spaniards and probably also Indians. Columbus was in the Cibao and the adelantado Bartolomé was in Xaraguá trying to quell the rebellions when Bobadilla arrived in Santo Domingo. One of the first sights to greet Bobadilla and his companions as they sailed into the Ozama River was a set of gallows on either bank, from which two of the Spanish rebels were hanging. The hanging of Spaniards, combined with the many complaints against Columbus, provoked Bobadilla to storm the fortaleza (which was defended by Diego Colón and the loyal warden of the fort) with a mob of discontented colonists and assume control of the colony. When Columbus arrived back in Santo Domingo after hearing of Bobadilla's actions, he and his brothers were thrown into the prison and then sent back to Spain in chains.[10] In this ignominious manner Columbus's governance of the Indies was ended, and a new era of quasi-imperial control began.

Little changed in Hispaniola during Bobadilla's governance; the population remained at about three hundred people, and no new Spanish or Indian uprisings took place. Bobadilla's single significant initiative seems to have been his independent decision to release the gold miners from their obligation to pay both the Crown's half and Columbus's tenth of the proceeds. Once this measure was in place, the recovery of gold increased dramatically, with possibly as much as 275 kilograms produced in 1501.[11] Although the exemption of the taxes was severely disapproved of (and quickly reinstated) by the Crown, it did demonstrate that Hispaniola was capable of producing the gold that Columbus had always claimed it could.

The real transformation of Spanish colonial life in Hispaniola began after the two-year interregnum of the interim governor Bobadilla. He was replaced in 1502, when the permanent governor appointed by Ferdinand and Isabela, Nicholás de Ovando, arrived in Santo Domingo with thirty ships and 2,500 settlers, most of them eager to strike out for the gold fields. Ovando was a military man, a member of the Order of Alcántara, and a loyal servant to Ferdinand. His task of restoring the Indies and its revenues to Crown control was daunting and faced a number of immediate challenges.

The most pressing initial problems echoed the complaints heard at La Isabela—sickness and hunger. The sudden arrival of 2,500 people in the tiny colony of three hundred placed a severe strain on the system. A great many of the newcomers left immediately for the gold fields of San Cristóbal and the Cibao, despite having no equipment for or experience in mining. The scarcity of food, the hard work, and the crowded conditions in the camps caused rampant illness among the immigrants. According to Las Casas, within a few months of arrival more than a thousand of the new settlers had died, and some five hundred remained desperately ill. Those who had brought clothes and tools fared better, as they were able to trade these items for food and land from the three hundred settlers already in the island, who were rich in Indians and land but poor in European goods, especially clothing.[12]

In October 1502, the ships that had brought Ovando and his company returned to Spain, carrying with them Bobadilla and Roldán. Almost as soon as they set sail a major hurricane swept across the island, destroying the settlement of Santo Domingo, wiping out the food supplies of the region, and sinking all but a few of the thirty ships in the fleet, including the vessel carrying Columbus's two old enemies. Both Roldán and Bobadilla were drowned in the disaster, giving some retrospective prescience to Columbus's claim in 1499: "But God, our Lord, who knows my intention very well. . . . will save me as he has done so far, because until today nobody who has maliciously attacked me has failed to be punished by Him."[13]

With the company considerably reduced, Ovando set about rebuilding Santo Domingo, this time on the west side of the Ozama, so as to provide easier access to the growing communities and gold mines in the interior. This was the first Spanish city in the Americas known to have been laid out in the rectilinear grid plan that was to become standard throughout the Spanish colonies, as we saw in chapter 6.

Ovando was still faced with the problem of labor to satisfy the needs of the surviving newly arrived settlers as well as the demands of government installations. The challege also remained of mitigating the economic power of the some three hundred settlers (the colombistas and roldanistas) already in the island who held the most important land and Indian repartimientos. Ovando used the institutions of encomienda and repartimiento to resolve both problems.

In reaction to the enslavement of the Taínos under Columbus, Ferdinand and Isabela had formally issued Instructions in 1501 reiterating that Indians were not slaves but rather Crown vassals. The Crown thus denied the roldanista assumption that Indians were private property, and it explicitly established a legal basis for a system of encomienda controlled by the governing officials. Allocations of Indian labor were awarded to meritorious settlers (and stripped from uncooperative settlers) at government sufferance, providing Ovando with a critically important means of social and economic control. He was able, with Crown sanction, to assign the best lands and greatest number of Indians to certain favored Spaniards (often of high social standing) and withhold them from others (often those original settlers who were not of high rank).[14]

What emerged was a peculiar series of accommodations between Crown interests in religious conversion of the Indians (which had been openly declared since the founding of La Isabela), the Crown's economic interests, the economic interests of the settlers, and Ovando's local problems of governance in a remote colony. The great losers in this process were the people who were at the center of these interests— the Taínos, who suffered unimaginable hardships and unrecoverable losses through the repartimiento and encomienda systems.

In the Public Instructions of Zaragoza issued to Ovando in March 1503, Ferdinand and Isabela repeated their concern that all the inhabitants of America be converted to Christianity by whatever means necessary.[15] One of these means was to be the *reducción* of Indians into towns built specifically for them, where they could live in Indian communities and learn the ways of Christianity and "civilized life." They were also to provide labor in mines and fields, but under contract and for a salary. At the same time, however, the monarchs issued Secret Instructions to Ovando himself, which were not to be made public. These stipulated that the reducciones of Indians, should, so far as possible, be located near the gold mines, to ensure a ready labor force.[16]

In implementing these instructions, Ovando had to be mindful of local conditions, and he must certainly have realized that the Spanish settlers would not passively accept the removal of repartimiento Indians to central towns, away from their control. Reports reached the Crown that the Indians would not stay in towns, and that when Spanish control relaxed, they took to the hills and resisted all attempts at conversion. By late 1503, in response to these reports, the Crown position had changed. Queen Isabela again wrote to Ovando, this time ordering the governor "to compel the Indians to have dealings with the Christian settlers on said Island, to work on their buildings, to mine and collect gold and other metals, and to work on their farms and crop fields."[17] The work was to be organized through the Taíno caciques, and although the same decree stipulated that the Indian laborers were to be paid a salary and rations, there is no indication that this was ever taken seriously in the colony.

Settlers already in Hispaniola when Ovando arrived held most of the Indian repartimientos, and the new colonists arriving with Ovando demanded their share as well. Possibly with this in mind, he embarked on a series of brutal military campaigns to subjugate the remaining Taíno cacicazcos not under Spanish control. These included the Isla Saona and Higuey in the southeastern part of the island, the rich province of Xaraguá in the west, the southwestern peninsula of Haniguayaba, and the northwestern part of the island, Guahaba.[18] These measures would extend Spanish control throughout the island and provide a plentiful new source of Indians to distribute to the recently arrived settlers.

The campaign was carried out in 1503 and 1504 with savage and unscrupulous efficiency. One of the most infamous acts of butchery was during Ovando's expedition to Xaraguá with 370 men to see the cacica Anacaona. He and his men were welcomed with feasts and festivities, which were attended by dozens of Anacaona's subordinate chiefs and their subjects from throughout the region. Having requested to speak to all of the assembled chiefs in a house, Ovando instead signaled his men to fall upon the group. They captured and bound eighty caciques and burned them alive in the house. "As for the Queen, the Lady Anacaona, to show her respect, they hanged her," Las Casas reports.[19] Ovando and his men then destroyed the rest of the town and its inhabitants.

With the Taíno polities thus destroyed and virtually all the Indians that the Spaniards could find assigned to individual settlers, Ovando set about establishing towns. Las Casas described the building of the towns in sorrowful terms: "The preparation of town sites in these various places was not done by Spaniards with shovels in their hands, nor by their sweat and labor; for none of them even knew how to level the ground. It was the Indians, constrained by them and terrorized by the massacres, who did all the work, laid out the sites, built the houses, and cleared the ground for cultivation; and so the Comendador Mayor [Ovando] began to follow the policy that Francisco Roldán had inaugurated, that the Admiral had tolerated, and that the Comendador Bobadilla had strengthened and extended."[20]

Fifteen towns were established around the island by Ovando, and each of them had jurisdictional responsibility for a certain amount of surrounding territory. Those Spaniards receiving encomiendas of Indians were also assigned to specific towns, and it was the clear intent of the Crown that Christians should live together and not be dispersed throughout the country. Isabela's Instructions to Ovando in 1501, which mandated the establishment of these settlements, specified that "it is our will that the Christians living in said island of Hispaniola, live together from now on, rather than being scattered through the countryside . . . you should ensure that none shall live outside of the towns that are established on the island, though each Spaniard can build on his property a hut or small house in which to take shelter when he goes to look it over or to cultivate it."[21]

Civilized life, in the eyes of the Spanish authorities, was life in towns. It was in these towns, however, that the original Columbian idea of a transplanted, civilized Spanish way of life was transformed in distinctively American ways that were often not those intended by the Spanish authorities.

Life in these sixteenth-century Hispaniolan towns was obviously very different from the Spanish experience at La Isabela. The immigrant population of the new towns was larger and more diverse than that of La Isabela and included women and children as well as men. As many as five thousand Spaniards may have resided in Hispaniola's fifteen towns in 1514, and between 1509 and 1514 approximately 10 percent of them were women.[22]

The factoría model had been abandoned, and the Crown now relied on tithes and taxes accruing from the colonists' production activities to make a profit. Gold mining remained the most profitable of these for the first decade of the century, bringing in as much as 450,000 *pesos de oro* a year,[23] but cattle ranching and agriculture (including sugar production) were also important. With this level of prosperity, shipping and communication between Spain and the Indies increased sharply both in intensity and frequency, providing for the entry of many more European goods into the colony (and a lucrative 7.5 percent government tax on goods). By 1508, at the peak of the gold rush, forty-five Spanish ships were calling annually at Santo Domingo.[24] The food supply had stabilized, and horses, cattle, and pigs had established themselves to such an extent that by 1507 there was no need to import any from Spain for breeding, and licenses were issued to hunt feral hogs.[25]

Most dramatically, however, there no longer existed effective, independent Taíno polities in Hispaniola, either as enemies, allies, or hosts of the Spaniards. Except for the Taínos who had fled their homes and lived as renegades in the remote hills, the Indians and their lands were all "owned" by individual Spaniards, and it was only through their forced labor that the economic boom of the early sixteenth century was made possible. The degree to which individuals were able to capture and profit from Taíno labor contributed to their social standing nearly as much as their origins did. Access to Taíno labor was thus hotly contested and jealously controlled for both economic and social reasons.

Such unrestrained and rampant exploitation of a population already overstressed by epidemic European diseases and more than a decade of warfare obviously could not go on indefinitely, and by 1508 the dwindling numbers of native people in Hispaniola could not meet Spanish demands for labor. Only sixty thousand Indians were counted by the royal treasurer in that year, reduced from possibly more than a million people just fifteen years earlier.[26] By 1510 their population was reported to have been 33,523, and by the 1514 Indian census and repartimiento there were only 26,334 Indians to be counted.

Two forces tried to intervene in this downward spiral, but neither was in time to change its course. The first was the Catholic Church: a vehement public protest against Spanish treatment of the Taínos was belatedly launched by members of the Dominican order in Hispaniola in 1511. Initiated by a fiery sermon given in Concepción de la Vega on 21 December by Fray Antonio de Montesinos, the Dominicans decried the annihilation of the Indians and attempted to change Spanish policy and reform the system of Indian labor.[27] Although their efforts resulted in the Laws of Burgos, passed in 1512, and doubtless served to mitigate Indian exploitation in other parts of Spanish America, they were too late to save the Taínos.

The Indians also attempted to take matters into their own hands. Throughout the years of forced labor, both Indians and Africans imported as slaves managed to escape the Spanish settlements and flee to remote mountain areas, where they lived as cimarrones, or fugitives. By

1520, their leaders were organizing successful attacks on Spanish settlements. The principal cacique of the cimarrones was Enriquillo, who had been educated as a child by Franciscan friars. Enriquillo operated in the south in the Baharuco (or Barauco) Mountains, and another cacique, Tamayo, led a smaller group of cimarrones in the north. Enriquillo consolidated both groups and fought the Spaniards in what was known as the Barauco War between 1519 and 1533. The Spaniards were unable to suppress the guerrilla warriors, and in 1533 they signed a peace treaty with Enriquillo. In exchange for his loyalty to the king and the cessation of the raids, the cimarrones were given full amnesty and freedom. Enriquillo himself was given a land grant and the honorific title of "Don."[28]

Although the outcome of the Barauco War was successful for the cimarrones, it did little to relieve the immediate plight of those few remaining Indians who were still held by Spanish encomienda holders (encomenderos). Like the Dominican protests, however, the cimarron resistance forced both church and Crown authorities to rethink their positions, and alter their policies.

The economic crisis provoked by the demise of the Indian labor force led to several developments that had profound implications for the direction of social and economic change in the Americas. One development was the radiation of the Spaniards outward to the other Caribbean islands and ultimately to the mainland, where they sought new resources and established settlements. In 1509, after Queen Isabela's death and at the end of Ovando's tenure as governor, Ferdinand granted permission to abduct the people of the Lucayas (Bahamas) and other parts of the Caribbean as slaves.[29]

Within ten years the islands were depopulated. As the Hieronymite priest Alonso de Zuazo wrote in 1518: "They brought in all the Indians they could catch in the Island of Giants [Curaçao], the Lucayas, and the Island of the Barbudos, and many other islands—as many as 15,000 persons. . . . Those who survived were branded in the face and sold as slaves . . . and so . . . these islands were deserted as useless, by men who wished to depopulate them and to kill the Indians who lived there . . . they were laid to waste, and inhabited only by wild animals and birds."[30]

In the same letter Zuazo noted that, despite the increase in the Indian population by forced immigration, there were in Hispaniola "no more than 11,000 [Indians], and to judge from the past, if no remedy is found, in three or four years there will be none left."

His words were sadly prophetic. In 1518 and 1519 those Indians who had survived the first few decades of the sixteenth century were dealt yet another major blow when an epidemic of *viruelas* (pox, probably small-pox or measles) savagely attacked the Indian population. Las Casas recounted the immense suffering that resulted and commented, "I don't believe that 1,000 souls were left alive and escaped from this misery, of the immense number of people that were on this island, which we saw with our own eyes."[31]

The solution to this loss of a labor force for the Spaniards spelled doom for the hundreds of thousands of African people brought unwillingly to the Americas as slaves, introducing another social and population element into the imperial arena, especially after 1520. Africans, both free and enslaved, had been in the Americas in small numbers since the early part of the century. Some of the first African slaves arrived in 1505, when Ferdinand sent a ship with miners, equipment, and seventeen black laborers.[32] By 1511, "everyone on Hispaniola was of the opinion that the work of one negro was worth that of four Indians."[33]

As a consequence, Africans were brought to Hispaniola in such large numbers that Las Casas, writing between 1550 and 1559, noted that there were already thirty thousand Africans on the island. "There were at that time [ca. 1500] on the island some ten or twelve negroes, sent by the King, who had been brought to make the fortress which is above and at the mouth of the river [Santo Domingo]. However, given this license [to bring in negroes], the end of it was that many more still followed, in such a manner that over 30,000 have already been brought to this island, and to all of the Indies, more than 100,000 according to what I believe; and for all of this the Indians have not been helped, nor have they been liberated."[34]

In spite of Las Casas's misgivings, African slavery continued to intensify on the island. The enslavement of African people was justified by reference to the same religious-legal arguments that prohibited the enslavement of Indians, the Bulls of Donation issued by Alexander VI in 1493. These papal bulls implied no obligation to evangelize and convert Africans, as Spain held no territorial presence in Africa. Furthermore, Africa was tainted by the hint of Islamic influence, which was sufficient justification for slavery. Curiously, once African slaves reached the American colonies they were subjected to the ministrations of the church, including evangelization and conversion, although conversion did not bring liberation.[35]

The interactions among Indian, African, and Spanish people in the early sixteenth-century Caribbean stimulated a genetic and cultural *mestizaje*—mixing—that remains a distinctive hallmark of Latin American criollo society. The earliest expressions of this process are found in the first Spanish towns of Hispaniola after La Isabela, where social and material life as known in Spain and intended at La Isabela was altered during the first turbulent decade of Spanish presence in America. Although many of the institutional aspects of these towns, such as governance, economy, and demography are documented in written accounts, other aspects equally influential in colonial life are not. These include changes in domestic organization, social relations, and the ideological constructs sustaining them. As we suggested in our introduction, many of these changes are seen most clearly in the material expressions of household life in these early Spanish-American towns, best revealed archaeologically. Let us now consider some of the changes that occurred in the material world of the Spaniards between La Isabela and the mid-sixteenth century by summarizing the archaeological data from La Isabela's successor towns (which we detail in chapter 10 of our *Evidence* volume).

Chapter 11

Destinies Converged

The genesis of European colonialism in America took place at La Isabela, and any thoughtful analysis of colonial development must take into account the contours of the original Columbian venture, its failure, and the recasting of Spain's economic and social policies in the Americas in response to that failure. We have maintained throughout this book that the trajectory of this first colony was profoundly shaped by the local experiences and actions of the non-elite residents of the colony, both Europeans and American Indians. We also adhere to the principle that the archaeological record is often the only direct source of information we have about cultural practice and daily life of nonliterate participants in the colonial arena. For this reason, archaeological evidence has been equally as important as documentary sources in our efforts to understand the culturally multifaceted criollo society that emerged from the crucible of late fifteenth-century Hispaniola. In this final chapter we shall compare and interpret the archaeological and historical data from some Spanish sites of the very early colonial period to articulate more precisely La Isabela's role in colonial development.

Although the sites of many of the towns established immediately

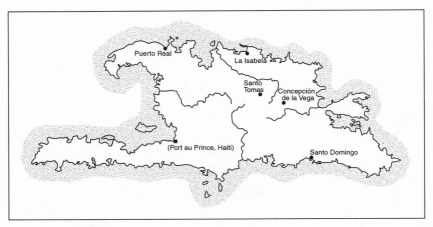

11.1. Locations of late fifteenth- and some early sixteenth-century Spanish settlements in Hispaniola.

after the failure of La Isabela have been located, only three of them—Santo Domingo, Concepción de la Vega (near the fort of Concepción), and Puerto Real (near present-day Cap Haitien)—have been the subject of systematic and extensive archaeological study (figure 11.1). We concentrate here on Concepción de la Vega and Puerto Real, because they were abandoned before the end of the sixteenth century and were never re-occupied. Although Santo Domingo is the largest and perhaps most intensively excavated of the early sixteenth-century settlements, it has been occupied continuously for the past five hundred years and is today a city of more than two million people. The processes of urbanization have taken a heavy toll on the remains of the sixteenth century.[1]

Less than two years after arriving at La Isabela, Columbus established the fortress of Concepción in the Cibao valley near present-day La Vega, in the territory of the Taíno cacique Guarionex. It is thought that the original fort was built at Guaricano, the town in which Guarionex resided. By 1498, however, a new fort had been built a league—two crossbow shots—away from Guaricano, because of increasing resistance to Spanish presence on the part of Guarionex's people. A Christian town, known as Concepción de la Vega, was soon established near the new fort.

Circumstances in Concepción de la Vega (as in all of Hispaniola) were dramatically altered after Ovando and his 2,500 settlers arrived in 1502. Large numbers of the newcomers went to the Cibao in search of gold, and Concepción de la Vega quickly developed into America's first boom town. Concepción grew during the first decades of the sixteenth century into one of the colony's largest cities, rivaling the official capital of Santo Domingo in size, wealth, and economic importance. There were forty-three encomenderos (landholders who also had rights to Indian labor) in Concepción de la Vega in 1514, and of these nineteen were married—ten to Indian women and nine to Spanish women. These encomenderos were assigned 2,450 Indian laborers through 47 caciques. Alonso de Zuazo commented that forty householders "kept horses, and would ride out as elegant and well-caparisoned as one might from Salamanca or any populous city in Spain."[2]

Concepción's fortunes rose and fell with the local resources the Spaniards exploited. Once it became clear that both the gold and the Caribbean Indian population were quickly disappearing, the town was gradually abandoned. Spaniards moved to the island's capital or emigrated to New Spain. By the 1540s the town was reduced to no more than a dozen *vecinos* (landholding citizens who were heads of households), and in 1562 an earthquake destroyed Concepción's standing structures, which the remaining residents took as a sign to abandon the settlement.

The areas of the fort, monastery, and *plaza de armas* of Concepción de la Vega were excavated by archaeologists of the Dirección Nacional de Parques of the Dominican Republic (DNP) between 1976 and 1994 (figure 11.2). The site was surveyed, to locate its boundaries and internal organization, by a University of Florida and DNP team from 1996 to 1999, and the hundreds of thousands of artifacts excavated by the DNP team before 1994 were also were catalogued and curated for the first time during this project.[3]

Puerto Real was established in 1503 as one of Ovando's chain of new towns intended to control the island. It was located in the former territory of Guacanagarí, Columbus's old ally, on the north coast of what is today Haiti, some eighty kilometers west of La Isabela. Unlike Concepción, Puerto Real was not located in an area of gold deposits, and it never achieved Concepción's wealth or prominence. It was also one of the most isolated Spanish settlements on the island. Puerto Real did, nevertheless, develop a stable economy based on farming, cattle ranching, and the production of hides for trade. The citizens of the town soon realized that the most lucrative outlet for their products were the Portuguese, English, and French corsairs who came to northern Hispaniola to trade illegally with Spanish citizens. The residents of Puerto

11.2. Ruins of the fortaleza de la Concepción, Concepción de la Vega.

Real entered quite willingly into arrangements with the corsairs as the best way to both sell their hides and acquire necessary goods, as we saw in chapter 5.

Little is known of Puerto Real's population before the repartimiento of 1514. There were thirty-five encomenderos in the town at that time, nineteen of whom were considered to be vecinos. Among those who were not vecinos were a blacksmith, a barber, and a public notary, and it is also known that a schoolteacher resided in the town. Of the five vecinos who were listed as married, three were married to Spanish women and two to Indian women.[4] At some time after 1527, when Las Casas began his *Historia*, he observed that Puerto Real "still exists but is almost abandoned [*cuasi perdida*]."[5] The contraband trade must have revived the population somewhat, as it was noted in 1561 that Puerto Real had "little more than twenty vecinos," a number repeated in 1567.[6] In 1578, however, in response to their repeated failures to halt the illegal trade between the citizens of Puerto Real and foreign corsairs, the Spanish authorities forcibly evacuated and burned the town.

Puerto Real was excavated by the University of Florida between 1979 and 1985, in conjunction with the Musée de Guahabá of Limbé, Haiti. The work included a systematic subsurface survey of the city as well as excavation of the church, the town's central plaza area, two domestic areas, and a tannery (figure 11.3).[7]

11.3. Excavation of the church and central plaza area at Puerto Real.

Concepción de la Vega and Puerto Real each mark important stages in the post-Columbian, post-Isabeline evolution of Spanish-American society. Concepción was a gold-rush boom town, flourishing because of the gold mines and the still-viable Taíno population in the early part of the century. Puerto Real's peak seems to have emerged somewhat later, as cattle ranching and contraband trade stabilized on the frontier. It persisted past the time when the Taínos and other Caribbean peoples were largely annihilated as self-sustaining, traditional societies, and the Spanish population of Puerto Real relied primarily on African labor. The archaeological records of the two towns clearly reflect these differences in economy and labor, but, more important, the records reveal some of the otherwise undocumented social and material adjustments that were made as part of the colonists' coping strategies.[8]

Concepción de la Vega and Puerto Real, revealed archaeologically, present dramatic contrasts to La Isabela. Obviously many of these contrasts can be understood from historically documented changes in governance, demography, and economic circumstances in both Spain and Hispaniola, but some differences cannot. As we noted earlier, pervasive changes in American social identities are suggested in the material world

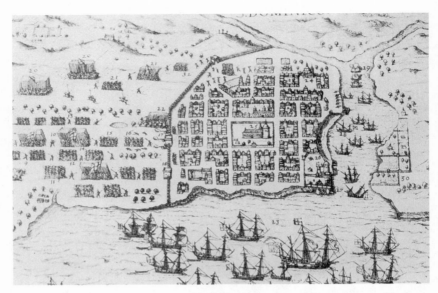

11.4. Plan of Santo Domingo, established in 1502. Detail from the 1586 Drake map of Santo Domingo. Manuscript copy, courtesy of the P. K. Yonge Library of Florida History, University of Florida.)

11.5. Ligurian Blue-on-Blue Italian majolica tableware, Concepción de la Vega. (Photo: James Quine.)

of the early Spanish colonists of Hispaniola, and these changes are nearly invisible without recourse to the archaeological record.

This record shows that certain Renaissance sensibilities were introduced abruptly in the early sixteenth-century colonies, replacing the essentially medieval patterns that had dominated La Isabela. After La Isabela, the symmetrical, rectilinear grid-plan town became the norm (figure 11.4), and tapia public architecture was abandoned in favor of brick and stone. While the objects and technologies at La Isabela usually came from Mudéjar Spain and the Islamic world, the material worlds of the colonists in the sixteenth-century towns were dominated by objects from Italy, Spain, and Northern Europe (figure 11.5). The Islamic styles that are so evident at La Isabela nearly disappear. These changes suggest a perspective different from the kind that governed life at La Isabela.

Archaeological remains also show that the population composition in the sixteenth-century settlements was different from that in La Isabela, which was overwhelmingly dominated by Spanish men. At both Concepción de la Vega and Puerto Real there is clear evidence that women and children were active in the life of the towns, both visibly through toys, jewelry, and items of clothing, and less visibly in the materials associated with household activities (figures 11.6 and 11.7). The presence of women is closely related to the other major demographic difference suggested in the sixteenth-century towns by archaeology—non-European (Indian and African) presence and influence.

Although the residents of the Ovando-era towns had access to a much wider variety of European items than did the colonists at La Isabela, they also incorporated American Indian elements into their households in a way that was not seen at La Isabela. By the middle of the century, non-European items were as common in the household inventories of these towns as European goods. They were, however, restricted primarily to women's domains of the kitchen and household. Food and food preparation in the "Spanish" households were a mélange of Iberian and American elements. Environmental archaeologists Elizabeth Reitz, Margaret Scarry, and Bonnie McEwan have suggested that the cuisine of Spanish colonists in the Americas was flexible and creative in the way it maintained ideal Iberian food preferences (as for mammal meat) while adjusting to foods and cooking traditions in the local environment (manioc, corn, turtles, fish, and manatees).[9] Some American and African household elements documented as having been adopted by Europeans in the sixteenth-century Caribbean, such as hammocks, cigars, and implements and vessels made from gourds, have persisted to the present in the region (figure 11.8).[10]

This wholesale integration of these non-Spanish elements in household areas controlled by women is undoubtedly related to the widespread occurrence of the Spanish-Indian intermarriage patterns that

11.6. Enameled floral-motif pendant, Concepción de la Vega. (Photo: James Quine.)

11.7. Lace bobbin and needle-case top, Puerto Real. The incised, half-circle object may be part of a gaming piece. (Photo: James Quine.)

began in the earliest days of the colony. Indian and African women who worked in Spanish households as servants were also undoubtedly influential in household management, even when Spanish women were the mistresses in homes.

Marriage between Spaniards and Indians was sanctioned by both the church and the Crown in the early Spanish colonies, and accommodation of elite American Indians often included intermarriage between

11.8. Criollo household of the nineteenth century. Native cassava, tobacco, and thatching are integrated with European styles of dress and ornamentation, ca. 1820. Louis de Frecinet: *Voyage autour de monde: Enterpris par ordre du roi, executé sur les corvettes de S. M. Uranie et la Physicienne, pendant les années 1817,1818,1819, et 1820.* Paris: Chez Pillet Aîné.)

Spanish conquistadors or soldiers and Indian cacicas and noble-women.[11] Such marriages were intended to legitimize Spanish claims to land and labor, although in some cases (as in Spanish Florida), they were entered into mistakenly through a misunderstanding of matrilin-eal descent rules.

Queen Isabela's instructions to Ovando on Indian policy in 1501 included the mandate to "induce some Christians to marry some Indian women and some Christian women with Indian men, so that both parties can communicate and teach each other, and the Indians will be instructed in the things of our Holy Catholic Church, as well as in how to work their land and manage their enterprises, so that they become men and women of reason." Ovando appears to have been unsympathetic to such marriages, castigating those who entered into them or even assisted in them.[12] The colonists, however, were not deterred. Even though a royal cédula (decree) formally asserting the legality of Spanish-Indian marriages was not issued until 4 January 1514, it was simply legitimizing what already existed in fact. The repartimiento of that same year, for example, recorded that slightly more than half (54 percent) of the island's 188 married encomenderos had Indian wives, including those of Concepción de la Vega and Puerto Real.[13] No information is given for those Spaniards who were not encomenderos or vecinos, but it can be assumed that the incidence of marriage with Indian women was perhaps even higher among economically less-privileged groups.[14]

A large number of Spanish men also lived in concubinage with Indian and African women, and the church tried vigorously—but with limited success—to make them marry. This contributed not only to the increase of the mestizo population but also to the social association of mixed blood with illegitimacy. These patterns of intermarriage and intermating that began in the first years of Spanish presence in Hispaniola persisted and spread throughout the entire Spanish-American empire, and they were profoundly influential in shaping Spanish-American society in a variety of ways, through the primary agency of women in households.[15]

The transformations that took place in the domestic life of Hispaniola's sixteenth-century towns are even more striking when compared to households of the same period in Spain. Spaniards in sixteenth-century Seville obviously did not incorporate American-Indian and African wives and domestic traditions into their households on a large scale, but they also did not abandon the medieval vessel forms so typical of La Isabela (and so scarce in Spanish-American towns after La Isabela) in favor of newer, Renaissance forms. Relatively little systematic archaeological work has been carried out in domestic sites of early sixteenth-century Spain, yet recent studies show that many of the Moorish-influenced medieval forms that were discontinued in the Americas after La Isabela were retained in Andalusian houses through the sixteenth century and beyond. Utilitarian jars, cooking pots, amphoralike storage jars, braziers, mortars, and oil lamps were common at sixteenth-century Andalusian sites, and many of these forms are still in fact being produced and used in Andalusia today.[16]

By the middle of the sixteenth century, virtually all Spanish-American households, regardless of presumed status, diverged clearly in a material sense from those of Spain at the time. The early production of European-style craft industries—principally in Mexico City after its conquest in 1521—introduced another new dimension into Spanish-American households. The crafting of glazed pottery, glassware, cloth-

11.9. Guadalajara polychrome vessel showing Aztec influence on Spanish table-ware pottery during the eighteenth century. (St. Augustine, Florida, SA–34–2. Florida Museum of Natural History, Gainesville.)

ing, metalwork, and jewelry and nearly the entire range of production activities typical of Spain at the time were established in many parts of Spanish America by the end of the sixteenth century.[17] Archaeological evidence has shown that during the second half of the sixteenth century these American goods were used in the Spanish households of the Caribbean, Florida, and Mexico largely to the exclusion of their Spanish-made counterparts, which continued to be used in Spain for centuries after they had largely disappeared in Spanish-American households.[18] Although goods produced by American craft guilds and laborers were predominantly in a European tradition, the labor force included many Indians whose influence is clearly seen in the decorative aspects of craft products (figure 11.9).[19]

By the time Puerto Real was abandoned in the third quarter of the sixteenth century, another transformation had occurred in the households of Spanish America. A hybrid European-American-African criollo material tradition seems to have emerged and reproduced itself, and that tradition not only described but was also created by the lives of the majority of people in the Spanish Americas.

As we (and others) have suggested, intermarriage and consensual relationships among Spaniards (mostly men) and Indians and Africans (mostly women) formed a crucial dynamic in creating and stabilizing the social milieus of the Spanish-American empire. These relationships fostered exchange and understanding among groups of "others," in which non-European women acted as the primary brokers of culture. This exchange—both cultural and genetic—redefined the notion of race in ways with which we are still struggling today, and it shaped a new social order for the Spanish empire around the ancient idea of *limpieza de sangre*, or purity of blood.

Spanish-African and Indian cohabitation led to a bewildering array of genetic and social admixture among these groups and their offspring. In confronting the actuality of the Americas and the experiences of the people who lived there in the sixteenth century, imperial Spanish ideology was forced to recast the concept of limpieza de sangre to mean purity of white Spanish blood, rather than the purity of old Christian blood that obsessed fifteenth- and sixteenth-century Spaniards. By the eighteenth century the notion of racial purity had produced the formal institutionalization of racial mixture into more than twenty-five categories, explicitly illustrated in colonial Mexico by nearly a thousand paintings (figure 11.10).[20]

Although these categories reflected a commitment to social hierarchy and racial prejudice, they nevertheless provided a legitimizing means of integrating virtually any combination of racial attributes into a recognized institutional structure. Furthermore, they were used very flexibly in social practice. In eighteenth-century Mexico, for example, individuals often identified themselves at different times as belonging to different racial categories depending on the relative advantages of a category in a specific situation. Regardless of imperial legal categories and distinctions, people in the Spanish Americas apparently regarded their racial identity "not so much as an indicator of group membership or even as a badge of self-definition within a static and rigid system, but rather as a component of [his] personal identity that could be manipulated and often changed."[21]

The social and institutional response to multiethnic and multicultural integration in the Spanish Americas is but one example of how local colonial actions shaped the course of empire. From La Isabela on-

Mulato con Española.
Morisco.

Morisco con Española
Chino.

Chino con India.
Salta atras.

9

lo

Lobo con China
Gibaro.

Gibaro con Mulata
Albarazado

Albarazado con Negr̄
Canbujo.

13

14

Sanbaigo con Loba
Calpamulato.

Calpamulato con Canbuja
Tente en el Aire.

Tente en el Aire, con Mulata
Note entiendo.

11.10. Detail of a late eighteenth-century painting from Mexico showing the various official categories of racial mixture. (Anonymous. Courtesy of the Museo del Virreinato, Mexico.)

ward, the organization of Spain's American project changed in response to local American experience and, for the most part, non-elite agency. Refusal of the first colonists either to adapt to American conditions at La Isabela or to accommodate Columbus's vision resulted in the abandonment of the factoría model and the shift to a mercantile empire. Even before this shift both Columbus and the Crown of Spain were forced to alter their policy toward the American Indians in ways they considered undesirable, owing to the alignment of Roldán and his "commoners" with the Taínos, and their adoption of an Indian way of life. The non-elite Europeans immigrants' rejection of the "natural" social order of fifteenth-century Spain based on nobility (hidalguía) introduced a different kind of social order in America that ultimately had cultural, economic, and ideological repercussions on both continents.

We have noted many instances of imperial policy being altered (or reversed) in response to the demands of the Spanish-American colonists or their outright refusal to conform to Crown edicts. These included reducing the Crown's share of income, permitting the use of the Indians as a source of labor, sanctioning Spanish-Indian intermarriage, acceding to and legitimizing cimmaron rebels, and abandoning large segments of territory when the authorities could not control the colonists' illegal trade. By the mid-sixteenth century, the structure and dynamic of colonial life were no longer either shaped or controlled primarily by a formal central authority but rather by the perspectives and actions of the second- and third-generation criollo residents.

Under these circumstances, it is quite likely that a sense of Spanish-American colonial identity distinct from identity as "Spanish" developed early in the Caribbean, particularly away from the colonial capitals (even though political independence did not occur until the nineteenth century). This is suggested in the many instances of rebellions by white, black, and Indian colonists—from Peru to Puerto Real—against Spanish imperial dominion within the first seventy-five years of colonization.[22] A sense of identity distinct from Spain is also suggested by the recognition and acceptance of mixed racial categories. And as historian Anthony Pagden has suggested, a distinct American identity is also implied by literature and art in the Spanish colonies, such as the works that celebrated the descent of criollos from American Indian rulers, thereby legitimizing them as an entity distinct from Spaniards.[23]

The differences between the imperial center in Spain and the imperial colonies in America in terms of social practice and its underlying

ideology, however, are underscored most tangibly in the material remains of life in Spanish-American households. Archaeological evidence
from La Isabela has revealed that the original colonial idea was one of
reproducing Spanish material and cultural practice in America, while
excavations at subsequent Spanish town sites in Hispaniola showed that
this idea was quickly abandoned or at least significantly altered. The
material aspects of life in those early sixteenth-century towns demonstrate a clear divergence from the material patterns of households in
Spain, both in the regular incorporation of African and Indian elements in the areas of Spanish colonial domestic life controlled by
women, and by the early dependence of colonists on crafts and commodities made in America rather than those imported from Spain. We
see this most clearly in the households of Spanish colonial residents,
particularly when the archaeological record is considered from the perspective of gender.

Much has been made of the "extinction" of the Taínos in the sixteenth-century Caribbean, and it is true that few pure-blooded Taínos
practicing their traditional ways of life remained at the end of the century. But by the same criteria, it can also be argued that the Spanish residents of Hispaniola in the early sixteenth century were also extin-
guished. What emerged instead was a way of life that incorporated
many Taíno traits and survivals, many African traits and survivals, and
many more European traits and survivals. The entangling of these elements with each other and with newly developed ideas in the early
Spanish colonies produced a society that was neither Spanish, Indian,
nor African but something newly expressed both in the ideology of
racial categories and in the material aspects of daily household life.
Neither Spain nor America could avoid this convergence. And we conclude by suggesting that it was within those households, especially in
women's domestic activities, that the social transformation of the Spanish colonies began, causing the convergence of Spain and America and
leading, ultimately, to the end of empire.

Names of Persons Known to Have Been at La Isabela

Abarca, Rodrigo[1]
Acosta, Alvaro de (constable)[2]
Aguado, Juan de (ship captain)[1]
Alonso, Fray (friar)[3]
Arenas, Pedro de (secular priest)[12]
Arévalo, Rodrigo de (Lanza de Jineta)[11]
Arroyo, [?] (commendador)[1]
Arteaga, Luis de (hidalgo from Verlenga, commander of La Magdalena
    ca. 1495)[10]
Ayala, Juan de (commander of Concepción fort ca. 1495)[10]
Ballester, Miguel (warden of Concepción fort, 1497)[1]
Barrantes, García (captain of garrison at Guarionex's town, 1497)[1]
Beltrán, [?] (Crown servant)[8]
Bobadilla, Francisco (captain in Lanzas de Jinetas)[11]
Buil, Fray (Franciscan friar, Catalan, Crown representative, and head of religious
    contingent)[1]
Borgoña, Fray (Franciscan friar)[10]
Cáceres, Lope (Lanza de Jineta)[11]
Campos, Sebastián de (commendador, Galician)[1]
Caño, Diego (Lanza de Jineta)[11]
Carvajal, Juan (provision master)[4]

Cas de Dios, Miguel de (vecino of Jaca)[4]
Chanca, Alvarez (physician)[1]
Callado, Gonzalo Gómez (soldier with Roldán in 1497)[1]
Colón, Bartolomé (adelantado, brother of Cristóbal)[1]
Colón, Diego (brother of Cristóbal)[1]
Coronado, Pedro (Lanza de Jineta)[11]
Coronel, Pedro Hernández, (constable; mayor of La Isabela)[8]
Cosa, Juan de la (vizcaino, navigator)[3]
Cuneo, Michel de (Italian noble from Savona)[2]
Duela, Juan de la (Franciscan friar)[5]
Escobar, Diego (warden of fort at La Magdalena, 1497)[1,10]
Estrada, Francisco de (Lanza de Jineta)[11]
Feriz, Gaspar (Aragonese, mutineer hanged)[13]
Fernández, María (only woman noted as present at founding)[2]
Fernando, Don [?] (hidalgo, left in 1495)[6]
García, Gil (bachiller, alcalde mayor)[8]
Gaspar, [?] (Crown servant)[8]
Gallego [?] (hidalgo of Madrid)[1]
Ginovés, Tenerin (contramaestre of the carabela Cardera)[2]
Girao, [?][1]
Gorvalán, Ginés de (ship captain, one of leaders of the 1494 entradas)[5]
Gonzalo, Arias (Lanza de Jineta)[11]
Hernández Coronel, Pedro (chief constable)[1]
Hojeda, Alonso de (hidalgo, captain, criado of duke of Medinaceli)[1]
Infante, Juan (Mercederian friar)[12]
Jorge, Fray (friar, left in 1495)[6]
Las Casas, Pedro de (father of Bartolomé, Seville)[1]
Ledesma, Alonso de (vecino of Ledesma)[4]
León, Chistóval de (Lanza de Jineta)[11]
León, Ponce de (hidalgo)[1]
Leyva, Diego de (Lanza de Jineta)[11]
Loaza [?] (Galician who died of hunger)[4]
Lujan, Juan de (criado of king)[1]
Luna, Alvaro (Captain in Lanzas de Jinetas)[11]
Madrid, Francisco (vecino of Madrid)[4]
Malaver, Alonso (Sevillian)[1]
Maldonado, Melchior (Sevillian)[1]
Marchena, Antonio (Catalan friar from Monserrat)[12]
Margarite, Pedro (captain, very important Aragonese hidalgo)[1]
Marquez, Diego (hidalgo, criado of Pisa, veedor)[1,2]
Mayorga, Luis[3]
Medel, Alonso (captain of the *Niña*)[2]
Mojica, Adrián de (hidalgo)[1,7]
Molina, [?][3]
Muliarte, Miguel (left in 1495)[6]

Navarro, Pedro[1]
Neyra, Angel de (secular priest, died in the Indies)[12]
Niño, Francisco (pilot of the *Niña*)[2]
Niño, Juan (master—quartermaster—of the *Niña*)[9]
Niño, Francisco (gromet on the *Niña*)[9]
Olano, Sebastián de (receptor)[2]
Olmedo, Francisco de (Lanza de Jineta)[11]
Ortíz, Alonso (Sevillian)[1]
Osorio, Diego (Lanza de Jineta)[11]
Pacheco, Gonzalo (Lanza de Jineta)[11]
Pané, Ramón (Hieronymite friar)[1,5]
Paolo, [?] (master of mining, went to Monte Plato to test marcochita sand, 1495)[6]
Peñalosa, Diego (notary)[4]
Peñalosa, Francisco de (captain of soldiers and uncle of Bartolomé de Las Casas)[1]
Pérez, Bartolomé (pilot of *San Juan*)[2]
Pérez, Rodrigo (Catalan friar from Monserrat)[12]
Pérez de Luna, Fernán (escribano)[2]
Pérez Martell, Alonso (master—quartermaster—of *San Juan*, Sevillian)[1]
Pérez Noño, Cristóbal (master—quartermaster—of the *Cardera*)[2]
Pisa, Bernal de (royal accountant)[1]
Quintela, Antonio de (Lanza de Jineta)[11]
Rambla, Gonzalo de la (soldier at Concepción, 1497)[1]
Rivera, Peraffan de (Sevillian)[1]
Rodríguez, Alonso (Contramaestre of the *Cardera*)[2]
Roldán, Francisco (escudero, alcalde of La Isabela, and criado of Columbus)[1]
Román, Antonio (Lanza de Jineta)[11]
Salamanca, Diego de (soldier with Roldán, 1497)[7]
Salas, Pedro de (Portuguese)[2]
Salcedo, Padre (priest)[3]
San Miguel, Francisco de (vecino of Ledesma)[4]
Sánchez de Carvajal, Alonso (ship captain and alderman from Baeza)[1]
Sepúlveda, Diego de (Lanza de Jineta)[11]
Serrano, Alonso (Lanza de Jineta)[11]
Solórsono, Juan (Mercederian friar)[12]
Tello, Gómez (veedor)[2]
Terreros, Pedro de (Columbus's personal steward)[9]
Tisín, Juan de (Franciscan friar)[5]
Torres, Antonio (ship and fleet captain)[1]
Torres, Cristóbal de (headwaiter to Columbus)[3]
Torres, Diego de (baile of Valencia)[6]
Tristán, Diego (hidalgo volunteer)[9]
Valdivieso, Pedro de (rebel with Roldán)[7]
Valenciano, Bernaldo (left in 1495)[6]

Vallejo, Alonso de (captain of soldiers)[1]
Villacorta, Pedro de (treasurer)[1]
Villalobos, Francisco (Sevillian)[1]
Zedo, Fermín (Sevillian goldsmith, took part in 1494 Pisa rebellion)[1]
Zuñiga, Francisco de (Sevillian)[1]

Sources

1. Las Casas, I, in Parry and Keith (1984:70–71, 222–29)
2. Varela (1986:17–19)
3. List of products received in tribute, in Parry and Keith (1984:212–13)
4. Columbus letter to Margarit, 1494, in Parry and Keith (1984 206–07)
5. Taviani (1991, vol. 1:129)
6. Royal Instructions to Aguado, 1495, in Parry and Keith (1984:207–08)
7. Las Casas on Roldán rebellion, in Parry and Keith (1984:224–25)
8. Columbus, "Torres Memorandum," 1494, in Jane (1930:74–113)
9. Morison (1942:396–97)
10. Relación of Fray Ramón Pané, in Keen (1959:153–69)
11. Ramos (1982:171–84)
12. Dobal (1987)
13. Las Casas I, CIX (1985, vol. 1:427).

NOTE ON HISTORICAL SOURCES

A tremendous amount of historical writing over several centuries has been devoted to narratives and interpretations of the Columbian enterprise. Basic primary sources pertaining to La Isabela, however, are relatively few, and they include the often self-aggrandizing letters and journal entries of Columbus himself as well as the eyewitness accounts of physician Diego Alvarez Chanca and expedition members Michel de Cuneo, Guillermo Coma, Simón Verde, and Juan de Bardi.[1] Several other contemporary (or nearly contemporary) accounts of the Columbian expeditions also provide important information about events during the first years of colonization, although the writers generally did not witness the events at first hand.

Probably the most important primary source for the earliest decades of Spanish presence in America are the writings of Sevillian-born Bartolomé de Las Casas, who wrote his multivolume *Historia de las Indias*, three hundred chapters long, between about 1527 and 1547 (although it was not published until 1875, when it was issued by the Real Academia de Madrid).[2] Las Casas's father had participated in the establishment of La Isabela as a member of Columbus's second expedition, and Bartolomé himself came to Hispaniola in 1502 as an encomendero (a recipient of a grant of land and labor from the Crown) and slave owner. He became a Dominican priest in 1510, and in 1514 he renounced his encomienda and began his lifelong campaign to fight exploitation and enslavement of the American Indians. The primary purpose of the *Historia* was undoubtedly to further this cause, but it also incorporated detailed narrative accounts of events in America between 1492 and 1520, including the only surviving excerpts from several parts of Columbus's diary. Las Casas's account is particularly important as a source for understanding the Taíno Indians, with whom he was deeply concerned.

An equally useful source of information about the early years of contact are the chronicles written by Peter Martyr d'Anghiera between 1493 and 1510.[3] Martyr d'Anghiera was an Italian humanist scholar who took up residence in 1487 at the court of Ferdinand and Isabela as a papal diplomat, protonotary apostolic, and chaplain to Isabela, and there he became a close friend of Columbus. He compiled his *Décadas del Nuevo Mundo* (or *De Orbe Novo*) from the correspondence of the Catholic Kings as well as from numerous interviews with members of the expeditions, including Columbus himself. The *Décadas* were published in several parts in Italy in 1504 and 1507 and in Seville in 1511.

A third indispensable source is the *Life of the Admiral Christopher Columbus*, written by Columbus's illegitimate but acknowledged son Ferdinand.[4] Ferdinand joined his father's fourth voyage in 1502 at the age of 13, and he spent most of his subsequent life in Spain as a scholar and bibliophile. He wrote his father's biography in Spain during the 1530s (the later years of Ferdinand's life), and it was first published in Italy in 1571, thirty-two years after Ferdinand's death. Along with his brother Diego and their uncle Bartolomé, Ferdinand was active in the efforts of the Columbus family throughout the first decades of the sixteenth century to reinstate not only Christopher's political rights but also their own hereditary rights to govern the Indies.[5] Although the tone of the biography is undoubtedly colored by the family agenda, the closeness of Ferdinand to his father and his access to his father's papers make it an important primary source nevertheless.

A fourth important source of first-hand information about the Columbian project is *Historia general y natural de las Indias*, by Gonzalo Fernández de Oviedo y Valdés, written before 1550. Oviedo served as a treasury official in several parts of the Caribbean from 1513 to 1547 and had first-hand knowledge about much of what he reported. The first part of his *Historia* was published in Madrid in 1526, and it is often suggested that Oviedo's somewhat unsympathetic treatment of the Taíno Indians (who were cast essentially as part of the flora and fauna of the region) served to inspire Las Casas to write his *Historia*.[6]

Other well-known chronicles essential to the study of the second Columbian voyage in particular and the Columbus era in general include the *Memorias del reinado de los Reyes Católicos*, written by Andrés Bernáldez, a Sevillian priest and friend of Columbus who died in 1513. Not published until 1856, it is considered to be the best source for the second voyage, although it is based in large part upon the letter of Dr. Chanca. Francisco López de Gómara's *Historia general de las Indias* is an often cited source for the contact period, but it is less useful with respect to La Isabela. Lopéz de Gómara was Hernán Cortés's chaplain, and although his *Historia* was published in Spain in 1553, it is often considered by modern historians to have been based on hearsay and often unreliable sources.[7]

Thousands of modern secondary works have been written about Columbus since 1600,[8] but considerably fewer modern secondary historical sources are concerned directly or specifically with La Isabela.[9] Although these modern works are historiographically interesting and often provide useful compilations of information, they have been used in this study primarily as background and context for the discussion of what is known directly from primary sources about La Isabela. The chronicles of Columbus and his expedition members as well as those of Martyr D'Anghiera, Las Casas, Ferdinand Colón, Bernáldez, and Oviedo assume primary importance, and these accounts are privileged throughout our discussions.

NOTES

Chapter 1

1. Ballesteros Beretta (1945, vol. 2: 188).
2. See Crosby (1986, 1972); Sauer (1966).
3. Elliott (1972) considers the intellectual, social, and economic impacts that the encounter with America had on Europe, suggesting that "in discovering America, Europe had discovered herself"(p. 53). Other researchers have emphasized the environmental and material impacts of the encounter. These include Crosby (1972); Hobhouse (1985); Langer (1975); and Viola and Margolis, eds. (1991).
4. Among those who have focused on La Isabela itself are Dobal (1988); Guerrero y Veloz Maggiolo (1988); Pérez de Tudela (1954, 1955); Puig Ortíz (1973); and Varela (1987). Puig Ortíz provides the most comprehensive treatment of the site through modern times.
5. For examples of this characterization, see Morison (1942:430−31); Moya Pons (1995:30−3); Phillips and Phillips (1992:199−200); Taviani (1991, vol. 1:126−28); Sauer (1966:74−75); Wilford (1991:171−72).
6. The most comprehensive studies include Ballesteros Beretta (1945); Morison (1942); Taviani (1991); Varela (1997); Watts (1985); Wilford (1991).
7. Among those who have addressed local circumstances in Hispaniola and their impact on the shape of the sixteenth-century Spanish imperial project are Floyd (1973), Moya Pons (1986, 1992), Pérez de Tudela (1954, 1955, 1956), and Stevens-Arroyo (1993).

8. A consideration of this debate is beyond the scope of this discussion, and much of it has been summarized by Axtell (1995); Benítez (1992); García Arévalo (1992); Patterson (1991); Quesada and Zavala (1991); Sale (1990); Sued-Badillo (1996); and most recently Summerhill and Williams (2000).

9. See, for example, Dobal (1988).

Chapter 2

1. For considerations of Portuguese expansion strategies and exploration in the context of early modern Europe see Diffie and Winius (1977:41–51); Parry (1990:131–45); Phillips, C. (1990); and Phillips, J. (1988:225–60).

2. See Diffie and Winius (1977:41–50) and MacAlister (1984:46–51) on the feitorias, and Pérez de Tudela (1954) on Columbus's familiarity with them.

3. Fernández Armesto (1987:212–13).

4. For a detailed analysis and discussion of the role of the Canary Islands and its products in Columbus's expeditions see Tejera (1998).

5. On Columbus's prior activity in the Canaries see Taviani (1985:3).

6. Useful sources on the history and influence of the Canary Islands, as well as on Spanish relations with the native peoples, include Abreu Galindo (1977); Aznar Vallejo (1983); Morales Padrón (1978); Tejera (1992); Tejera and Aznar Vallejo (1992).

7. See Parry (1990:146–48).

8. On the military and religious conquest of the Canary Islands by Spain see Alvarez Delgado (1980); Stevens Arroyo (1993:521–23).

9. Stevens Arroyo (1993:529–30), Aznar Vallejo (1983), and Tejera (1992) offer useful discussions of Spanish-Guanche interaction.

10. An early argument for this impact was offered by Fernández Armesto (1987).

11. For a recent summary of Muslim influences in Spain see Vernet (1992), and for the society of *convivencia* see Mann et. al (1992).

12. See discussion by Stevens Arroyo (1993:517).

13. On Columbus's desire for commerce with Asia see, for example, Pérez de Tudela (1983); Taviani (1985:393–96).

14. Reproduced in Parry and Keith (1984:18–20).

15. For further analyses and discussion of these themes, see Pérez de Tudela (1954, 1956, 1983).

16. See Varela (1987b, 1988) for information on Columbus's Genoese connections.

17. Among the most useful of these are Ballesteros Beretta (1945); Dunn and Kelley (1989); Fuson (1987); Morison (1940, 1942:211–335); Taviani (1985); and Varela (1986:43–203).

18. See Wilson (1990:70–71).

19. Columbus, 1493 letter to Santangel in Parry and Keith (1984:60).

20. The wreck of the *Santa María* and the events surrounding the short-lived settlement of La Navidad are discussed further in chapter 4, as well as in Deagan (1987); Hodges (1985); Morison (1940); Ramos (1989); Taviani (1991, vol. 2:95–114). Columbus's accounts are included in the *Diario de Colón* in Parry and Keith (1984: 45–51) and in Varela (1986:150–62).

21. Columbus in Parry and Keith (1984:48).

22. Columbus in Parry and Keith (1984:53).

23. Columbus discusses the Indians present on his first voyage and their fates in his 1493 letter to Santangel in Parry and Keith (1984:60); Las Casas in Parry and Keith (1984:66); and Bernáldez in Jane (1930:314, 325).

24. Colorful accounts of this procession are given both by Las Casas I, XC (1985, vol. 1:366–70). Translated in Parry and Keith (1984:65–66) and by Fernando Colón in Keen (1959:100–101).

25. See, for example, discussion by Kamen (1991:36–47).

26. These are printed in Navarrete (1954–64, vol. 2:66–72) and appear in English in Parry and Keith (1984:71–74).

27. Columbus, "Torres Memorandum," 1493, in Parry and Keith (1984:183–84). Las Casas I, LXXXII (1985, vol. 1:346).

28. Ferdinand Colón in Keen (1959:109).

29. Las Casas I, LXXXII (1985, vol. 1:345–47), also in Parry and Keith (1984:70), and Ferdinand Colón in Keen (1959:109).

30. Royal letter to Fonseca, 1493, in Parry and Keith (1984:75).

31. Varela (1986:17–18).

32. For a comprehensive overview of the Lanzas and their roles in Spain and at La Isabela see Ramos (1982).

33. Varela (1986:19).

34. For a recent biography of Buil and summary of his role at court see Dobal (1991). Dussel (1969:30) also provides useful information on Buil and his role in the expedition.

35. Considerations of La Isabela's religious contingent have been offered by Dobal (1991:47–49); Errasti (1998:25–26); Fita y Colomé (1884); and Taviani (1991, vol. 1:129).

36. On women at La Isabela and in fifteenth-century Hispaniola see Varela (1986:6); Ferdinand Colón in Keen (1959:149); and Chiarelli and Luna Calderón (1987:207).

37. Las Casas in Parry and Keith (1984:70).

38. Rumeu de Armas (1989, vol. 2:447).

39. For more detailed discussion of these animals and other products of the Canaries, see Tejera (1998:94–105).

40. Columbus to the sovereigns, 1499, in Parry and Keith (1984:233).

41. Discussions of these events by Chanca can be found in Parry and Keith (1984: 85–86), and by Martyr D'Anghiera, *Décadas*, in Gil and Varela (1984:59).

42. Martyr D'Anghiera, *Décadas*, in Gil and Varela (1984:59).

Chapter 3

1. Dunn and Kelley (1989:90–91, 96–97).

2. Chanca in Parry and Keith (1984:78); Martyr D'Anghiera in MacNutt (1970, vol. 1:81). Recent Taíno scholarship has indicated that the ethnic and cultural groups in the Caribbean at the time of contact were considerably more varied than the early

chroniclers indicated. At least three groups are thought to have occupied Hispaniola, only one of which was "Taíno" (who produced a certain style of pottery known as Chican). Others included the Macorijes of north-central Hispaniola, who spoke a different language, and the Ciguayo of the northeastern coastal region, who were also apparently distinct from the Taíno. This issue is considered in detail in our *Archaeology* volume, chapter 2.

3. The most important single source of written information about Taíno cosmology and belief systems is the report of the Hieronymite friar Ramón Pané, commissioned by Columbus in 1494 to live among the Taínos and learn about their customs and beliefs. A great deal of information about the Taínos has also been generated by archaeological research at Taíno sites, and a number of authors have synthesized and integrated this work with documentary information. We draw extensively throughout this chapter on the contributions of those researchers. The most comprehensive synthesis is perhaps that provided in three parts by William Keegan (1994, 1996b, 2000). Other major archaeological studies and syntheses include Alegría (1983, 1997a, 1997b); Anderson-Córdova (1990); Arrom (1988a); Bercht et al., eds. (1997); Cassá (1975); Gerbi (1985); Pantel, ed. (1983); Rouse (1992, 1986, 1948); Sturtevant (1961); Veloz Maggiolo (1993, 1997); and Wilson (1990, 1997c).

4. See Feinman and Neitzel's comparative study of chiefdoms worldwide (1984).

5. Detailed considerations of Taíno population estimates can be found in Cook (1993); Henige (1978); Moya Pons (1992; 1987:181–89); Newson (1993:248–54); and Wilson (1990:90–92). Low estimates of one hundred thousand are offered by Mira Caballos (1997:34) and Rosenblatt (1954:102). Mid-range estimates of four hundred thousand are given by Moya Pons (1987:187; 1992), and of five hundred thousand by Anderson-Córdova (1990). David Watts (1978), following Las Casas, suggests three million to four million (1985, vol. 2, ch.1), and a high estimate of six million to eight million Taínos for the Greater Antilles is offered by Cook and Borah (1971).

6. These problems of perception and communication, combined with the disruption of traditional Taíno society within one generation of contact, conspired to render a reliable Caribbean source of analogy for archaeological interpretation largely inaccessible. This in turn has led some scholars to argue that accurate reconstruction and understanding of the past is unobtainable. For more in-depth discussion of these issues and their impact on our historical understanding of the Taínos, see Alegría (1997b); Greenblatt (1991); Hulme (1986:2–12); Pagden (1982:10–26); Stevens-Arroyo (1997); Todorov (1984).

7. The history of native Caribbean culture is complex and not fully understood. It has been constructed primarily by archaeologists on the basis of ceramic sequences and chronologies, and the study of Taíno prehistory has been absorbed with tracing origins and migration and diffusion routes. The intent of our discussion here is not to consider Taíno prehistory in detail but rather to provide temporal and geographical contexts for a consideration of Taíno society at the time of contact.

8. See, for example, studies by Chanlatte and Nargones (1983) and Roe (1997).

9. Recent discussion of the early migrations to the Caribbean can be found in Keegan (2000), Wilson (1997a:17), and Veloz Maggiolo (1997:37).

10. A comprehensive and comparative study of Taíno ball courts can be found in Alegría (1983).

11. On Taíno ceramic, ritual, and artistic traditions see Bercht et al., eds. (1997); García Arévalo (1977); Rouse (1948); and Rouse and Arrom (1991). On intensification of social stratification see Alcina Franch (1983); Keegan (1997); Keegan et al. (1998); Wilson (1990).

12. Rouse (1992:17, 108–109); see also Keegan (2000); Veloz Maggiollo (1993).

13. Wilson (1997a); Veloz Maggiolo (1997). For a comprehensive treatment of the entire spectrum of native Caribbean cultures see Wilson, ed. (1997c).

14. Dunn and Kelley (1989:428).

15. Columbus to the Catholic Kings, 1493, in Jane (1930:260).

16. See Stevens-Arroyo (1997:104).

17. Columbus, 1492, in Morison (1963:128); Cuneo, 1493, in Parry and Keith (1984:91); Bernáldez in Jane (1930: 323).

18. See, for example, Harrington (1921:416–17).

19. Bernáldez in Jane (1930:323); Cuneo in Parry and Keith (1984:91); Columbus in Jane (1960:124).

20. Cuneo in Parry and Keith (1984:91); Las Casas I, LIV (1985:263); Oviedo y Valdés (1959, vol. 1:89).

21. Columbus in Morison (1963:128).

22. Chanca in Parry and Keith (1984:87).

23. Martyr D'Anghiera, *Décadas*, book 9. This account is translated in Arrom (1999:47).

24. Pané in Ferdinand Colón (Keen 1959:154). On metal composition, see Rouse and Arrom (1991:511).

25. Las Casas I, CXX (1985, vol. 1:417). The lower and upper Macorix were two of twenty-seven "provinces" listed by Las Casas in his *Apologética* (1958, vol. 1:17); Wilson suggests this location (1990:103).

26. See Veloz Maggiolo et. al (1981) and Veloz Maggiolo (1993) for discussions of the distinctions among Upper and Lower Macorijes, the Ciguayos and their associated archaeological complexes.

27. See Martyr D'Anghiera, *Décadas*, in Gil and Varela (1984:106–107).

28. Chiefdoms in this context follow the criteria of Carneiro (1981) and Feinman and Neitzel (1984). Other useful recent sources on chiefdoms in general are Earle, ed. (1991) and Redmond, ed. (1997). For an assessment of the work on Taíno social and political organization see Wilson (1990:28–34), and for arguments on avunculocal residence see Keegan and Maclachlan (1989) and Keegan (1997).

29. These schema are offered in Charlevoix (1730) and Casimir de Moya (1909) in Vega (1987:12); Rouse (1948:529); and Vega (1987). The versions of Charlevoix, Casimir de Moya, and Rouse are based on Las Casas and Oviedo, while Vega draws upon information recorded by the cartographer Andrés de Morales. Las Casas and D'Anghiera both also recorded numerous subregions or provinces in the island, possibly related to political divisions within the chiefdoms. These are summarized by Wilson (1990:108–09).

30. Moya Pons (1987:107).

31. On characteristics of Taíno chiefs, see Alegría (1979); Rouse (1948:529–30; 1992:16–17); Wilson (1990:31–32). Columbus's comments of 1493 are recorded in Parry and Keith (1984:61).

32. Wilson (1990:116–22).

33. On Taíno warfare, see Rouse (1948: 532–33). Such comments about Carib cannibalism as those offered by Chanca (in Parry and Keith (1984:77–81) are considered and reinterpreted by Keegan (1996a) and Patterson (1991). For a contrasting view to Keegan and Patterson see Allaire (1997).

34. Columbus to Santangel (in Parry and Keith 1984:61); Cuneo (in Parry and Keith 1984:92).

35. Columbus, *Diario*, in Jane (1930:198); Las Casas I, LVIII (1985, vol. 1:274); Bernáldez in Jane (1930:323).

36. Las Casas I, CV (1985, vol. 1:156–58). See also Chanca in Jane (1930:323).

37. Alegría (1985:3) and Rouse (1948:524–25) discuss the ethnohistorical and archaeological evidence for this assertion.

38. Martyr D'Anghiera, *Décadas*, in Gil and Varela (1984:60).

39. Alegría (1985).

40. On Taíno agriculture and food crops, see Newsom (1993), Sturtevant (1961), Vega (1997), and Wing (1983, 1989b). A very comprehensive illustration of fruits used by the Taínos is provided by Vega (1997).

41. Corn cultivation and preparation by the Taínos is discussed in Newsom and Deagan (1994), Sturtevant (1961), and Rouse (1948:523).

42. Bernáldez in Jane (1930:328). For detailed considerations of Taíno hunting and fishing, see also Wing (1989a–b) and Rouse (1948:524).

43. Columbus in Jane (1930:188–89).

44. Additional discussion of Taíno trading activities can be found in Rose (1987:328–29); Rouse (1992:17); and Wilson (1990:49–51).

45. Las Casas I, LVII (1985, vol. 1:272).

46. Examples of such items can be seen in Taylor et al. (1997) and Vega (1973).

47. Taíno ritual has received a great deal of attention from modern scholars, who have relied heavily on the accounts of Ramón Pané and Bartolomé de Las Casas. Among those who discuss Taíno religion and ritual are Arrom (1988, 1989,1999); García Arévalo (1977, 1983, 1997); Oliver (1997); Rouse (1992:13–15, 118–21); Siegel (1997); and Stevens-Arroyo (1988). The most comprehensive treatments of Pané and the scholarship surrounding his work can be found in Arrom (1989; 1999).

48. Quoted by Ferdinand Colón in Keen (1959:153).

49. Las Casas, *Apologética*, chapter 167 (1958:417).

50. On Taíno and Orinoco origin myths see Arrom (1989; 1997, 1999); Oliver (1997); Stevens-Arroyo (1988).

51. The Taíno supreme deity and his family, as well as the pantheon of Taíno lesser gods are considered in more detail by Arrom (1975; 1989:18–19; 1991); Pané (1988; 1999) and in Keen 1959:154); and Rouse and Arrom (1991:511–12).

52. Keen (1959:159–60, 163). Examples of zemis in Taíno art can be seen in Bercht et al., eds. (1997); García Arévalo (1977); Rouse (1992:117).

53. Examples of these from La Isabela are described and discussed in our *Archaeology* volume, chapter 2.

54. In Keen (1959:152).

55. Alegría (1997:24) discusses hallucinogens used by the Taínos, and sexual imagery is considered by Oliver (1997) and Stevens-Arroyo (1988).

56. Martyr D'Anghiera, *Décadas*, book 2, in MacNutt (1970:317).

57. Alegría (1985, 1997).

58. For a description of such a game, see Las Casas I, CIV (1985, vol. 1:442).

59. For synthetic discussions of Taíno art see Arrom (1989); Arrom and García Arévalo (1988); Bercht et al., eds. (1997); Montás, Borrell, and Moya (1988); Rouse and Arrom (1991).

60. The symbolic content of Taíno ceramics are considered by a number of authors, among whom are Cusick (1988); García Arévalo (1990a); and Roe (1997).

61. Arrom (1989:21) interprets the three-pointed stones as symbols of the principal deity. McGinnis (1997) offers alternative interpretations.

62. García Arévalo (1990a) considers Spanish appreciation of Taíno artistry.

63. The schema for Taíno political divisions are discussed above, and their relation to the people of the La Isabela region is considered in greater depth in our *Archaeology* volume, chapter 2. As Samuel Wilson has emphasized, however, these asserted boundaries are ambiguous and shifting, based as they are on fragmentary documentary and archaeological data, each frozen at its own moment. Many modern writers assume that La Isabela was in a peripheral part of the territory governed by Guarionex. Evidence for Taíno towns in the vicinity of La Isabela is offered and assessed by Caro Alvarez (1973); Guerrero and Veloz Maggiolo (1988); Ortega and Guerrero (1988); Taviani (1991, vol. 2:161); and Veloz Maggiolo (1990).

64. Chanca in Parry and Keith (1984:86–87).

65. Las Casas I, LXXXVII (1985, vol. 1:362–63); Ferdinand Colón in Keen (1959:121); Cuneo in Gil and Varela (1984:243); Chanca in Parry and Keith (1984:86).

66. Columbus in Parry and Keith (1984:180).

67. Archaeology at the Perenal and Bajabonico sites is discussed in our *Archaeology* volume, chapter 2. Additional information about Taíno towns in the vicinity of La Isabela is offered and assessed by Caro Alvarez (1973); Guerrero and Veloz Maggiolo (1988); Ortega and Guerrero (1988); Taviani (1991, vol. 2:161); and Veloz Maggiolo (1990). See also Campos Carrasco et al. (1992:25).

68. See Wilson (1990:82–89); Sauer (1966:83–85, 88).

Chapter 4

1. We have unabashedly borrowed the title of this chapter from Samuel Eliot Morison's treatment of life in Hispaniola (Morison 1942:481), since it captures the essence of the documentary accounts of events at La Isabela between 1493 and 1498. These provide a critical context not only for the guiding questions of our archaeological research in the town but also for evaluating and interpreting the results of that research. We have chosen here to recount the events in a chronological sequence, both to provide a narrative and historical structure for the chapters that follow and to assess the changing circumstances of human practice and experience through La Isabela's short life. The presentation includes heavy and possibly distracting dependence on direct quotations. We adopted this approach intentionally, however, because

of the considerable ambiguity and contradiction among the primary sources about the sequences and causes of events during those first years of settlement. Modern historians have tended to be equally varied in their interpretations of those sources, and have often been selective in the passages used as a basis for narration and interpretation. Reproduction and citation of the passages upon which we have drawn are included here to permit a more critical analysis of our own conclusions.

2. In Parry and Keith (1984:86).

3. On the geography and geology of the site, see Díaz del Olmo et al. (1991).

4. This is described by Martyr D'Anghiera in Gil and Varela (1984:61–62).

5. Authors critiquing Columbus's choice of site include Gabb (1881:66); Keith and Thompson (1985:33–34); Morison (1942:430–31); Phillips and Phillips (1992:199–200); Taviani (1991, vol. 1:126–28); Sauer (1966:74–75).

6. Columbus in Varela (1987:735); Chanca in Parry and Keith (1984:86).

7. Cruxent (1990).

8. Columbus, "Torres memorandum," in Jane (1930:84).

9. Columbus, "Torres memorandum," in Jane (1930:78, 80, 82).

10. For discussions of animal-borne and other diseases at La Isabela, and the implications of these, see Cook (1993; 1998:15–39); Guerra (1985, 1988); and Lawren (1987).

11. Oviedo y Valdés (1959, vol. 2:50); Las Casas, *Apologética* (1958, ch. 20). Francisco Guerra (1978) reviews the debate over the origins of syphilis.

12. Las Casas I, LXXXVIII (1985, vol. 1:363). Also in Collard (1971:88).

13. Coma in Gil and Varela (1984:199).

14. Las Casas records this discontent and its consequences, I, XCII, in Collard (1971:49).

15. This first expedition to the interior is documented by Las Casas, I, XC, in Collard (1971:51); Martyr D'Anghiera in Gil and Varela (1984:65); Ferdinand Colón in Keen (1959:122); and Michel de Cuneo in Parry and Keith (1984:89). Chanca's hopeful comments about the quantity of gold is reproduced in Parry and Keith (1984:88), and Cuneo's gleeful observation is in Parry and Keith (1984:89).

16. Columbus's communiqué to the sovereigns carried by Torres (the "Torres Memorandum") is translated and reproduced in Parry and Keith (1984:179–85) and Jane (1930:74–113).

17. See Parry and Keith (1984:187).

18. Las Casas I, XCII (1985, vol. 1:377). Also in Collard (1971: 49).

19. Las Casas, I, XC (1985:367).

20. This *entrada* is recounted by Las Casas I, XC (1985, vol. 1:367–68), and later (in 1601) by Antonio de Herrera, translated by John Stevens (1740) and reproduced in Parry and Keith (1984:192).

21. For more detailed accounts of these events see Didiez Burgos (1971) and Guerrero and Veloz Maggiolo (1988).

22. Columbus in Varela (1987a:738).

23. Las Casas I, XC, in Collard (1971:49); Varela (1987a:739).

24. Columbus in Varela (1987a:738–39).

25. Columbus's account of these events can be found in Parry and Keith

(1984:204). See also the comments of Las Casas (I, XC) in Collard (1971:50) and of Ferdinand Colón in Keen (1959:128).

26. In Parry and Keith (1984:204).

27. Wilson provides a more detailed consideration of these events (1990:82–89).

28. On Margarite's behavior see Ferdinand Colón in Keen (1959:147–48); and Las Casas I, CVII, in Collard (1971:56–57).

29. The disaffection and departure of Margarite, and the fatal damage his men did to the Taínos are recounted by Las Casas I, C (1985, vol. 1:399–400).

30. Martyr D'Anghiera, *Decadas*, in Parry and Keith (1984:208).

31. On the alliance see Dídiez Burgos (1971:25); Las Casas I, C (1985:401); and Ferdinand Colón in Keen (1959:148).

32. See Parry and Keith (1984:185–87).

33. In Keen (1959:149).

34. The original request appears in Parry and Keith (1984:187).

35. These events are recounted by Las Casas I, C (1985:400) and by Martyr D'Anghiera in Parry and Keith (1984:209). Concepción (1981:13–14) and Dídiez Burgos (1971:27) provide modern interpretations.

36. Las Casas I, C (1985:400).

37. Cuneo in Morison (1963:226).

38. Various accounts of the capture are provided by Martyr D'Anghiera in Parry and Keith (1984:208–10); Taviani (1991, vol. 1:165–67); and Wilson (1990:84–88).

39. On the 1495 campaign in the Cibao see Ferdinand Colón in Keen (1959:148–49); Martyr D'Anghiera in Parry and Keith (1984:210–11); and Las Casas I, CIV (1985, vol. 1:413).

40. Ferdinand Colón in Keen (1959:149).

41. Ferdinand Colón in Keen (1959:149) and Martyr D'Anghiera in Gil and Varela (1984:84) claimed that Caonabo died on the voyage to Spain. Las Casas asserted that his death occurred as he was chained in the ships that sank in La Isabela's harbor during the 1495 hurricane; Las Casas I, CII (1985, vol. 1:408).

42. Sauer (1966:89).

43. Ferdinand Colón in Keen (1959:149–50).

44. See discussions of tribute and its impacts in Moya Pons (1987:17) and Wilson (1990:91–97).

45. The famine is discussed by Las Casas I, CVI (1985, vol. 1:419); Martyr D'Anghiera in Parry and Keith (1984:209); and Ferdinand Colón in Keen (1959:150).

46. Martyr D'Anghiera in Parry and Keith (1984:209).

47. Las Casas I, CIII (1985, vol. 1:409); Martyr D'Anghiera in Parry and Keith (1984:211); Morison (1942:490–91).

48. These are reproduced in Parry and Keith (1984:206–08).

49. Aguado's actions are described by Ferdinand Colón in Keen (1959:170–72) and by Las Casas I, CVIII (1985, vol. 1:424–25).

50. Las Casas I, CVIII (1985, vol. 1:425).

51. Las Casas I, CVIII (1985, vol. 1:425).

52. Las Casas I, CX (1985, vol. 1:430–31); Martyr D'Anghiera in Parry and Keith (1984:211).

53. Keen (1959:169); see also Las Casas I, CXI (1985, vol. 1:432–33).

54. Las Casas I, CXI (1985, vol. 1:432).

55. See also Moya Pons (1992:131).

56. Chanca in Parry and Keith (1984:86–87); Columbus, "Torres Memorandum," in Parry and Keith (1984:180).

57. See, for example, Chanca in Parry and Keith (1984:86–87); Ferdinand Colón in Keen (1959:127); Cuneo in Parry and Keith (1984:89–91).

58. See Las Casas I, CXIII (1985, vol. 1:438–39) and Roldán's complaints as recorded by Las Casas I, CXVII (1985:449).

59. Las Casas I, CXIII (1985, vol. 1:439).

60. On the orders for abandonment see Gil and Varela (1984:86, notes); Las Casas I, CXIII (1985, vol. 1:438–40); Martyr D'Anghiera in Gil and Varela (1984:86–87).

61. Las Casas I, CXIII (1985, vol. 1:439–40).

62. Martyr D'Anghiera in Gil and Varela (1984:86–87).

63. Las Casas I, CXIII and CXXIII (1985, vol. 1:439, 469); Martyr D'Anghiera in Gil and Varela (1984:86).

64. See Las Casas I, CXVII (1985, vol. 1:448).

65. For an ethnohistorical analysis of that visit, see Wilson (1990: 25–29).

66. Las Casas I, CXV (1985, vol. 1:444); Martyr D'Anghiera in Gil and Varela (1984:89).

67. Martyr D'Anghiera in Gil and Varela (1984:90).

68. These interactions are recounted by Las Casas I, CXV (1985, vol. 1:445–46) and Martyr D'Anghiera in Gil and Varela (1984:90–91).

69. Roldán in Parry and Keith (1984:228); Las Casas I, CXVII–CXIX (1985, vol. 1:448–57).

70. Las Casas provides a detailed and colorful account of these events; Las Casas I, CXVII–CXIX (1985, vol. 1:448–57), translated in Parry and Keith (1984:231).

71. Las Casas I, CXVII (1985, vol. 1:451).

72. Roldán in Parry and Keith (1984:229); Columbus to the sovereigns in Parry and Keith (1984: 233).

73. Martyr D'Anghiera in Gil and Varela (1984:95).

74. For discussion of these difficulties see Wilson (1990:102–08).

75. Las Casas I, CXIX (1985, vol. 1:455–56).

76. Roldán to Cisneros in Parry and Keith (1984:229); Las Casas in Parry and Keith (1984:227).

Chapter 5

1. Las Casas I, CVII (1985, vol. 1:378).

2. Ober (1893:253).

3. Las Casas, I, CX (1985, vol. 1:429), writes about using La Isabela's stones; other comments are provided by Caro Alvarez (1973:50) and Schomburgk (1853, cited in Puig Ortíz 1973).

4. Las Casas I, CVX (1985, vol. 1:105).

5. Las Casas II, XIV (1985, vol. 2:254). On royal revenues from pig hunting see Juan Gil (1986:46).

6. The Hawkins event is documented in a series of letters and memorials reproduced by Irene Wright (1929:60–71).

7. Hakluyt (1962, vol. 2:135–36).

8. For a comprehensive treatment of the *devastaciones* of the Banda del Norte, see Hernández Tapia (1970:283–94).

9. Hernández Tapia (1970:316).

10. Moya Pons (1995:63).

11. Moya Pons (1995:15–16).

12. Moya Pons discusses Canary Island settlers (1995:78–80); on the timber trade at La Isabela see Puig Ortíz (1973:57) and Ober (1893:242).

13. Casimir de Moya's Atlas is reproduced in Demorizi (1979); plate IV shows the area of La Isabela. Other useful nineteenth-century descriptions of the site can be found in Colvocorresses in Thatcher (1903:284); and Ober (1893:243–44).

14. Thatcher (1903:288); see also Ober (1893:248–49) and Puig Ortíz (1973:58–59).

15. Reproduced in Palm (1945:299).

16. In Palm (1945:299).

17. Ober (1908:253).

18. The 1891 report and map produced by Lt. Colvocoresses and his colleagues is reproduced in Thatcher (1903:283–87) and is translated into Spanish by Dobal (1988).

19. Ober (1893:248–58).

20. Ober (1893:246). These items were among those excavated in 1892 by the Junta para la Celebración del Centenario and loaned to the Columbian Exposition in Chicago.

21. The excavation is described in Puig Ortíz (1973:63). Puig Ortíz's book on La Isabela is the most comprehensive treatment of activities at the site between 1890 and 1960.

22. These excavations are considered in greater detail in our *Archaeology* volume, chapter 4.

23. Puig Ortíz (1973:66).

24. Puig Ortíz (1973:67); Ober (1908:253).

25. Reproduced in Demorizi (1980:179–84).

26. Incháustegui (1939:101); Demorizi (1980:179–84).

27. Caro Alvarez (1973); Palm (1945); Puig Ortíz (1973:72–74).

28. Rafael Cantisano, personal communication to José Cruxent, El Castillo, 1990.

29. What little is known of these excavations is recorded by Caro Alvarez (1973:50) and Palm (1955, vol. 2:19).

30. Goggin (1968:24).

31. Cruxent (1990:253).

32. This and other oral-history transcripts related to La Isabela are on file at the Parque Nacional de la Isabela and at the Florida Museum of Natural History, University of Florida, Gainesville.

33. See Brache (1985:87).

34. Maruta Devora (lifelong resident of El Castillo), personal communication to José Cruxent, El Castillo, February 1990.

35. Puig Ortíz (1973:75–76).

36. Their results are discussed and interpreted in Dobal (1988).

37. These events and the archaeological activities related to them are recounted in Puig Ortíz (1973:79–85).

38. The dais was mapped in 1985 by researchers from Texas A and M University, reported in Keith and Thompson (1985:7–8).

39. These excavations and their results are reported in Chiarelli and Luna Calderón (1987); Dobal (1988:102–04); Guerrero and Ortega (1983); and Luna Calderón (1986).

40. Keith and Thompson (1985).

41. Chiarelli and Luna Calderón (1987).

42. See Campos Carrasco et al. (1992:31–33); Cantisano (1988).

43. Deetz (1993:164–65).

44. The methods, controls, and results of both the surveys and excavations at La Isabela are detailed in our *Archaeology* volume, chapter 4.

45. The details of analysis methodology and results can be found in our *Archaeology* volume, chapter 4 and appendix 2.

Chapter 6

1. The University of Florida's survey of Las Coles, and the subsequent excavations carried out there by Cruxent, are detailed in our *Archaeology* volume, chapter 3.

2. The operation and products of the kiln are discussed in chapter 9, and they are documented in our *Archaeology* volume, chapter 10.

3. For discussion of the co-evolution of defensive systems and firearms in Europe, see Pepper and Adams (1986).

4. Mumford (1961:308, 360).

5. Mumford (1961:360). See also Gutkind (1967:254–57).

6. Some of the most comprehensive of the many recent studies of Spanish-American urbanism include CEHOPU (1989); Crouch, Garr, and Mundigo (1982); García Fernández (1989); García Zarza (1996); Rodríguez and Ibáñez, eds. (1992); and Zendegui (1977).

7. García Zarza (1996:43–71) reviews many of the various theories concerning the origins of the American grid-plan town.

8. These are discussed by Beresford (1967) and Morris (1979:93–112). Gutkind (1967:240–46) concentrates on *bastides* established in medieval Spain.

9. Mumford (1961:330).

10. Dechert (1983) and Morris (1979:121–50) consider the fifteenth-century Italian architectural treatises. On Vitrivius and his influence see Argan (1969:18–22) and Stanislawski (1947).

11. Dechert (1983:1–2, 19).

12. Taviani (1985:448). On Columbus's associations with books and bookselling, see Taviani (1985:445–52).

13. See, for example, Nitz (1997:112–14).

14. Guillermo Coma in Gil and Varela (1984:199); Las Casas I, LXXXVIII, in Collard (1971:47).

15. Authors who have interpreted documentary accounts as indicating that La Is-

abela had a grid plan layout include Dobal (1988:59); García Zarza (1996:73–74); Nitz (1997); Puig Ortíz (1973); Solana (1986:13); and Varela (1987:738). For one of the few contrary opinions see Palm (1955:1:52).

16. Columbus, translated in Parry and Keith (1984:180). In Varela's transcription (1986:209) the phrase used by Columbus was "*porque non ha de ser sino albarradas.*" *Albarradas* can refer to dry-laid walls or earthen defense walls used provisionally in the country (Real Academia Española 1995).

17. In Gil and Varela (1984:199).

18. Material distributions and excavations in the suspected vicinity of the wall are documented and interpreted in our *Archaeology* volume, chapter 5.

19. For a very early statement of this principle, see Thomas Aquinas, *Summa theologica* (1995, second part of the second part, question 84, article 3).

20. Guillermo Coma in Gil and Varela (1984:199).

21. These sources of evidence and their interpretation are detailed in our *Archaeology* volume, chapter 5.

22. Las Casas I, LXXXVIII, in Collard (1971:47).

23. Columbus's 1493 observations on the on the quarry are recorded in Varela (1987a:738). Columbus's comments about the stone near Monte Cristi are recorded by Las Casas in Parry and Keith (1984:52).

24. General surveys of tapia construction and its history can be found in Hassan and Hill (1986:75) and Norton (1997). Córdoba de la Llave (1990:302–03) discusses tapia use in fifteenth-century Andalusia, and the Carmona city walls of tapia are documented by Pavón (1992:305–06). For more detailed descriptions of tapia construction methods at La Isabela, see our *Archaeology* volume, chapter 6.

25. For other examples of stonework at La Isabela see Puig Ortíz (1973:21, 36, 45) and our *Archaeology* volume, chapter 6.

26. These spikes and nails are analyzed and documented in our *Archaeology* volume, chapter 6.

27. Coma's letters were incorporated by Syllacio into a pamphlet published in 1494. This is translated in Morison (1963:243).

28. Carlé et al. (1984:32–33).

29. Additional details of architectural and construction techniques for the Casa de Colón and all the other principal buildings at La Isabela are documented in our *Archaeology* volume, chapter 6.

30. Described by Las Casas CXVII–CXIX (1985, vol. 1:448–57).

31. See Beresford (1967); Morris (1979:93–112); Mumford (1961:330); and Gutkind (1967:240–246).

32. Houses in Andalusia are discussed by Pavón (1992:122–23), and Boone (1980:95) provides comparative information on fifteenth-century Qsar es-Seghir.

33. Martyr D'Anghiera in Gil and Varela (1984:61).

34. The church at Puerto Real is documented by Willis (1984; 1995:158–59), and information about frontier churches in Spanish Florida can be found in Saunders (1990) and in Jones and Shapiro (1990).

35. Cruxent suggests that the thickness and quantity of plaster recovered during the excavation of the church may indicate that the roof was made of plaster. This is explored further in our *Archaeology* volume, chapter 6.

36. See Kubler (1940, 1948) and Saunders (1990).

37. Aquinas (1995, second part of the second part, question 84, article 3); Kubler (1948:242).

38. This stone is illustrated by Puig Ortíz (1973:36), who also shows other stones from La Isabela (1973:21, 29, 45).

39. Rouse and Cruxent (1963: figure 54A).

40. Ober (1893:325–29). See also Dobal (1987).

41. The Catholic Kings to Columbus, 1493, in Parry and Keith (1984:74).

42. Carlé et al. (1984:45–46).

43. Las Casas I, LXXXVII (1985, vol. 1:363); Syllacio, 1494, Morison translation (1963:243).

44. Las Casas I, CXVII (1985, vol. 1:432).

45. The disturbances to the alhóndiga have made interpretation of the structure's configuration at its north end problematical. There was clearly a focus on metallurgy in that area, and the evidence for construction and organization is detailed in our *Archaeology* volume, chapter 10.

46. See our *Archaeology* volume, chapter 6.

47. Gibbs's observations are recorded in Puig Ortíz (1973:58–59), and those of Heneken are reproduced in Palm (1945:299).

48. Michel de Cuneo in Gil and Varela (1984:243).

49. The archaeological evidence for these and other structures at La Isabela is presented in detail in our *Archaeology* volume, chapter 6.

50. Information on houses in Córdoba is provided by Córdoba de la Llave (1990); on those of Qsar es-Seghir by Boone (1980:95); and on those of Benialí by Butzer et al. (1986:378).

51. In Oliveira Marques (1971:117).

Chapter 7

1. Cuneo in Parry and Keith (1984:90–91).

2. Ramos Gómez (1992:80–81).

3. Nicoló Syllacio, 1494, Morrison translation (1963:243).

4. Ferdinand Colón in Keen (1959:130–31).

5. Cuneo in Parry and Keith (1984:89–91). See also chapter 3 and Vega (1997).

6. Chanca, 1494, in Parry and Keith (1984:86).

7. Ferdinand Colón in Keen (1959:127).

8. Cuneo in Parry and Keith (1984:90–91).

9. Columbus to the sovereigns, 1499, in Parry and Keith (1984:233); Cuneo in Parry and Keith (1984:90).

10. Chanca in Parry and Keith (1984:86–87).

11. Ferdinand Colón in Keen (1959:127).

12. See, for example, Gerbi (1985:12–22).

13. Las Casas I, LXXXII (1985, vol. 1:346–47).

14. Crown to Aguado, 1495, translated in Parry and Keith (1984:206).

15. On grains in the later medieval European diet see Braudel (1970:130–32). The

nutritional aspects of the rations for La Isabela are discussed in detail in our *Archaeology* volume, chapter 7.

16. Las Casas I, CVIII (1985, vol. 1:425).

17. Forty proveniences from the site that were thought to represent relatively undisturbed fifteenth-century soil deposits were separated by flotation, but this effort produced fewer than one hundred identifiable bones. Elizabeth Reitz, who studied the faunal remains from those contexts, was unable to draw reliable conclusions about the Spanish diet on the basis of this sample. The recovery and analyses of these materials is discussed in more detail in our *Archaeology* volume, chapter 7.

18. These were studied by Lee Ann Newsom at the Florida Museum of Natural History, who, like Reitz, was unable to draw any reliable conclusions about plant use by the Spaniards from the extremely small sample. The plant data are presented in more detail in our *Archaeology* volume, chapter 7).

19. Late medieval Iberian ceramics in Andalusia are documented in Amores and Chisvert (1993); Lister and Lister (1987:93–114); and McEwan (1988; 1992). Those from Qsar es-Seghir in Morocco are illustrated in Myers (1989) and Redman (1986:190–200). Additional typological and technical information about the Spanish ceramics from La Isabela can be found in our *Archaeology* volume, chapter 7.

20. See Deagan (1996) for summary and discussion of the evidence from such sites.

21. Martínez Llopis (1995:169–71); McEwan (1988:63–64).

22. Spanish domestic sites of the approximate period of La Isabela have been reported by Bonnie McEwan (1988; 1992) and Amores and Chisvert (1993).

23. According to Las Casas I, CVIII (1985, vol. 1:425).

24. In Keen (1959:179–81).

25. Documented in our *Archaeology* volume, chapter 7.

26. See, for example, those in Ruempol and Van Dongen (1991:145–46); also Museum of London (1993:128–31).

27. Tannahill (1973 226–27).

28. Reitz and Scarry (1985) archaeologically document a similar subsistence situation for sixteenth-century St. Augustine in Florida.

29. On late medieval household furnishings in Europe, see Braudel (1979:283–84). Córdoba de la Llave (1990:296–97) documents fifteenth-century interiors in Córdoba, and Paz Aguiló (1982:272–74) addresses palace interiors of that era.

30. As discussed by Lister and Lister (1987:25–26, 110).

31. These are illustrated by Frothingham (1963: plates 9a,16a).

32. Oliveira Marques (1971:136–39). Braudel's assertion appears in Braudel (1979:328).

33. Documented in our *Archaeology* volume, chapter 8.

34. Amores and Chisvert (1993:288) discuss the lebrillo and its functions in Seville during the early modern period. A useful discussion can also be found in Lister and Lister (1989).

35. Ferdinand Colón in Keen (1959:128).

36. In Parry and Keith (1984:180–81).

37. Las Casas II, CLIV (1985: 83). Translated in Parry and Keith (1984:248).

38. Guerra (1985, 1988) is a leading scholar of animal-transmitted diseases in post-Columbian America; Reiter's syndrome has been suggested by Weissman (in Phillips and Phillips 1992:200) and intestinal dysentery by Sauer (1966). For a comprehensive review of this evidence see Cook (1998:28–38).

39. Las Casas, II, VI (1985, vol. 2:226).

40. Las Casas I, CXV (1985, vol. 1:444).

41. Columbus in Jane (1930:98). Las Casas, I, LXXXVIII (1985, vol. 1:363), translated in Collard (1951:47) discusses the establishment of hospitals at La Isabela.

42. Columbus to the sovereigns, 1493, in Parry and Keith (1984:182).

43. Lister and Lister (1987:30–31, 78).

44. See, for example discussion by Anderson (1979:140).

45. Las Casas II,VI (1985, vol. 2:226).

46. Las Casas II, I (1985, vol. 2:205), translated in Parry and Keith (1984:252).

47. On the use of lacings in Spanish clothing see Anderson (1979:89–92).

48. For more detailed discussion and illustration of Spanish jewelry of this period see Muller (1972); Deagan (2002, chapter 6); and our *Archaeology* volume, chapter 8.

49. These events are recounted by Columbus in Parry and Keith (1984:40) and by Las Casas I, LVII (1985, vol. 1:288).

50. Columbus quoted by Las Casas, in Parry and Keith (1984:40, 44, 47, 60).

51. An analytical and comparative discussion of jewelry items from La Isabela can be found in our *Archaeology* volume, chapter 8.

52. Spaer (1992) archaeologically documents such bracelets in the Islamic world.

53. The bracelets from Portuguese Morocco are reported by Redman (1986:204) and Boone (1980:148–49). Muller (1972:25) documents Queen Isabela's use of *manillas*.

54. Díaz-Plaja (1995:240–44) discusses late medieval pastimes among the Spanish elite.

55. In Parry and Keith (1984:220).

56. See, for examples and discussion, Sarriá Rueda (1994) and Carrión Gútiz (1994).

57. See Díaz-Plaja (1995:229–30) and Oliveira Marques (1971:242–51) for discussion of these activities among the later fifteenth-century Iberian elite.

58. Díaz-Plaja (1995:239–49) and López Cantos (1992:269–71) discuss both the Spaniards' attachments to and sanctions against gambling.

Chapter 8

1. On the *Patronato Real* see Haring (1947:103, 180) and Hanke (1949). For introductions to the role of the church in Caribbean colonization in general see Hanke (1935) and MacAlister (1984:133–83).

2. On the first contingent of priests in America, see Arranz-Márquez (1992:19–32); Dobal (1987, 1991); Errasti (1998:25–26); Taviani (1991, vol. 1:129).

3. Las Casas I, LXXXVI (1985, vol. 1:358).

4. Ferdinand Colón in Keen (1959:121).

5. See, for example, Dídiez-Burgos (1971:29).

6. Accounts of the excavation of the human remains at La Isabela can be found in Chiarelli and Luna Calderón (1987); Guerrero y Ortega (1983); Luna Calderón (1986); Vargiu (1990).

7. Chiarelli and Luna Calderón (1987:206–09).

8. For discussion of this phenomenon see Oliveira Marques (1971:271–73).

9. For discussion of these precepts see (for example) Aries (1975) and Oliveira Marques (1971:270–75).

10. Columbus to the sovereigns, 1494, in Jane (1930:96). See also Ramos (1982).

11. Columbus to the sovereigns, 1493, in Parry and Keith (1984:61).

12. See discussions in LaRocca (1989).

13. Las Casas I, LXXXII (1985, vol. 1:346).

14. Columbus in Parry and Keith (1984:184); see also Varela (1982:160).

15. These are detailed and illustrated in our *Archaeology* volume, chapter 9.

16. For descriptions and examples see Lemos (1991); Brown (1978:35–36); Lavin (1965:41–43).

17. Documentation of these guns and their ammunition at La Isabela are provided in our *Archaeology* volume, chapter 9.

18. In Díaz-Plaja (1995:186–87).

19. Ramos (1982:28–33) provides a comprehensive discussion of the escuderos in general and the Lanzas de Jinetas at La Isabela in particular. Ramos considers in detail the organization, arrival, and activities of the lanzas in La Isabela, as well as the disciplinary problems they caused there.

20. Ramos (1982:28).

21. See Lunenfeld (1970).

22. Las Casas I, LXXXII (1985, vol. 1:346).

23. Columbus, "Torres Memorandum," in Parry and Keith (1984:183); also Ramos (1982).

24. Las Casas I, CXVIII (1985, vol. 1:454).

25. Description and illustration of horse equipment from La Isabela is found in our *Archaeology* volume, chapter 9.

26. Several varieties and patterns of rivets were identified at La Isabela, and these are illustrated and discussed in our *Archaeology* volume, chapter 9.

Chapter 9

1. Las Casas, I, LXXXII (1985, vol. 1:345–47).

2. Ferdinand Colón in Keen (1959:109).

3. For a detailed analysis of Spanish attitudes to labor, see Bennassar (1979).

4. Las Casas I, LXXXVIII (1985, vol. 1:363).

5. Ferdinand Colón in Keen (1959:128).

6. Chanca in Parry and Keith (1984:86–87).

7. Columbus, 1494, in Varela (1989:738).

8. See Glick (1997); Lister and Lister (1987:21–23).

9. Córdoba de la Llave provides information about the pottery guilds in late fifteenth-century Córdoba, as well as a description of a casa tejar (1990:303–04).

10. These and other tools are discussed and illustrated in chapter 10 of our *Archaeology* volume.

11. Morison (1942:490–91) interprets the original accounts of the June 1495 hurricane and subsequent ship construction in this way; these are provided by Las Casas I, CIII (1985, vol. 1:409), and Martyr D'Anghiera in Parry and Keith (1984:211).

12. The large body of literature on shipbuilding techniques in late fifteenth-century Spain has been synthesized very usefully by Roger Smith (1993:50–93).

13. The Molasses Reef wreck is reported by Keith (1987), and the Emmanuel Point wreck by Smith et al. (1995).

14. These are discussed and illustrated in our *Archaeology* volume, chapter 10.

15. In Parry and Keith (1984:186).

16. Craddock (1995:110–11) discusses the recovery and refinement of placer gold. For a sixteenth-century description of this process see Hoover and Hoover (1950:297–99).

17. This mercury is best illustrated in Deagan (1992a).

18. In Parry and Keith (1984:187).

19. Diderot (1959:Plate 136) and Hoover and Hoover (1950:427–32) illustrate early mercury production. For examples of mercury on sixteenth-century shipwrecks see Smith et al. (1995:117–18), and for eighteenth-century shipwreck mercury see Borrell (1983).

20. For illustration of these medieval and early modern assaying crucibles, see Smith and Gnudi (1990:291–92,137–40) and Hoover and Hoover (1950:229).

21. Craddock (1995:221–24) discusses the refinement of galena, and the archaeological evidence for these processes is found in our *Archaeology* volume, chapter 10.

22. For a discussion of various metallurgy furnace types see Craddock (1995:167–203).

23. See, for example, Cotter (1957:12); Craddock (1995:207–08); Schmidt (1997:111); Agricola in Hoover and Hoover (1950:276). It is also conceivable that the pit may have functioned as a cupellation furnace to melt larger amounts of smelted metal, although there is very little evidence for cupels (crucibles) in the vicinity of the furnace.

24. See Córdoba de la Llave (1990:226–28).

25. Examples of Spanish forges in fifteenth-century Córdoba are discussed and illustrated by Córdoba de la Llave (1990:230), and forges from later colonial New Mexico are illustrated by Simmons and Turley (1980:46–48).

26. For examples and discussion see Hassan and Hill (1986:165–66); Lister and Lister (1987:52–53); Myers (1989:86–97).

27. Lister and Lister (1987:52).

28. Córdoba de la Llave (1990:325) discusses the organization of potters' guilds in fifteenth-century Córdoba. The ceramics produced and found archaeologically at La Isabela are treated in detail in our *Archaeology* volume, chapters 7 and 8.

29. Late medieval pottery workshop organization is detailed by Córdoba de la Llave (1990:324–30) and Lister and Lister (1987:254–65).

30. Suggested by Myers (1989:88).

31. Columbus, "Torres Memorandum," in Parry and Keith (1984:184).

32. Morison (1942:397).

33. Columbus, "Torres Memorandum," in Parry and Keith (1984:184). See also the discussions by numismatist Alan Stahl (1995:190–92).

34. Stahl (1992, 1995). The coins from La Isabela are also discussed and illustrated in our *Archaeology* volume, chapter 10.

35. Stahl (1992:5).

36. Counting-token designs, dating, and use are discussed by Van Beek (1986), and information about the merchants' weights represented at La Isabela is taken from Kisch (1965:129–34).

37. These instructions are reproduced in Parry and Keith (1984:71–75).

38. Chanca in Parry and Keith (1984:87).

39. Las Casas I, LVI (1985, vol. 1:269).

40. The archaeological evidence upon which this assertion is based is presented and discussed in our *Archaeology* volume, chapter 2.

41. This list is reproduced in Parry and Keith (1984:212–13).

42. See for example, Las Casas's version of Columbus's *Diario*, Las Casas I, LXXXII (1985, vol. 1:346), in Parry and Keith (1984:30–33). Bernardo Vega also summarizes information on the use of hawk's bells (1979:42–45).

43. These include burial sites in the Dominican Republic reported by Vega (1979) and García Arévalo (1990a).

44. These bell fragments appear identical to examples recovered in the artifact cache at Sabana Yegua, in the San Juan de la Maguana region of the Dominican Republic. That site is thought to date to the early contact period, reported by Vega (1979). The bells from La Isabela are illustrated in our *Archaeology* volume, chapter 10.

Chapter 10

1. See, for example, the comments of Las Casas I, CXLVII (1985, vol. 2:64).

2. Stevens-Arroyo (1993:530–31). See also the discussions by Floyd (1973:39–44), Moya Pons (1986:19–27), and Pérez de Tudela (1955) on the role of the roldanistas in shaping a criollo sensibility and way of life.

3. These instructions are reproduced in Parry and Keith (1984:217–21).

4. Royal instructions to Columbus for the third voyage, in Parry and Keith (1984:217–20).

5. See MacAlister (1984:157–64) for a synthesis of the many discussions of the evolution of repartimiento and encomienda in the Americas.

6. For useful discussions of these events and their immediate consequences see Las Casas I, CLX (1985, vol. 2:103) and Moya Pons (1986:31–32).

7. Las Casas I, CLXXVI (1985, vol. 1:172). Translated in Parry and Keith (1984:235).

8. The site of Nueva Isabela has been located and partially excavated by Marcio Veloz Maggiolo and Elpidio Ortega, but little remains of the original settlement. See Veloz Maggiolo and Ortega (1992).

9. Floyd (1973:44) and Sauer (1966) offer detailed discussions of these developments.

10. For a dramatic report of these events see the account of Las Casas, in Parry and Keith (1984:234–42).

11. Calculated by Sauer (1966:105).

12. Las Casas II, VI (1985:226).

13. Columbus's letter to the Crown on the Roldán rebellion, 1499, translated in Parry and Keith (1984:233).

14. For a detailed analysis of this process see Moya Pons (1986:36–44, 47–48).

15. These Instructions are reproduced in Parry and Keith (1984:260–62).

16. Moya Pons (1986:149).

17. In Parry and Keith (1984:263).

18. Las Casas II, IX–X (1985, vol. 2:235–42).

19. Las Casas II, IX (1985, vol. 2:237).

20. Las Casas II, X (1985, vol. 2:241).

21. Royal instructions to Ovando, 1501, in Parry and Keith (1984:256).

22. For the most detailed analysis of these historically known economic and social factors operating in Hispaniola in the decades following La Isabela, see Moya Pons (1986). Konetske (1945:145) provides documentation on the immigration of Spanish women to Hispaniola during this period.

23. Calculated by Floyd (1963:68–69).

24. Chaunu and Chaunu (1955, vol. 2:20–23).

25. Sauer (1966:156–57).

26. According to Las Casas II, XLII (1985, vol. 2:346). Moya Pons (1986:181–89) provides a modern interpretation of Taíno decline during this period, and Arranz-Márquez (1991) reproduces and interprets the 1514 repartimiento records.

27. See Pérez (1984) for the text of Montesino's sermon, and Hanke (1949) for additional discussion of this theme.

28. On Enriquillo and the Barauco (Baharuco) War, see Deive (1989:30–42), Mira Caballos (1997:313), and Marté (1981:359–60). Las Casas's comments on the cimarrones can be found in Las Casas III, CXXV–CXXVII (1985, vol. 3:265–78).

29. Las Casas II, XLIII (1985, vol. 2:346–48).

30. Alonso de Zuazo to Chievres, in Parry and Keith (1984:274).

31. Las Casas III,CXXVII (1985, vol. 3:270).

32. Fox (1940:23–24).

33. Deive (1980:31).

34. Las Casas III, CXXIX (1985, vol. 3:275).

35. See discussions by Klein (1989:88–89).

Chapter 11

1. For reports and descriptions of archaeological work in Santo Domingo, see Council (1976); García Arévalo (1978); Olsen et al. (1998); Ortega (1982); Ortega and Cruxent (1976); Ortega and Fondeur (1978a, 1979).

2. The 1514 repartimiento is analyzed and reported by Arranz Márquez (1991), and Alonso de Zuazo's description of Concepción is reproduced in Parry and Keith (1984:274).

3. For a summary of these activities and their results see Deagan (1999) and Woods (1999). The work at Concepción de la Vega is also treated in greater detail in our *Archaeology* volume, chapter 11.

4. Arranz-Márquez (1991:92–93).

5. Las Casas II, IX (1985, vol. 2:241).

6. Lyon (1995:460–62).

7. The work at Puerto Real is summarized by the authors in Deagan, ed. (1995) and Ewen (1991). An expanded discussion of the archaeology at the site is also included in chapter 11 of our *Archaeology* volume.

8. The archaeological data from these two sites are examined in detail in chapter 11 of our *Archaeology* volume, and we summarize those results in this discussion.

9. Reitz and McEwan (1995); Reitz and Scarry (1985).

10. For a wide-ranging discussion of these survivals in the Dominican Republic see Vega (1981).

11. For a few of the many discussions of this phenomenon in the early Spanish colonies see Deagan (1985:304–05; 1996); Floyd (1973:59–61); Morner (1967:37); Socolow (2000:32–78).

12. The 1501 Instructions for the government of the Indians are reproduced in Parry and Keith (1984:260), and discussion of Ovando's responses can be found in Rosenblatt (1954, vol. 2:53–54) and Moya Pons (1987:41–42). Other scholars, such as Kenneth Andrews (1973), have pointed to the difficulties that some of these marriages caused the Spanish men in the union through the inheritance of Indians under his Indian wife's control. Such inheritance complicated the assignment of Indains by the governor to other Spaniards in repartimiento, and this economic- political issue may have been at the root of opposition to Spanish and Indian marriages.

13. Arranz Márquez (1991:596–97).

14. See, for example, Pedro Carrasco's analysis of Spanish-Indian marriages by social group for Puebla in 1534 (1997:88).

15. Morner (1967:40–42) discusses the association of mestizo blood with illegitimacy. For documentation and discussion of intermarriage patterns in other parts of Spanish America see Esteva-Fabregat (1995); Morner (1967); Nash (1980); Rosenblatt (1954, vol. 2).

16. See Amores and Chisvert (1993); Coll Conesa and Más Belén (1998); Lister and Lister (1987); and McEwan (1988, 1992). This theme is also expanded in our *Archaeology* volume, chapter 11.

17. See, for example, Santiago Cruz (1960).

18. See Deagan (1987a); Fairbanks (1973); Goggin (1968); Lister and Lister (1987).

19. For example, see Toussaint (1967).

20. For a comprehensive review and illustration of the Casta paintings representing these "racial" combinations see García Saíz (1989).

21. On the flexibility of self-identified racial categories in Spanish colonial America, and the European classifications of people in America represented by the Casta paintings, see Boyer (1997), Chance (1978:130–31), and Katzew (1996).

22. Brading (1991) offers a comprehensive analysis of creole identity and the rise of creole patriotism throughout Spanish America. Other specific treatments can be found in Hamilton and Hodges (1995), Hernández Tapia (1970), and Pagden (1987).

23. See Pagden (1990:91–115; 1993).

Notes on Historical Sources

1. The chronicles of Columbus and his companions have been synthesized in Varela (1982), Gil and Varela (1984), Oviedo and Valdés (1959), and Las Casas (1985). See also Collard (1971), (MacNutt 1970), and Jane (1930).

2. The history of Las Casas's *Historia* (and of Las Casas himself) is recounted in detail by Lewis Hanke (1952). We have relied primarily on the three-volume 1985 edition of the *Historia* published in Santo Domingo in commemoration of the *V Centenario del Descubrimiento de América* (Ediciones del Continente), which is well annotated and organized and has a very useful index.

3. We have used the edition edited by Gil and Varela (1984). Contextual background on Martyr D'Anghiera is provided by Gil and Varela (1984:17–39). For portions of the *Décades* in English, see MacNutt (1970).

4. Published and annotated in English by Keen (1959).

5. These proceedings are compiled in the *Pleitos de Colón;* see Navarrete (1934).

6. On Oviedo's *Historia,* see Friede and Keen (1971). Wilson offers a useful assessment of Oviedo from an ethnohistorical perspective (1990:11–12).

7. Taviani (1991, vol. 2:13).

8. Some of the more useful scholarly syntheses of these secondary works on Columbus can be found in Ballesteros Beretta (1945); Floyd (1973); Gil and Varela (1984); Morison (1963, 1946); Peréz Tudela Bueso (1954, 1955a–b); Phillips and Phillips (1992); Taviani (1983, 1985, 1986, 1991); Todorov (1984); Varela (1982, 1986, 1997); and Wilson (1990).

9. The few modern studies of La Isabela itself include Caro Álvarez (1973); Chiarelli, ed. (1987); Dobal (1988); Domínguez Compañys (1947); Guerrero and Veloz Maggiolo (1988); Ortega and Guerrero (1988); Palm (1945); Puig Ortíz (1973).

REFERENCES

Abreu Galindo, Fray José. 1977. *Historia de la conquista de las siete islas de Canaria*. Santa Cruz de Tenerife: Ediciones Goya.

Alcina Franch, José. 1983. La cultura Taína como sociedad en transición entre los niveles tribal y de jefaturas. In *La cultura Taína: Seminario sobre la situación de investigación de la cultura Taína*, edited by A. G. Pantel. Madrid: Biblioteca del V Centenario, pp. 69–80.

Alegría, Ricardo. 1983. Aspectos de la cultura de los indios Taínos de las Antillas mayores en la documentación ethno-histórica. In *La cultura Taína: Seminario sobre la situación de investigación de la cultura Taína*, edited by A. G. Pantel. Madrid: Biblioteca del V Centenario, pp. 123–40.

————. 1985. *Ball courts and ceremonial plazas in the West Indies*. Yale University Publications in Anthropology, 79. New Haven: Yale University Press.

————. 1997a. An introduction to Taíno culture and history. In *Taíno: Pre-Columbian art and culture from the Caribbean*, edited by Fatima Bercht, Estrellita Brodsky, John Alan Farmer, and Dicey Taylor. New York: El Museo del Barrio and the Monacelli Press, pp. 18–33.

————. 1997b. The study of aboriginal peoples: Multiple ways of knowing. In *The indigenous people of the Caribbean*, edited by S. Wilson. Gainesville: University Presses of Florida, pp. 9–19.

Allaire, Louis. 1997. The Caribs of the Lesser Antilles. In *The indigenous people of the*

Caribbean, edited by S. Wilson. Gainesville: University Press of Florida, pp. 177–85.

Alvarez Delgado, J. 1980. Primera conquista y cristianización de La Gomera: Algunos problemas históricos. *Anuarios de estudios Atlánticos* 6:455–92.

Amores Carredano, Fernando, and Nieves Chisvert, Jiménez. 1993. Tipología de la cerámica común bajomedieval y moderna sevillana (s. XV–XVII) I. La loza quebrada de relleno de bóvedas. SPAL *(Revista de prehistoria y arqueología de la Universidad de Sevilla)* 2:269–325.

Anderson, Ruth M. 1979. *Hispanic costume, 1480–1530*. New York: Hispanic Society of America.

Anderson-Córdova, Karen. 1990. Hispaniola and Puerto Rico: Indian acculturation and heterogeneity, 1492–1550. Ph.D. dissertation, University of Puerto Rico. Ann Arbor: University Microfilms.

Andrén, Anders. 1998. *Between artifacts and texts: Historical archaeology in global perspective.* Translated by Alan Crozier. New York: Plenum Press.

Aquinas, Thomas. 1995. *Summa theologica (1225–1274).* Translated by the Fathers of the English Dominican Province, 1947. Chicago: Benzinger Brothers. Hypertext version 1995, New Advent (http://www.newadvent.org).

Argan, Guilio C. 1969. *The rennaissance city.* New York: George Braziller.

Aries, Phillippe. 1975. *Western attitudes toward death.* Baltimore: Johns Hopkins University Press.

Arnold, Barto, and Robert Weddle. 1978. *The nautical archaeology of Padre Island, Texas.* New York: Academic Press.

Arranz Márquez, Luis. 1991. *Repartimiento y encomienda en la isla Española.* Santo Domingo: Fundación García Arévalo.

———. 1992. La iglesia y el descubrimiento de América. Volume 1 of *Historia de la iglesia en Hispanoamerica y en las Filipinas.* Madrid: Biblioteca de autores cristianos.

Arrom, José Juan. 1988. *Fray Ramón Pané: Relación acerca de las antiguedades de los indios: El primer tratado escrito en América* 8th edition. Mexico City: Siglo Veintiuno Editores.

———. 1989. *Mitología y artes prehispánicas de las Antillas* 2d edition. Mexico City: Siglo Veintiuno Editores.

———. 1997. The creation myths of the Taíno. In *Taíno: Pre-Columbian art and culture from the Caribbean*, edited by Fátima Bercht, Estrellita Brodsky, John Alan Farmer, and Dicey Taylor. New York: El Museo del Barrio and the Monacelli Press, pp. 68–79.

———. 1999. Introductory study. In *An account of the antiquities of the Indians* by Fray Ramón Pané. Translated by Susan Griswold, with Introductory Study, Notes, and Appendices by J. J. Arrom. Durham and London: Duke University Press, pp. xi–xxix.

———, and Manuel García Arévalo. 1986. *Cimarrón.* Santo Domingo: Fundación García Arévalo.

———. 1988. *El murciélago y la lechuza en la cultura Taína.* Serie Monográfica, 24. Santo Domingo: Fundación García Arévalo.

Auth, Susan H. 1976. *Ancient glass in the Newark Museum.* Newark: Newark Museum.

Avery, George. 1997. Pots as packaging: The Spanish olive jar and Andalusian transatlantic commercial activity, 16th–18th centuries. Unpublished Ph.D. dissertation (Anthropology), University of Florida, Gainesville.

Axtell, James. 1995. Columbian encounters: 1992–1995. *The William and Mary Quarterly* 52, no. 4:649–69.

Aznar Vallejo, Eduardo. 1983. *La integración de las Islas Canarias en la corona de Castilla (1487–1526): Aspectos administrativos, sociales y económicos.* Seville: Ediciones Universidad de Sevilla.

Ballesteros Beretta, Antonio. 1945. *Cristóbal Colón y el descubrimiento de América.* 2 volumes, 4 and 5 of *Historia de América y de los pueblos americanos.* Barcelona and Buenos Aires: Salvat Editores.

Bell, R. C. 1969. *Board and table games from many civilizations.* Oxford: Oxford University Press.

Benítez, Fernando. 1992. *1992, que celebramos, que lamentamos.* Mexico City: Ediciones Era.

Bennassar, Bartolomé. 1979. *The Spanish character: Attitudes and mentalities from the sixteenth to the nineteenth century.* Translated by Benjamin Keen. Berkeley: University of California Press.

Benzoni, Girolamo. 1857. La historia del mondo nuovo, 1565. Translated and edited by W. H. Smythe as Hakluyt Society Publications, 21. *History of the New World.* London: Hakluyt Society.

Bercht, Fátima, Estrellita Brodsky, John Alan Farmer, and Dicey Taylor, editors. 1997. *Pre-Columbian art and culture from the Caribbean.* New York: El Museo del Barrio and the Monacelli Press.

Beresford, M. W. 1967. *New towns of the middle ages.* Guildford, England: Lutterworth Press.

Boone, James. 1980. Artifact deposition and demographic change: An archaeological case study of medieval colonialism in the age of expansion. Ph.D. dissertation, SUNY Binghamton. Ann Arbor: University Microfilms.

Borrell, Pedro. 1983. *The quicksilver galleons.* Santo Domingo: Museo Casas Reales.

Bourne, Edward. 1907. Columbus, Ramón Pané, and the beginnings of American anthropology. *Proceedings of the American Antiquarian Society* 17:310–48.

Boyd-Bowman, Peter. 1973. *Patterns of Spanish emigration to the New World (1493–1580).* Council on International Studies, Special Studies, 34. Buffalo: State University of New York.

Boyer, Richard. 1997. Negotiating *calidad:* The everyday struggle for status in Mexico. In *Diversity and social identity in colonial Spanish America: Native Americans, Africans, and Hispanic communities during the middle period,* edited by Donna Ruhl and Kate Hoffman. *Historical archaeology* 31, no. 1:1–103. Society for Historical Archaeology, pp. 64–73.

Brache, Anselmo B. 1985. *Constanza, Maimón y Estero Hondo (testimonios e investigación sobre los acontecimientos).* Santo Domingo: Taller Editora.

Brading, D. A. 1991. *The first America.* Cambridge: Cambridge University Press.

Braudel, Fernand. 1979. *The structures of everyday life.* Volume 1 of *Civilization and Capitalism, 15th–18th Century.* New York: Harper and Rowe.

Brill, Robert. 1992. Preliminary remarks on the analysis of glasses from La Isabela, Dominican Republic. Paper prepared for the American Association for the Advancement of Science annual meeting, Chicago, 1992.

————. 1999. *The scientific study of ancient glass*, 2 volumes. Corning, N.Y.: Corning Museum of Glass.

————, I. L. Barnes, S. C. Tong, E. C. Joel, and M. J. Murtaugh. 1986. Laboratory studies of some European artifacts excavated on San Salvador island. In *Proceedings of the first San Salvador Conference: Columbus and his world*, edited by D. Gerace. San Salvador, Bahamas: College Center of the Finger Lakes, pp. 247–92.

Brown, Ian. 1979. Bells. In *Tunica treasure*, edited by J. Brain. Boston and Salem: Peabody Museums, pp. 197–205.

Brown, M. L. 1980. *Firearms in colonial America*. Washington, D.C.: Smithsonian Institution Press.

Butzer, Karl, and Elisabeth Butzer. 1989. Historical archaeology of medieval Muslim communities in the Sierra of Eastern Spain. In *Medieval archaeology*, edited by C. Redman. Binghamton: SUNY Center for Medeival and Early Renaissance Studies, pp. 217–36.

————, Elisabeth Butzer, and J. F. Mateu. 1986. Medieval Muslim communities of the Sierra de Espadán. *Viator: Medieval and Rennaissance Studies* 17:339–413.

Campos Carrasco, Juan M. 1987. Arqueología medieval en la ciudad de Sevilla: Planeamientos, metodologías y estado actual de las investigaciones. II Congreso de Arqueología Medieval Española. Madrid: Asociación Española de Arqueología Medieval.

————, Florentino Pozo Blázquez, Blas Calero Ramos, and Fernando Díaz del Olmo. 1992. *La Isabela umbral de América: Guía de interpretación*. Santo Domingo: Agencia Española de Cooperación Internacional.

Cantisano, Rafael. 1988. La Isabela—Solar de America. Paper presented at the Conferencia Quinto Centenario de la Universidad Nacional Pedro Henríquez Ureña y el Ohio State University. 7 December 1988. Santo Domingo.

Carlé, María del C., María de Fauve, N. B. Ramos, P. de Forteza, and I. J. Las Heras. 1984. *La sociedad hispanomedieval: La ciudad*. Buenos Aires: Editorial Gedisa.

Carneiro, Robert. 1981. The chiefdom: Precursor of the state. In *The transition to statehood in the New World*, edited by R. Cohen and E. R. Service. Philadelphia: Institute for the Study of Human Issues, pp. 205–23.

Caro Alvarez, J. A. 1973. La Isabela, Santo Domingo, R. D. *Boletín del Museo del Hombre Dominicano* 3:48–52.

Carrasco, Pedro. 1997. Indian-Spanish marriages in the first century of the colony. In *Indian Women of Early Mexico*, edited by Susan Schroeder, Stephanie Wood, and Robert Haskett. Norman: University of Oklahoma Press, pp. 87–104.

Carrión Guítiez, Manuel. 1994. La encuadernación española. In *Historia ilustrada del libro español de los incunables al siglo XVII*, edited by Hipólito Escolar. Madrid: Fundación Germán Sánchez Ruipérez, pp. 395–446.

Cassa, Roberto. 1975. *Los Taínos de la Española*. Santo Domingo: Universidad Autónoma de Santo Domingo.

Centro de estudios históricos de obras públicas y urbanismo (CEHOPU) (various authors). 1989. *La ciudad hispanoamericana: El sueño de un orden*. Madrid: Ministerio de Fomento.

Chance, John K. 1978. *Race and class in colonial Oaxaca.* Palo Alto: Stanford University Press.

Chanlatte-Baik, Luis, and Yvonne Narganes. 1983. *Catálogo arqueología de Vieques: Exposición 13 Marzo–22 Abril 1983.* Río de Piedras: Universidad de Puerto Rico Museo de Antropología, Historia y Arte.

Charlevoix, Père Pierre-François Xavier de. 1730. *Histoire de l'Isle Espagnole ou de Saint-Domingue.* 2 volumes. Paris: Chez Hippolyte-Louis Guerin.

Chaunu, Huguette, and Pierre Chaunu. 1957. *Seville et l'Atlantique (1504–1650).* Volume 2. Paris: Ecole Pratique des Hautes Etudes and Armand Colin.

Chiarelli, B. 1987. La Isabela. Special issue of *International journal of anthropology* 2, no. 3:195–253. Florence.

———, and Fernando Luna Calderón. 1987. The excavation of La Isabela, first European city in the New World. *International journal of anthropology* 2, no. 3:199–209. Florence.

Cohen, Jeremy. 1997. Preliminary report on the 1996 field season at Concepción de la Vega, Dominican Republic. Project report submitted to the Dirección Nacional de Parques, Santo Domingo. On file, Florida Museum of Natural History, Gainesville.

Coll Conesa, Jaume, and Bienvenido Más Belén. 1998. Cerámica moderna. In *Sobre cuatro casas andaluzas y su evolución,* edited by Pedro Jiménez and Julio Navarro, *Platería* 14:51–64. Murcia: Ayuntamiento de Murcia.

Collard, André, translator and editor. 1971. *Las Casas: History of the Indies.* New York: Harper and Row.

Concepción, Mario. 1981. *La Concepción de la Vega: Relación histórica.* Sociedad de Geografía Dominicana, volume 16. Santo Domingo: Editorial Taller.

Cook, Noble David. 1993. Disease and depopulation of Hispaniola, 1492–1518. *Colonial Latin American review* 2:213–45.

———. 1998. *Born to die: Disease and New World conquest, 1492–1650.* Cambridge: Cambridge University Press.

Cook, Sherburne, and Woodrow Borah. 1971. *Essays in population history,* volume 1, *Mexico and the Caribbean.* Berkeley: University of California Press.

Córdoba de la Llave, Ricardo. 1990. *La industria medieval de Córdoba.* Córdoba: Caja Provincial de Ahorros de Córdoba.

Cotter, John. 1957. *New discoveries at Jamestown.* National Park Service. Washington, D.C.: U.S. Government Printing Office.

Council, R. Bruce. 1976. Archaeology of the Convento de San Francisco. Unpublished M.A. thesis, Department of Anthropology, University of Florida.

Craddock, Paul. 1995. *Early metal mining and production.* Washington, D.C.: Smithsonian Institution Press.

Crosby, Alfred. 1972. *The Columbian exchange.* Westport, Conn.: Greenwood Press.

———. 1986. *Ecological imperialism: The biological expansion of Europe, 900–1900.* Cambridge: Cambridge University Press.

Crouch, Dora. 1991. Roman models for Spanish colonization. In *Columbian Consequences,* volume 3, *The Spanish borderlands in pan-American perspective,* edited by D. H. Thomas. Washington, D.C.: Smithsonian Institution Press, pp. 21–36.

————, Daniel J. Garr, and Axel I. Mundigo. 1982. *Spanish city planning in North America*. Cambridge, Mass.: MIT Press.

Cruxent, José M. 1989. Relación y noticias acerca de la Isabela. *Ysabela* 1, no. 1:12–18. Santo Domingo.

————. 1990. The origin of La Isabela. In *Columbian Consequences*, volume 2, *Archaeological and historical perspectives on the Spanish borderlands east*, edited by David Hurst Thomas. Washington, D.C.: Smithsonian Institution Press, pp. 251–60.

————, and Kathleen Deagan. 1992. New insights from the first Euro-American town, La Isabela. Paper presented at the 1992 annual meeting of the American Association for the Advancement of Science, Chicago, 18 February 1992.

Cusick, James G. 1989. Change in pottery as a reflection of social change: A study of Taíno pottery before and after contact at the site of En Bas Saline, Haiti. Unpublished M.A. thesis, Department of Anthropology, University of Florida, Gainesville.

Deagan, Kathleen. 1981. Downtown survey: The discovery of 16th century St. Augustine in an urban area. *American Antiquity* 46, no. 3:626–33.

————. 1983. *Spanish St. Augustine: The archaeology of a colonial creole community*. New York: Academic Press.

————. 1985. Spanish-Indian interaction in sixteenth-century Florida and the Caribbean. In *Cultures in Contact*, edited by W. Fitzhugh. Washington, D.C.: Smithsonian Institution Press and the Anthropological Society of Washington, pp. 281–318.

————. 1987a. *Artifacts of the Spanish colonies: Florida and the Caribbean*. Volume 1. Washington, D.C.: Smithsonian Institution Press.

————. 1987b. Columbus's lost colony. *National Geographic* 172, no. 5:672–76.

————. 1989. Report on the 1989 sub-surface test program at La Isabela, Dominican Republic. On file, Dirección Nacional de Parques, Santo Domingo, and the Florida Museum of Natural History, Gainesville.

————. 1990. Overview and introduction: Spanish colonization and settlement in the circum- Caribbean region. In *Columbian Consequences*, volume 2, *Archaeological and historical perspectives on the Spanish borderlands east*, edited by David Hurst Thomas. Washington, D.C.: Smithsonian Institution Press, pp. 225–50.

————. 1992a. La Isabela, foothold in the New World. *National Geographic* 181, no. 1:40–53.

————. 1992b. Preliminary report on laboratory analyses of the archaeological collections from La Isabela. On file, Dirección Nacional de Parques, Santo Domingo, and the Florida Museum of Natural History, Gainesville.

————. 1996. Colonial transformations: Euro-American cultural genesis in the early Spanish-American colonies. *Journal of anthropological research* 52, no. 2:135–60.

————. 1998. Transculturation and Spanish-American ethnogenesis: The archaeological legacy of the quincentenary. In *Studies in culture contact: Interaction, culture change, and archaeology*, edited by James G. Cusick. Center for Archaeological Investigations, Occasional Paper No. 25, pp. 23–43. Carbondale: Center for Archaeological Investigations.

————. 1999. Summary final report on archaeological resources at the Parques

Nacionales Concepción de La Vega and La Isabela, República Dominicana. On file, Dirección Nacional de Parques, Santo Domingo, and the Florida Museum of Natural History, Gainesville.

———. 2002. *Artifacts of the Spanish colonies,* volume 2, *Portable personal possessions.* Washington, D.C.: Smithsonian Institution Press.

———, editor. 1995. *Puerto Real: The archaeology of a sixteenth-century Spanish town in Hispaniola.* Gainesville: University Press of Florida.

Deagan, Kathleen, and José Cruxent. 1993. From contact to criollos: The archaeology of Spanish colonization in Hispaniola. In *The meeting of two worlds: Europe and the Americas, 1492–1650,* edited by Warwick Bray. Proceedings of the British Academy, 81. Oxford: Oxford University Press, pp. 67–104.

———. 1995. The first European artifacts in the Americas: La Isabela, 1493–1498. In *The scientific study of artefacts from post-medieval Europe and beyond,* edited by D. Hook and D. Gaimster. Occasional Papers of the British Museum, 109. London: The British Museum, pp. 2–12.

———. 1997. Medieval foothold in the Americas. *Archaeology* 51, no. 3:54–59.

———. 2002. *Archaeology at La Isabela: America's first European town.* New Haven and London: Yale University Press.

———, and Ricardo Fernández-Sardina. 1993. Excavations in the La Isabela Poblado, 1990–1991. Report submitted to the National Endowment for the Humanities, the National Geographic Society, and the Dirección Nacional de Parques de la República Dominicana. MS on file, Florida Museum of Natural History, Gainesville.

Deagan, Kathleen, and Elizabeth Reitz. 1995. Merchants and cattlemen: The archaeology of a commercial structure at Puerto Real. In *Puerto Real: The archaeology of a sixteenth-century Spanish town in Hispaniola,* edited by K. Deagan. Gainesville: University Press of Florida, pp. 231–84.

Dechert, Michael S. 1983. *City and fortress in the works of Francesco di Giorgio: The theory and practice of defensive town architecture.* 3 volumes. Ph.D. dissertation, Catholic University of America. Ann Arbor: University Microfilms.

Deetz, James. 1993. *Flowerdew Hundred: The archaeology of a Virginia plantation, 1617–1864.* Charlottesville: University of Virginia Press.

Deive, Carlos Esteban. 1980. *La esclavitud del negro en Santo Domingo, 1492–1844.* Santo Domingo: Ediciones del Museo del Hombre Dominicano.

———. 1983. El chamanisimo Taíno. In *La cultura Taína: Seminario sobre la situación de investigación de la cultura Taína,* edited by A. G. Pantel. Madrid: Biblioteca del V Centenario, pp. 81–88.

———. 1989. *Los guerrilleros negros.* Santo Domingo: Fundación Cultural Dominicano.

Demorizi, Emilio Rodríguez. 1975. *Noticias de Puerto Plata.* Sociedad Dominicana de Geografía, volume 8. Santo Domingo: Editora Educativa Dominicana.

———. 1980. *Lugares y monumentos históricos de Santo Domingo.* Santo Domingo: Editora Taller.

———, Editor. 1979. *Atlas de la isla y de la ciudad de Santo Domingo de Casimiro N. de Moya* (1890). Sociedad Dominicana de Geografiá, volume 13. Santo Domingo: Editora Taller.

De Vorsey, Louis, Jr., and John Parker. 1985. *In the wake of Columbus: Islands and controversy.* Detroit: Wayne State University Press.

Díaz del Olmo, Fernando, Juan Campos Carrasco, Ricardo L. Domínguez, and Florentino Pozo Blázquez. 1991. La Isabela: Proyecto de actuación territorial. Apoyo a la restauración arqueológica y puesta en valor arqueoambiental. Technical report, Agencia Española de Cooperación Internacional, Santo Domingo.

Díaz-Plaja, Fernando. 1995. *La vida cotidiana en España medieval.* Crónicas de la Historia, 11. Madrid: Editorial EDAF.

Diderot, Denis. 1959. *A Diderot pictorial encyclopedia of trades and industry (1752).* 2 volumes. New York: Dover Books.

Didiez Burgos, Ramón J. 1971. *El milagro en el fuerte de Santo Tomás.* Santo Domingo: Sociedad Dominicana de Geografía.

Diffie, Bailey, and George D. Winius. 1977. *Foundations of the Portuguese empire, 1415–1580.* Minneapolis: University of Minnesota Press.

Dobal, Carlos. 1987. *La Isabela: Jerúsalem Americana.* Santiago: Universidad Católica Madre y Maestra.

——. 1988. *Cómo pudo ser la Isabela?* Santiago: Universidad Católica Madre y Maestre.

——. 1991. *El primer apóstol del Nuevo Mundo.* Santiago: Universidad Católica Madre y Maestre.

Dominguez, Lourdes. 1978. La transculturación en Cuba (sigs. 16–17). *Cuba arqueológica,* pp. 33–50. Havana.

——. 1984. *Arqueología colonial Cubana: Dos estudios.* Havana: Editorial de Ciencias Sociales.

Domínguez-Companys, F. 1947. *La Isabela, primera ciudad fundada por Colón en América.* Havana: Gonzáles.

Dunn, Oliver, and James E. Kelley, Jr., Editors. 1989. *The diario of Christopher Columbus's first voyage to America, 1492–1493.* Norman: University of Oklahoma Press.

Dunnell, Robert C. 1991. Methodological impacts of catastrophic depopulation on American archaeology and ethnology. In *Columbian Consequences,* volume 3, *The Spanish borderlands in pan-historical perspective,* edited by David H. Thomas. Washington, D.C.: Smithsonian Institution Press. pp. 561–80.

Dussel, Enrique D. 1969. *El episcopado hispanoamericano.* 9 volumes. Cuernavaca: Centro intercultural de documentación.

Earle, Timothy. 1984. The evolution of chiefdoms. *Current anthropology* 30, no. 1:84–88.

——, editor. 1991. *Chiefdoms: Power, economy, and ideology.* Cambridge: Cambridge University Press.

Egan, Geoff, and Frances Pritchard. 1991. *Dress accessories c. 1150–1450.* London: Museum of London.

Elliot, J. H. 1972. *The Old World and the New, 1492–1650.* Cambridge: Cambridge University Press.

Errasti, Mariano. 1998. *Los primeros Franciscanos en América.* Santo Domingo: Fundación García-Arévalo.

Esteva-Fabregát, Claudio. 1995. *Mestizaje in Ibero-America.* Translated by John Wheat. Tucson: University of Arizona Press.

Ewen, Charles. 1991. *From Spaniard to Creole: The archaeology of Hispanic-American cultural formation at Puerto Real, Haiti.* Tuscaloosa: University of Alabama Press.

Fairbanks, Charles. 1973. The cultural significance of Spanish ceramics. In *Ceramics in America*, edited by I. Quimby. Charlottesville: University of Virginia Press, pp. 141–74.

Feinman, Gary, and Jill Neitzel. 1984. Too many types: An overview of sedentary pre-state societies in the Americas. In *Advances in archeological method and theory*, edited by M. Schiffer. Volume 7. New York: Academic Press, pp. 39–102.

Fernández Armesto, Felipe. 1987. *Before Columbus: Exploration and colonization from the Mediterranean to the Atlantic.* New York: Clarendon Press.

Fernández Gómez, Fernando and Juan Campos Carrasco. 1988. Panorama de la arqueología medieval en el casco antiguo de Sevilla. III Congreso de Arqueología Medieval Española. Huesca: Asociación Española de Arqueología Medieval.

Fita y Colomé, Fidel. 1884. *Fray Bernal Boyl, colección de documentos raros e inéditos relacionados a este varón ilustre.* Volume 19. Madrid: Boletín de la Real Academia Española de la Historia.

Fletcher, Richard. 1992. *Moorish Spain.* London: Weidenfield and Nicolson.

Floyd, Troy. 1973. *The Columbus dynasty in the Caribbean, 1492–1526.* Albuquerque: University of New Mexico Press.

Foster, George. 1960. *Culture and conquest.* Viking Fund Publications in Anthropology, 27. New York: Wenner-Gren Foundation.

Fox, John. 1940. *The beginning of Spanish mining in America: The West Indies and Castillo de Oro.* Unpublished Ph.D. dissertation, University of Michigan, Ann Arbor.

Friede, Juan, and Benjamin Keene, editors. 1971. *Bartolomé de las Casas in history.* DeKalb: Northern Illinois University Press.

Frierman, Jay D. 1975. *Medieval ceramics, VI to XIII centuries.* Los Angeles: Frederick S. Wight Art Gallery, University of California.

Frothingham, Alice. 1963. *Spanish glass.* London: Faber and Faber.

Fuson, Robert. 1987. *The log of Christopher Columbus.* Camden, Maine: International Marine Publishing Company.

Gabb, William M. 1881. *On the topography and geology of Santo Domingo.* Transactions of the American Philosophical Society, new series, volume 15. Philadelphia.

García Arévalo, Manuel. 1977. *El arte Taíno de la República Dominicana.* Santo Domingo: Museo del Hombre Dominicano.

———. 1978. La arqueología indo-hispano en Santo Domingo. In *Unidades y variedades: Ensayos en homenaje a José M. Cruxent*, edited by Erika Wagner and Alberta Zucchi. Caracas: Centro de Estudios Avanzados, pp. 77–127.

———. 1983. El murciélago en la mitología y el arte Taíno. In *La cultura Taína: Seminario sobre la situación de investigación de la cultura Taína*, edited by A. G. Pantel. Madrid: Biblioteca del V Centenario, pp. 109–18.

———. 1990a. Transculturation in contact-period and contemporary Hispaniola. In *Columbian Consequences*, volume 2, *Archaeological and historical perspectives on the Spanish borderlands east*, edited by David Hurst Thomas. Washington, D.C.: Smithsonian Institution Press, pp. 269–80.

———. 1990b. *Dimensión y perspectiva del quinto centenario del descubrimiento de América.* Santo Domingo: Comisión Dominicana Permanente para la Celebración del

Quinto Centenario del Descubrimiento y Evangelización de América.

————. 1992. La presencia indígena en La Isabela. Paper presented at the Fourteenth International Congress for Caribbean Archaeology, San Juan, Puerto Rico.

————. 1997. The bat and the owl: Nocturnal images of death. In *Taíno: Pre-
Columbian art and culture from the Caribbean*, edited by Fátima Bercht, Estrellita
Brodsky, John Alan Farmer, and Dicey Taylor. New York: El Museo del Barrio
and the Monacelli Press, pp. 112–23.

García Fernández, J. L. 1989. Trazas urbanas hispanoamericanas y sus antecedentes. In *La ciudad hispanoamericana: El sueño de un orden*. Madrid: Centro de
Estudios Históricos de obras Públicas y urbanismo, Ministerio de Fomento.

García Saíz, Concepción. 1989. *Las castas (The Mexican castes)*. Mexico City: Olivetti.

García Zarza, Eugenio. 1996. *La ciudad en cuadrícula o hispanoamericana: Origen, evolución
y situación actual*. Salamanca: Universidad de Salamanca.

Gartley, Richard T. 1979. Afro-Cruzan pottery—A new style of colonial earthenware from St. Croix. *Journal of the Virgin Islands Archaeological Society* 8:47–61.

Gerbi, Antonello. 1985. *Nature in the New World: From Christopher Columbus to Gonzálo
Fernández de Oviedo*. Translated by Jeremy Moyle. Pittsburgh: University of Pittsburgh Press.

Gies, Frances, and Joseph Gies. 1994. *Cathedral, forge, and waterwheel: Technology and in-
vention in the Middle Ages*. New York: Harper Collins.

Gil, Juan. 1986. Las cuentas de Cristóbal Colón. In *Temas colombinas*, edited by Juan
Gil and Consuelo Varela. Publicaciones de la Escuela de Estudios Hispano-
Americanos, 324, pp. 1–75. Seville: Escuela de Estudios Hispano-Americanos.

————, and Consuela Varela, editors. 1984. *Cartas de particulares a Colón y relaciones
coetáneas*. Madrid: Alianza Editorial.

Glick, Thomas F. 1997. *Irrigation and hydraulic technology: Medieval Spain and its legacy*.
Varorium Collected Study Series. Aldershot, England: Ashgate Publishing.

Goggin, John. 1960. *The Spanish olive jar: An introductory study*. Yale University Publications in Anthropology, 62. New Haven: Yale University Press.

————. 1968. *Spanish majolica in the New World*. Yale University Publications in Anthropology, 72. New Haven: Yale University Press.

————. 1952. Field Notes. "West Indies." 14 Sept. 1952. Box 10, Goggin manuscript collection, P. K. Yonge Library, University of Florida, Gainesville.

González, Justo. 1969. *The development of Christianity in the Caribbean*. Grand Rapids:
William B. Eerdmans.

González Martí, Manuel. 1944. *Cerámica del levante español: Siglos medievales*, volume 1,
Loza. Barcelona: Editorial Labor.

Greenblatt, Stephen. 1991. *Marvelous possesions: The wonder of the New World*. Chicago:
University of Chicago Press.

Guerra, Francisco. 1978. The dispute over syphilis: Europe versus America. *Clio
Médica* 13:39–62. Amsterdam.

————. 1985. La epidemia americana de influenza en 1493. *Revista de Indias*
45:325–47.

————. 1988. The earliest American epidemic: The influenza of 1493. *Social science
history* 12:305–25.

Guerrero, José G., and Elpidio Ortega. 1983. La Isabela, primera ciudad del Nuevo Mundo aún no ha muerto, In *Hoy: Isla abierta*, no. 117, pp. 6–9. Santo Domingo.

Guerrero, José G., and Marcio Veloz Maggiolo. 1988. *Los inicios de la colonización en América*. Serie V Centenario, 1. San Pedro Macorís: Universidad Central del Este.

Gutkind, E. A. 1967. *Urban development in southern Europe: Spain and Portugal*. Volume 3 of *International history of city development*. New York: Free Press and Macmillan.

Hakluyt, Richard, editor. 1962. *Hakluyt's voyages*. 8 volumes. London: Everyman's Library.

Hamilton, Jennifer, and William Hodges. 1995. The aftermath of Puerto Real: Archeology at Bayahá. In *Puerto Real: The archaeology of a sixteenth-century Spanish town in Hispaniola*, edited by K. Deagan. Gainesville: University Press of Florida, pp. 377–418.

Hanke, Lewis. 1935. *The first social experiments in America: A study in the development of Spanish Indian policy in the sixteenth century*. Cambridge: Harvard University Press.

———. 1949. *The Spanish struggle for justice in the conquest of America*. Washington, D.C.: American Historical Association.

———. 1952. *Bartolomé de Las Casas, historian: An essay in Spanish historiography*. Gainesville: University of Florida Press.

Haring, Clarence H. 1947. *The Spanish empire in America*. New York: Harcourt, Brace, and Jovanavitch.

Harrington, M. R. 1921. Cuba before Columbus. *Indian notes and monographs*, parts 1–2. New York: National Museum of the American Indian.

Hassan, Ahmed Y., and David R. Hill. 1986. *Islamic technology: An illustrated history*. Cambridge: Cambridge University Press, and Paris: UNESCO.

Heath, Barbara. 1988. Afro-Caribbean ware: A study of ethnicity on St. Eustatius. Ph.D. dissertation, University of Pennsylvania. Ann Arbor: University Microfilms.

Henige, David. 1978. On the contact population of Hispaniola: History as higher mathematics. *Hispanic American historical review* 58, no. 2:219–37.

———. 1991. *In search of Columbus: The sources for the first voyage*. Tucson: University of Arizona Press.

Hernández Tapia, Concepción. 1970. Despoblaciones de la isla de Santo Domingo en el siglo XVII. *Anuario de Estudios Americanos* 27:281–320. Madrid.

Herrera y Tordesillas, Antonio. 1973. *The general history of the vast continent and islands of America (1725–1726)*. Translated by J. Stevens. New York: AMS Press.

Hobhouse, Henry. 1985. *Seeds of change: Five plants that transformed mankind*. New York: Harper and Row.

Hodges, William. 1985. The search for La Navidad. Typescript, Musée de Guahabá, Limbé, Haiti.

———. 1995. How we found Puerto Real. In *Puerto Real: The archaeology of a sixteenth-century Spanish town in Hispaniola*, edited by K. Deagan. Gainesville: University Press of Florida, pp. 9–33.

———, and Eugene Lyon. 1995. A general history of Puerto Real. In *Puerto Real: The archaeology of a sixteenth-century Spanish town in Hispaniola*, edited by K. Deagan,

Gainesville: University Press of Florida, pp. 83–112.

Hoffman, Charles. 1986. Archaeological investigations at the Long Bay site, San Salvador, Bahamas. In *Proceedings of the first San Salvador Conference: Columbus and his world*, edited by D. Gerace. San Salvador, Bahamas: College Center of the Finger Lakes, pp. 237–45.

Hoffman, Paul. 1980. The historian and historic sites archaeology. In *Forgotten places and things: Archaeological perspectives on American history*, edited by Albert Ward. Albuquerque: Center for Anthropological Studies, pp. 37–41.

Hoover, Herbert, and Lou Hoover. 1950. *De re metallica* (Georgius Agricola, 1556). New York: Dover Books.

Hulme, Peter. 1986. *Colonial encounters: Europe and the native Caribbean, 1492–1797*. London: Routledge.

Icháustegui, J. Marino. 1939. *Curso de geografía e historia (República Dominicana)*. Santiago: Editorial El Diario.

———. 1958. *Reales cédulas y correspondencia de Gobernadores de Santo Domingo*. 5 volumes. Madrid: Colección histórico-documental trujilloniana.

Jane, Cecil, translator and editor. 1930. *The voyages of Christopher Columbus*. London: Argonaut Press.

———, translator. 1960. *The journal of Christopher Columbus*. New York: Clarkson Potter.

Jones, B. Calvin, and Gary Shapiro. 1990. Nine mission sites in Apalachee. In *Columbian Consequences*, volume 2, *Archaeological and historical perspectives in the Spanish borderlands east*, edited by David H. Thomas. Washington, D.C.: Smithsonian Institution Press, pp. 491–510.

Kamen, Henry. 1991. *Spain, 1469–1714: A society of conflict*. New York: Longman.

Karcheski, Walter, Jr. 1990. *Arms and armor of the conquistador, 1492–1600*. Gainesville: Florida Museum of Natural History.

Karsten, Peter, and John Modell, editors. 1992. *Theory, method, and practice in social and cultural history*. New York: New York University Press.

Keegan, William. 1992. *The people who discovered Columbus*. Gainesville: University Press of Florida.

———. 1996a. Columbus was a cannibal: Myth and the first encounters. In *The Lesser Antilles in the age of European expansion*, edited by R. Paquette and S. Engerman. Gainesville: University Press of Florida, pp. 17–32.

———. 1996b. West Indian archaeology, 2: After Columbus. *Journal of archaeological research* 5, no. 2:265–94.

———. 1997. No man (or woman) is an island: Elements of Taíno social organization. In *The indigenous people of the Caribbean*, edited by S. Wilson. Gainesville: University Press of Florida, pp. 109–17.

———. 2000. West Indian archaeology, 3: Ceramic Age. *Journal of archaeological research* 8 no. 2:135–67.

———, and Morgan Maclachlan. 1989. The evolution of avunculocal chiefdoms: A reconstruction of Taíno kinship and politics. *American anthropologist* 91:613–30.

———, and Bryan Byrne. 1998. Social foundations of Taíno *caciques*. In *Chiefdoms and chieftaincy in the Americas*, edited by Elsa Redmond. Gainesville: University Press of Florida, pp. 217–44.

Keen, Benjamin, translator. 1959. *The life of the Admiral Christopher Columbus by his son, Ferdinand.* New Brunswick, N.J.: Rutgers University Press.

Keith, Donald. 1987. The Molasses Reef wreck. Unpublished project report, Institute for Nautical Archaeology, Texas A and M University, College Station.

————, and Bruce Thompson. 1985. The INA / Morning Watch Research archaeological survey of La Isabela, Dominican Republic. Unpublished manuscript, Institute for Nautical Archaeology, Texas A and M University, College Station.

Kirkman, James. 1974. *Fort Jesus: A Portuguese fortress on the east African coast.* Oxford: Clarendon Press.

Kisch, Bruno. 1965. *Scales and weights: A historical outline.* Yale studies in the history of science and medicine, 1. New Haven: Yale University Press.

Klein, Herbert. 1989. *Slavery in the Americas.* Second edition. Chicago: Elephant Paperbacks. First published in 1969.

Konetzke, Richard. 1945. La emigración de mujeres españolas a América durante la época colonial. *Revista internacional de sociología* 3, no. 9:123–44.

Krantz, Frederick, editor. 1988. *History from below.* Oxford: Blackwell.

Kubler, George. 1940. *The religious architecture of New Mexico in the colonial period and since the American occupation.* Colorado Springs: Taylor Museum.

————. 1948. *Mexican architecture of the sixteenth century.* New Haven: Yale University Press.

LaRocca, Donna. 1989. The renaissance spirit. In *Swords and hilt weapons,* by Michael Coe et al. London: Weidenfeld and Nicolson, pp. 44–57.

Las Casas, Bartolomé de. 1951. *Historia de las Indias,* edited by Agustín Millares Carlo. 3 volumes. Mexico City: Fondo de Cultura Económica.

————. 1958. *Apologética historia sumaria.* Madrid: Biblioteca de Autores Españoles.

————. 1985. *Historia de las Indias.* Serie V Centenario de Descubrimiento de las Américas. 3 volumes. Santo Domingo: Ediciones del Continente.

Lavin, James. 1965. *A history of Spanish firearms.* New York: Arco Publishing.

Lawren, Bill. 1987. Swine flu and the discovery of America. *Omni Magazine* 9, no. 4:18.

Lister, Florence, and Robert Lister. 1983. One pot's pedigree. In *Collected papers in honor of Charlie R. Steen, Jr.,* edited by A. Ward. Papers of the Archaeological Society of New Mexico, no. 8. Albuquerque: Archaeological Society of New Mexico, pp. 167–87.

————. 1987. *Andalusian ceramics in Spain and New Spain.* Albuquerque: University of New Mexico Press.

López Cantos, Angel. 1992. *Juegos, fiestas y diversiones en la América española.* Colecciones MAPFRE, Relaciones entre España y América, 10. Madrid: Editorial MAPFRE.

López-Penha, José Ramón Báez. 1992. *Por qué Santo Domingo es así.* Santo Domingo: Sociedad Dominicana de Bibliófolos.

Luna Calderón, Fernando. 1986. El cementerio de la Isabela: Primera villa europea del Nuevo Mundo: Estudio de antropología física. *Primera jornada de antropología* 1, no. 1:10–17. Santo Domingo: Museo del Hombre Dominicano y la Universidad Autónoma de Santo Domingo.

Lunenfeld, Marvin. 1990. *The council of the Santa Hermandad: A study of the pacification forces of Ferdinand and Isabella.* Coral Gables: University of Miami Press.

Lyon, Eugene. 1995. Chronology of contacts and other events affecting Puerto Real and its vicinity, 1513–1609. In *Puerto Real: The archaeology of a sixteenth-century Spanish town in Hispaniola*, edited by K. Deagan. Gainesville: University Press of Florida, pp. 457–76.

MacNutt, Frances, translator and editor. 1970. *De Orbe Novo*, by Peter Martyr D'Anghiera. 2 volumes. New York: Burt Franklin.

Major, R. H., translator. 1857. *Letters of Christopher Columbus with other original documents relating to his four voyages to the New World.* Reprinted 1961. New York: Corinth Books.

Mann, Vivian, Thomas F. Glick, and Jerrilyn Dodds, editors. 1992. *Convivencia: Jews, Muslims, and Christians in medieval Spain.* New York: George Braziller and the Jewish Museum.

Marcano, E., and R. Tavares. 1981. La formación Isabela, pleistoceno temprano. Publicaciones Especiales del Museo del Hombre Dominicano. (No number.) Santo Domingo: Museo del Hombre Dominicano.

Marté, Roberto, Editor. 1981. *Santo Domingo en los manuscritos de Juan Bautista Muñoz.* Santo Domingo: Fundación García Arévalo.

Martínez-Llopis, M. 1995. *Historia de la gastronomía española.* Huesca: Val de Onsera (España), Ministerio de Agricultura, Pesca y Alimentación.

Mathewson, Duncan. 1972. Jamaican ceramics: An introduction to 18th-century folk pottery in the West African tradition. *Jamaica Journal* 6, no. 2:54–56.

McAlister, Lyle. 1984. *Spain and Portugal in the New World.* Minneapolis: University of Minnesota Press.

McEwan, Bonnie, 1988. An archaeological perspective on sixteenth-century Spanish life in the Old World and the Americas. Unpublished Ph.D. dissertation, University of Florida, Gainesville.

———. 1992. The roles of ceramics in Spain and Spanish America during the sixteenth century. *Historical archaeology* 26, no. 1:92–108.

McGinnis, Shirley. 1997. Zemi three-pointer stones. In *Taíno: Pre-Columbian art and culture from the Caribbean*, edited by Fátima Bercht, Estrellita Brodsky, John Alan Farmer, and Dicey Taylor. New York: El Museo del Barrio and the Monacelli Press, pp. 92–105.

McGuire, Randall, and Robert Paynter, editors. 1991. *The archaeology of inequality.* Oxford: Blackwell.

Mira Caballos, Esteban. 1997. *El Indio Antillano: Repartimiento, encomienda y esclavitud (1492–1542).* Seville: Muñoz Moya Editor.

Mitchem, Jeffrey M., and Bonnie McEwan. 1988. New data on early bells from Florida. *Southeastern Archaeology* 7, no. 1:39–48.

Montás Onorio, Pedro Borrell, and Frank Moya Pons. 1988. *Arte Taíno.* Santo Domingo: Banco Central de la República Dominicana.

Morales Padrón, Francisco. 1978. *Canarias: Crónicas de su conquista (transcripción, estudios, notas).* Seville: Editorial el Museo Canario.

Morison, Samuel E. 1940. The route of Columbus along the north coast of Haiti and the site of La Navidad. *Transactions of the American Philosophical Society*, volume 31, part 4:239–85. Philadelphia.

————. 1942. *Admiral of the ocean sea.* Boston: Little, Brown.

————, translator and editor. 1963. *Journals and other documents on the life and voyages of Christopher Columbus.* New York: Heritage Press.

Morner, Magnus. 1967. *Race mixture in the history of Latin America.* Boston: Little, Brown.

Morris, A. E. J. 1979. *History of urban form before the industrial revolution.* Second edition. London: George Godwin.

Moya Pons, Frank. 1987. *Después de Colón: Trabajo, sociedad y política en la economía de oro.* Madrid: Alianza Editorial.

————. 1992. The politics of forced Indian labor in La Española. *Antiquity* 66, no. 250:130–39.

————. 1995. *The Dominican Republic: A national history.* New Rochelle, N.Y.: Hispaniola Books.

Muller, Patricia. 1972. *Jewels in Spain.* New York: Hispanic Society of America.

Mumford, Lewis. 1961. *The city in history.* New York: Harcourt, Brace, and World.

Museum of London. 1993. *London Museum medieval catalogue.* Reprint of 1940 edition. Ipswich: Anglia Publishing.

Musty, John. 1974. Medieval pottery kilns. In *Medieval pottery from excavations,* edited by V. I. Evison, H. Hodges, and J. G. Hurst. New York: St. Martin's Press, pp. 41–66.

Myers, Emlen. 1989. Ceramic technologies of medieval northern Morocco. In *Medieval archaeology,* edited by Charles Redman. Binghamton: SUNY Center for Medieval and Early Renaissance Studies, pp. 75–96.

————, and Jacqueline Olin. 1992. Analysis of the earliest Euro-American ceramics in the Americas: La Isabela. Paper presented at the 1992 annual meeting of the American Association for the Advancement of Science, Chicago, 18 February 1992.

Myers, Emlen, Kathleen Deagan, José Cruxent, and Jacqueline Olin. 1992. Characterization of the first European pottery in America: La Isabela, 1493–1498. Paper presented at the British Museum, November 1992.

Nash, June. 1980. Aztec women: The transition from status to class in empire and colony. In *Women and colonization: Anthropological perspectives,* edited by Mona Etienne and Eleanor Leacock. New York: Praeger, pp. 134–48.

National Academy of Sciences. 1980. *Recommended dietary allowances.* Committee on Dietary Allowances, Food and Nutrition Board. Washington, D.C.: National Academy of Sciences.

Navarrete, Martín Fernández de, Compiler. 1864–1884. *Colección de documentos inéditos relativos al descubrimiento, conquista, y organización de las antiguas posesiones españolas de América y Oceanía.* 42 volumes. Madrid: Real Academia de la Historia.

————. 1934. *Viajes de Cristóbal Colón.* Reprint of the 1825 edition. Madrid: Biblioteca de Autores Españoles.

————. 1954–1964. *Colección de los viajes y descubrimientos que hicieron por mar los españoles desde fines del siglo XV.* In *Obras Escogidas,* edited by Carlos Seco Serrano. 5 volumes. Madrid: Biblioteca de Autores Españoles.

Newsom, Lee Ann. 1993. *Plant use by Saladoid and Taíno people of the Caribbean.* Ph.D.

dissertation, University of Florida, Gainesville. Ann Arbor: University Micro-films.

————, and Kathleen Deagan. 1994. *Zea mays* in the West Indies: The archaeological and early historic record. In *Corn and culture in the New World*, edited by S. Johannessen and C. Hastorf. Boulder: Westview Press, pp. 203–17.

Newson, Linda. 1993. The demographic collapse of the native peoples of the Americas, 1492–1650. In *The meeting of two worlds*, edited by W. Bray. Proceedings of the British Academy, 81:247–88. Oxford: Oxford University Press.

Niel, W. Keith. 1955. *Spanish guns and pistols*. New York: Bell.

Nitz, Hans-Jurgen. 1997. Los principios de planificación en la fundación de la ciudad real de Santa Fe de Granada (1491), una aportación al modelo de ciudad colonial española en América. *Cuadernos geográficos* 27:11–129. Granada: Universidad de Granada.

Norton, John. 1997. *Building with earth*. London: Intermediate Technology Publications.

Ober, Frederick. 1893. *In the wake of Columbus*. Boston: D. Lothrop.

————. 1908. *A guide to the West Indies and Bermuda*. New York: Dodd and Mead.

Oliver, José. 1997. The Taíno cosmos. In *The indigenous people of the Caribbean*, edited by S. Wilson. Gainesville: University Press of Florida, pp. 140–53.

Oliveira Marques, A. H. de. 1971. *Daily life in Portugal in the late middle ages*. Madison: University of Wisconsin Press.

Olsen, Harold Bogaert, Eugenio Pérez Montás, and Esteban Prieto Vicioso, Editors. 1998. *Arqueología y antropología física en la Catedral de Santo Domingo*. Santo Domingo: Centro de Altos Estudios Humanísticos y del Idioma Español.

Ortega, Elpidio. 1980. *Introducción a la loza común o alfarería en el período colonial de Santo Domingo*. Santo Domingo: Fundación Ortega-Alvarez.

————. 1982. *Arqueología colonial en Santo Domingo*. Santo Domingo: Fundación Ortega-Alvarez.

————, and J. M. Cruxent. 1976. Informe preliminar sobre las excavaciones en las rutas del Convento de San Francisco. *Actas del XLI Congreso Internacional de Americanistas* 3:674–89.

Ortega, Elpidio, and Carmen Fondeur. 1978a. *Arqueología colonial en Santo Domingo*. Santo Domingo: Fundación Ortega-Alvarez.

————. 1978b *Estudio de la cerámica del período indo-hispano de la antigua Concepción de la Vega*. Serie Científica 1. Santo Domingo: Fundación Ortega-Alvarez.

————. 1979. *Arqueología de la Casa del Cordón*. Serie Científica II. Santo Domingo: Fundación Ortega-Alvarez.

Ortega, Elpidio, and José Guerrero. 1982. *Estudio de 4 nuevos sitios paleoarcaicos en la isla de Santo Domingo*. Santo Domingo: Museo del Hombre Dominicano.

————. 1988. *La Isabela y la arqueología en la ruta de Colón*. San Pedro de Macorís: Universidad Central del Este.

Oviedo y Valdés, Gonzalo Fernández de. 1959. *Historia general y natural de las Indias*. Madrid: Biblioteca de Autores Españoles.

————. 1851–1855. *Historia general y natural de las Indias*. 4 volumes. Madrid: Imprenta de la Real Academia de la Historia.

Pagden, Anthony. 1982. *The fall of natural man: The American Indian and the origins of comparative ethnography.* Cambridge: Cambridge University Press.

———. 1987. Identity formation in Spanish America. In *Colonial identity in the Atlantic World,* edited by N. Canny and A. Pagden. Princeton: Princeton University Press, pp. 14–94.

———. 1993. *European encounters with the New World.* New Haven: Yale University Press.

———. 1992. Fabricating identity in Spanish America. *History today* 42 (May 1992): 44–50.

Palm, Erwin. 1945. Excavations at La Isabela, white man's first town in the Americas. *Acta Americana* 3:298–303.

———. 1955. *Los monumentos arquitectónicos de la Española.* 2 volumes. Ciudad Trujillo: Publicaciones de la Universidad de Santo Domingo.

Pané, Ramón. 1988. *Relación acerca de las antiguedades de los Indios.* Biblioteca de Clásicos Dominicanos, 2. Santo Domingo: Ediciones de la Fundación Corripio.

———. 1999. *An account of the antiquities of the Indians.* Translated by Susan Griswold, with Introductory Study, Notes, and Appendices by J. J. Arrom. Durham and London: Duke University Press.

Pantel, A. Gus. 1983. Orígenes y definiciones de la cultura Taína: Sus antecedentes tecnológicos en el precerámico. In *La Cultura Taína,* edited by A. Gus Pantel. Madrid: Biblioteca del V Centenario, pp. 9–14.

Parry, J. H. 1981. *The age of reconnaissance: Discovery, exploration, and settlement, 1450–1650.* Berkeley: University of California Press.

———. 1990. *The Spanish seaborne empire.* Berkeley: University of California Press. First published 1966.

Parry, John, and Robert Keith, editors. 1984. *The Caribbean.* Volume 2 of *The New Iberian world.* 5 volumes. New York: Times Books.

Patterson, Thomas. 1991. Early colonial encounters and identities in the Caribbean: A review of some recent works and their implications. *Dialectical anthropology* 16:1–13.

Pavón, Basilio. 1992. *Ciudades Hispanomusulmanas.* Madrid: Editorial MAPFRE.

Paz Aguiló, María. 1982. Mobiliario. In *Historia de las artes aplicadas e industriales en España,* edited by Antonio Bonet Correa. Madrid: Ediciones Cátedra, pp.271–321.

Pepper, Simon, and Nicholas Adams. 1986. *Firearms and fortifications.* Chicago: University of Chicago Press.

Pérez, Fray Juan Manuel. 1984. *Estos ¿no son hombres?* Santo Domingo: Fundación García-Arévalo.

Pérez de Tudela Bueso, Juan. 1954. La negociación Colombina de las Indias. *Revista de Indias* 14, nos. 57–58:289–357.

———. 1955. La quiebra de la factoría y el nuevo poblamiento de la Española. *Revista de Indias* 15, no. 60:208–10.

———. 1956. *Las armadas de Indias y los orígenes de la política de colonización (1492–1505).* Madrid: Ediciones Atlas.

———. 1983. *Mirabilis in altis: Estudio crítico sobre el origen y significado del proyecto del descubridor de Cristóbal Colón.* Madrid: Instituto Gonzálo Fernández de Oviedo.

Phillips, Carla Rahn. 1986. *Six galleons for the king of Spain.* Baltimore: Johns Hopkins University Press.

———. 1990. The growth and composition of trade in the Iberian empires, 1450–1750. In *The rise of merchant empires*, edited by James D. Tracey. Cambridge: Cambridge University Press, pp. 34–101.

Phillips, J. R. S. 1988. *The medieval expansion of Europe.* Oxford: Oxford University Press.

Phillips, William, and Carla Rahn Phillips. 1992. *The worlds of Christopher Columbus.* Cambridge: Cambridge University Press.

Pichardo, Bernardo. 1944. *Reliquias históricas de la Española.* Second edition. Santiago: Editorial El Diaro.

Pike, Ruth. 1966. *Enterprise and adventure: The Genoese in Seville and the opening of the New World.* Ithaca: Cornell University Press.

Puig Ortíz, José A. 1973. *Por la valorización histórica de las ruinas de La Isabela, primera ciudad del Nuevo Mundo.* Santo Domingo: Editora del Caribe.

Quesada, Juan Rafael, and Magda Zavala, editors. 1991. *500 años: Holocausto o descubrimiento?* San José, Costa Rica: Editorial Universitaria.

Ramos, Demetrio. 1982. *El conflicto de las lanzas de jinetas.* Santo Domingo: Ediciones Fundación García-Arévalo.

———. 1989. *Colón no pudo volver. La fundación de la Navidad.* Madrid: Ediciones de Cultura Hispánica.

Ramos Gómez, Luis. 1992. Huellas de la relación mantenida por españoles e indios en La Isabela hasta la partida de Antonio de Torres, en el febrero de 1494. *Revista Española de antropología Americana* 22:75–88.

Real Academia Española. 1995. *Diccionario de la lengua Española. Electronic edition.* Madrid: Espasa Calpe.

Redman, Charles. 1986. *Qsar es-Seghir: An archaeological view of medieval life.* New York: Academic Press.

Redmond, Elsa, editor. 1997. *Chiefs and chieftaincy in the Americas.* Gainesville: University Press of Florida.

Reitz, Elizabeth. 1992. The Spanish colonial experience and domestic animals. *Historical Archaeology* 26, no. 1:84–91.

———, and Bonnie G. McEwan. 1995. Animals and the environment at Puerto Real. In *Puerto Real: The archaeology of a sixteenth-century Spanish town in Hispaniola*, edited by K. Deagan. Gainesville: University Press of Florida, pp. 287–334.

Reitz, Elizabeth J., and C. Margaret Scarry. 1985. *Reconstructing historic subsistence with an example from sixteenth-century Spanish Florida.* Society for Historical Archaeology Special Publication Series, no. 3. No place: Society for Historical Archaeology.

Rodríguez, Viquiera, and P. M. Ibañez, editors. 1992. *Las ciudades del encuentro.* Mexico City: Editorial Lumisa.

Roe, Peter. 1997. Just wasting away: Taíno shamanism and concepts of fertility. In *Taíno: Pre-Columbian art and culture from the Caribbean*, edited by Fátima Bercht, Estrellita Brodsky, John Alan Farmer, and Dicey Taylor. New York: El Museo del Barrio and the Monacelli Press, pp. 124–56.

Roosevelt, Anna. 1980. *Parmaná: Prehistoric maize and manioc subsistence along the Amazon and Orinoco.* New York: Academic Press.

Rose, Richard. 1987. Lucayan lifeways at the time of Columbus. In *Proceedings of the first San Salvador Conference: Columbus and his world*, edited by D. Gerace. San Salvador, Bahamas: College Center of the Finger Lakes, pp. 321–40.

Rosenblatt, Angel. 1954. *La población indígena y el mestizaje en América, 1492–1950*. 2 volumes. Buenos Aires: Editorial Nova.

Rouse, Irving. 1939. *Prehistory in Haiti*. Yale University Publications in Anthropology, 21. New Haven: Yale University Press.

————. 1941. *Culture of the Ft. Liberté region, Haiti*. Yale University Publications in Anthropology, 24. New Haven: Yale University Press.

————. 1948. The Arawak. In *Handbook of South American Indians*, volume 4, *The circum-Caribbean tribes*, edited by J. Steward. Bureau of American Ethnology Bulletin 143, no. 4:507–46.

————. 1982. Ceramic and religious development in the prehistoric Greater Antilles. *Journal of New World archaeology* 5, no. 2:45–55.

————. 1986. *Migrations in prehistory*. New Haven: Yale University Press.

————. 1992. *The Taínos: Rise and decline of the people who greeted Columbus*. New Haven: Yale University Press.

————, and J. J. Arrom. 1991. The Taínos: Principal inhabitants of Columbus' Indies. In *Circa 1492: Art in the age of exploration*, edited by Jay Levenson. Washington, D.C.: National Gallery of Art, and New Haven: Yale University Press, pp. 509–13.

Rouse, Irving, and José Cruxent. 1963. *Venezuelan archaeology*. New Haven: Yale University Press.

Rouse, Irving, and Clark Moore. 1984. Cultural sequence in southwestern Haiti. *Bureau National d'Ethnologie Bulletin* 1:25–38. Port au Prince.

Ruempol, A. P., and A. G. van Dongen. 1991. *Pre-indusriele Gebruiksvoorwerpen / Pre-industrial utensils*. Rotterdam: Museum Boymans–van Beuningen.

Rule, Margaret. 1983. *The "Mary Rose": The excavation and raising of Henry VIII's flagship*. London: Conway Maritime Press.

Rumeu de Armas, A. 1989. *Manuscrito del libro copiador de Cristóbal Colón*. 2 volumes. Madrid: Editorial Testimonio.

Sale, Kirkpatrick, 1990. *Conquest of paradise*. New York: Penguin Books.

Salméron, Africa León, and Navidad de Diego y Gonzales. 1915. *Compéndio de indumentaria española*. Madrid: Imprenta de San Francisco de Sales.

Sankalia, H., and M.G. Dikshit. 1952. *Excavations at Brahmapuri (1945–46)*. Deccan College Monograph Series, 5. Poona: Deccan College Postgraduate and Research Institute.

Santiago Cruz, Francisco. 1960. *Las artes y los gremios en la Nueva España*. Mexico City: Editorial Jus.

Sarría Rueda, Amalia. 1994. Los inicios de la imprenta. In *Historia ilustrada del libro español de los incunables al siglo XVII*, edited by Hipólito Escolar. Madrid: Fundación Germán Sánchez Ruipérez, pp. 35–94.

Sauer, Carl. O. 1966. *The early Spanish main*. Berkeley: University of California Press.

Saunders, Rebecca. 1990. Ideal and innovation: Spanish mission architecture in the Southeast. In *Columbian Consequences*, volume 2, *Archaeological and historical perspectives on the Spanish borderlands east,* edited by David Hurst Thomas. Washington, D.C.: Smithsonian Institution Press, pp. 527–42.

Schmidt, Peter. 1997. *Iron technology in East Africa: Symbolism, science, and archaeology.* Bloomington: Indiana University Press.

Scott, Elizabeth, editor. 1994. *Those of little note: Gender, race, and class in historical archaeology.* Tucson: University of Arizona Press.

Siegel, Peter. 1997. Ancestor worship and cosmology among the Taíno. In *Taíno: Pre-Columbian art and culture from the Caribbean,* edited by Fátima Bercht, Estrellita Brodsky, John Alan Farmer, and Dicey Taylor. New York: El Museo del Barrio and the Monacelli Press, pp. 106–11.

Simmons, Joe J. 1988. Wrought-iron ordnance: Revealing discoveries from the New World. *International journal of nautical archaeology and underwater exploration* 17, no. 1:25–34.

Simmons, Marc, and Frank Turley. 1980. *Southwestern colonial ironwork.* Santa Fe: Museum of New Mexico Press.

Sivaramakrishnan, K. 1995. Situating the subaltern: History and anthropology in the Subaltern Studies Project. *Journal of historical sociology* 8, no. 4:395–429.

Smith, G. Charles. 1986. A study of colono ware and non-European ceramics from sixteenth-century Puerto Real, Haiti. Unpublished M.A. thesis, University of Florida, Gainesville.

———. 1995. Indians and Africans at Puerto Real: The ceramic evidence. In *Puerto Real: The archaeology of a sixteenth-century town in Hispaniola,* edited by Kathleen Deagan. Gainesville: University Press of Florida, pp. 335–74.

Smith, Cyril S., and Martha Teach Gnudi, translators and editors. 1990. *The Pirotechnia of Vannoccio Biringuccio* (1540). New York: Dover Books.

Smith, Roger C. 1993. *Vanguard of empire.* New York: Oxford University Press.

———, James Spirek, John Bratten, and Della Scott-Ireton. 1995. *The Emmanuel Point ship archaeological investigations, 1992–1995.* Tallahassee: Florida Department of State, Division of Historical Resources.

Solana, Francisco de, editor. 1986. *Historia y futuro de la ciudad iberoamericana.* Madrid: Consejo Superior de Investigaciones Científicas, Centro de Estudios Históricos, Universidad Internacional Menéndez Pelayo.

South, Stanley, Russell Skowronek, and Richard Johnson. 1988. *Spanish artifacts from Santa Elena.* Occasional Papers of the South Carolina Institute of Archaeology and Anthropology, Anthropological Studies, 7. Columbia, S.C.: South Carolina Institute of Archaeology and Anthropology.

Spaer, Maude. 1994. The Islamic glass bracelets of Palestine: Preliminary findings. *Journal of glass studies* 34:44–62. Corning, N.Y.

Stahl, Alan. 1992. The coinage of La Isabela, 1493–1498. *Numismatist* 105:1399–1402.

———. 1995. Coins from the excavations at La Isabela, D.R., the first European colony in the New World. *American journal of mumismatics,* second series, 5–6:189–207.

Stanislawski, Daniel. 1947. Early Spanish town planning in the New World. *Geographical review* 27, no. 1:94–105.

Stearns, Peter, editor. 1988. *Expanding the past: A reader in social history.* New York: New York University Press.

Stevens-Arroyo, Anthony. 1988. *Cave of the Jagua: Mythological world of the Taínos.* Albuquerque: University of New Mexico Press.

———. 1993. The inter-Atlantic paradigm: The failure of Spanish medieval colonization in the Canary and Caribbean islands. *Comparative studies in society and history* 35, no. 3:515–43.

———. 1997. Canary Islands and the Antillean. In *La sorpresa de Europa*, edited by Antonio Tejera Gaspar. Santa Cruz de Tenerife: Universidad de la Laguna, pp. 83–107.

Sturtevant, William. 1961. Taíno agriculture. In *The evolution of horticultural systems in South America: Causes and consequences—A symposium*, edited by H. Wibert. Anthropological Supplement 2. Caracas: Sociedad de Ciencias Naturales La Salle, pp. 69–73.

Sued-Badillo, Jalil. 1996. The theme of the indigenous in the national projects of the hispanic Caribbean. In *Making alternative histories*, edited by Peter Schmidt and Thomas Patterson. Santa Fe, New Mexico: School for American Research Press, pp. 25–46.

Tannahill, Reay. 1973. *Food in history.* New York: Stein and Day.

Taviani, Emilio Paolo. 1983. *Cristóbal Colón: Génesis del gran descubrimiento.* 2 volumes. Barcelona: Editorial Teide.

———. 1985. *Christopher Columbus: The grand design.* Translated by William Weaver. London: Orbis.

———. 1986. *I viaggio di Colombo: La grande scoperta.* 2 volumes. Novara: Istituto Geográfico de Agostini.

———. 1991. *The voyages of Columbus.* 2 volumes. Translated by Mark Beckwith and Luciano Farina. Novara: Istituto Geográfico de Agostini.

Taylor, Dicey, Marco Biscione, and Peter Roe. 1997. Epilogue: The beaded zemi in the Pigorini Museum. In *Taíno: Pre-Columbian art and culture from the Caribbean*, edited by Fátima Bercht, Estrellita Brodsky, John Alan Farmer, and Dicey Taylor. New York: El Museo del Barrio and the Monacelli Press, pp. 158–69.

Tejera Gaspar, Antonio. 1992. *Majos y europeos: El contacto de culturas en Lanzarote en los siglos XIV y XV (un precedente americano).* Serie Informes, no. 33, Las Palmas, Tenerife: Universidad de la Laguna.

———. 1998. *Los cuatros viajes de Colón y las Islas Canarias.* La Gomera: Cabildo de la Gomera.

———, and Eduardo Aznar Vallejo. 1992. Lessons from the Canaries: First contact between Europeans and Canarians, c. 1312–1477. *Antiquity* 66, no. 250:120–29.

Thatcher, John B. 1903. *Christopher Columbus: The life, his works, his remains.* 2 volumes. New York: G. P. Putnam's Sons.

Todorov, Tzvetlan. 1984. *The conquest of America.* New York: Harper and Row.

Toussaint, Manuel. 1967. *Colonial art in Mexico.* Translated by Elizabeth W. Weismann. Austin: University of Texas Press.

United States Department of Agriculture. 1992. Composition of foods: Raw, processed, prepared. Microform. Nutrition Monitoring Division, coordinated by Lynn E. Dickey. Washington, D.C.: United States Department of Agriculture.

Van Beek, Bert. 1986. Jetons—Their use and history. Translated by Robert Shulman. In *Persepctives in Numismatics*, edited by Saul Needleman. Chicago: Ares Publishers, pp. 195–220.

Vargiu, Rita. 1990. Rapporto preliminare sullo studio della denzione del materiale scheletrico proveniente dal sito di La Isabela. Unpublished report submitted to the Dirección Nacional de Parques, República Dominicana. On file, Parque Nacional de La Isabela.

Varela, Consuelo, editor. 1982. *Cristóbal Colón: Textos y documentos completos.* Madrid: Editorial Alianza.

———, editor. 1986. *Cristóbal Colón: Los cuatro viajes testimonio.* Madrid: Editorial Alianza.

———. 1987a. La Isabela, vida y ocaso de una ciudad efímira. *Revista de Indias* 47, no. 181:733–44.

———. 1987b. Florentine's friendship and kinship with Christopher Columbus. In *Proceedings of the first San Salvador Conference: Columbus and his world,* edited by D. Gerace. San Salvador, Bahamas, Center College of the Finger Lakes, pp. 33–43.

———. 1988. *Colón y los Florentinos.* Madrid: Editorial Alianza.

———. 1997. *Cristóbal Colón: Un retrato de un hombre.* Madrid: Editorial Alianza.

Vega, Bernardo. 1973. Un cinturón tejido y una careta de madera de Santo Domingo en el período de transculturación. *Boletín del Museo del Hombre Dominicano* 3:199–226.

———. 1979. *Los metales y los aborígenes de la Hispaniola.* Santo Domingo: Museo del Hombre Dominicano.

———. 1981. La herencia indígena en la cultura dominicana de hoy. In *Ensayos sobre la cultura dominicana.* Serie Conferencia , 10. Santo Domingo: Museo del Hombre Dominicano, pp. 9–53.

———. 1987. *Los casicasgos de la Española.* Second edition. Santo Domingo: Museo del Hombre Dominicano.

———. 1997. *Las frutas de los Taínos.* Santo Domingo: Fundación Cultural Dominicana.

Veloz Maggiolo, Marcio. 1990. Las poblaciones indígenas de la Isabela. *Ysabela* 1, no. 4:19–28. Santo Domingo.

———. 1993. *La isla de Santo Domingo antes de Colón.* Santo Domingo: Banco Central de la República Dominicana.

———. 1997. The daily life of the Taíno people. In *Taíno: Pre-Columbian art and culture from the Caribbean,* edited by Fátima Bercht, Estrellita Brodsky, John Alan Farmer, and Dicey Taylor. New York: El Museo del Barrio and the Monacelli Press, pp 34–45.

———, and José Guerrero. 1986. Las Antillas del descubrimiento: Arqueología y etnología. *Hoy: Isla abierta,* 11 October 1986. Santo Domingo.

———, and Elpidio Ortega. 1980. Nuevos hallazgos arqueológicos en la costa norte de Santo Domingo. *Boletín del Museo del Hombre Dominicano* 9, no. 13:11–48. Santo Domingo.

————. 1992. *La fundación de la villa de Santo Domingo.* Serie Historia de la Ciudad, 1. Santo Domingo: Colección Quinto Centenario.

Vernet, Juan. 1992. The legacy of Islam in Spain. In *Al Andalús. The art of Islamic Spain,* edited by Jerrilyn Dodd. New York: Metropolitan Museum of Art, pp. 173–89.

Vicens Vives, Jaime. 1969. *An economic history of Spain.* Princeton: Princeton University Press.

Vigon, J. 1945. *La historia de la artillería española.* Madrid: Instituto Jerónimo Zurita.

Viola, Herman, and Carolyn Margolis, editors. 1991. *Seeds of Change.* Washington, D.C.: Smithsonian Institution Press.

Walker, Jeffrey. 1997. Taíno stone collars, elbow stones, and three-pointers. In *Taíno: Pre-Columbian art and culture from the Caribbean,* edited by Fátima Bercht, Estrellita Brodsky, John Alan Farmer, and Dicey Taylor. New York: El Museo del Barrio and the Monacelli Press, pp. 80–91.

Watts, David. 1978. *The West Indies: Patterns of development, culture, and environmental change since 1492.* Cambridge: Cambridge University Press.

Watts, Pauline Moffat. 1985. Prophecy and discovery: On the spiritual origins of Christopher Columbus's "Enterprise of the Indies." *American historical review* 90, no. 1:73–102.

Wilford, John Noble. 1991. *The mysterious history of Columbus.* New York: Alfred Knopf.

Williams, Maurice. 1986. Sub-surface patterning at 16th-century Spanish Puerto Real, Haiti. *Journal of field archaeology* 13, no. 3:283–96.

————. 1995. Spatial patterning and community organization at Puerto Real. *In Puerto Real: The archaeology of a sixteenth-century Spanish town in Hispaniola,* edited by K. Deagan. Gainesville: University Press of Florida, pp. 115–40.

Willis, Raymond. 1976. The archeology of 16th-century Nueva Cádiz. Unpublished M.A. thesis, Department of Anthropology, University of Florida, Gainesville.

————. 1984. Empire and architecture at 16th-century Puerto Real, Hispaniola. Ph.D. dissertation, University of Florida, Gainesville.

————. 1995. Empire and architecture at Puerto Real: The archeology of public space. In *Puerto Real: The archaeology of a sixteenth-century Spanish town in Hispaniola,* edited by K. Deagan. Gainesville: University Press of Florida, pp. 141–66.

Wilson, Samuel. 1990. *Hispaniola: Caribbean chiefdoms in the age of Columbus.* Tuscaloosa: University of Alabama Press.

————. 1997a. The Caribbean before European conquest: A chronology. In *Taíno: Pre-Columbian art and culture from the Caribbean,* edited by Fátima Bercht, Estrellita Brodsky, John Alan Farmer, and Dicey Taylor. New York: El Museo del Barrio and the Monacelli Press, pp. 15–17.

————. 1997b. The Taíno social and political order. In *Taíno: Pre-Columbian art and culture from the Caribbean,* edited by Fátima Bercht, Estrellita Brodsky, John Alan Farmer, and Dicey Taylor. New York: El Museo del Barrio and the Monacelli Press, pp. 46–55.

————, editor. 1997c. *The indigenous people of the Caribbean.* Gainesville: University Presses of Florida.

Wing, Elizabeth. 1983. La adaptación humana a los medioambientes de las Antillas. In *La cultura Taína: Las culturas de América en la época del descubrimiento*, edited by A. G. Pantel. Madrid: Biblioteca del V Centenario, pp. 87–105.

———. 1989a. Evidences for the impact of traditional Spanish animal uses in parts of the New World. In *The walking larder*, edited by J. Clutton-Brock. London: Orwin Hyman, pp. 72–79.

———. 1989b. Human exploitation of animal resources in the Caribbean. In *Biogeography of the West Indies*, edited by C. Woods. Gainesville: Sandhill Crane Press, pp. 137–52.

Woods, Alfred. 1999. Report on fieldwork at Concepción de la Vega, Dominican Republic: 1996 through 1998. Project report on file, Dirección Nacional de Parques, Santo Domingo, and the Florida Museum of Natural History, Gainesville.

Wright, Irene, editor. 1929. *Spanish documents concerning English voyages to the Caribbean, 1527–1568*. London: Hakluyt Society.

Zendegui, Guillermo. 1977. *La planificación urbana en las colonias españolas*. Washington, D.C.: Organization of American States.

ACKNOWLEDGMENTS

A project as lengthy and as complex as that of La Isabela was possible only through the cooperation and assistance of a great many agencies and individuals in the Dominican Republic, the United States, Venezuela, and Spain. Their support was crucial to all aspects of the project, those detailed in this book as well as those in our companion volume.

Funding for the research and analysis upon which this book is based has been provided by grants from the U.S. National Endowment for the Humanities (RO−21831−89 and RK20135−94), from the National Geographic Society Research Committee and *National Geographic* magazine, from the University of Florida Division of Sponsored Research and the University of Florida Institute for Early Contact Period Studies, and from the Florida Museum of Natural History. The excavations undertaken by Cruxent were supported by the Dirección Nacional de Parques de la República Dominicana (DNP), with major assistance from the Instituto Española de Cooperación Internacional. The Universidad Nacional Experimental Francisco de Miranda of Venezuela and the University of Florida each generously allocated the time of Cruxent and Deagan, respectively, to this project for nearly a decade.

It is owing to the commitment and vision of the Dirección Nacional de Parques de la República Dominicana that the project at La Isabela was conceived and successfully completed. The original impetus and energy for the program reported in this book was provided by Eugenio Pérez Montás and the late Manuel Valverde Podestá, the director of the DNP from 1986 to 1988. Pérez Montás was instrumental in forging the international collaboration at La Isabela, and he provided important advice and assistance throughout the project. We would also like to acknowledge his professional assistance in interpreting the architectural remains from La Isabela.

The commitment of the DNP to La Isabela was continued by Cristián Martínez, director of the Park Service from 1988 to 1992, and we are grateful for his unswerving support during that critical period. The Dirección Nacional de Parques has consistently supported the research and interpretive programs at the site since then, financing the excavations directed by Cruxent, providing housing for the foreign participants in the project, and furnishing research facilities at the site.

Archaeologist Manuel García Arévalo has not only been one of the collaborating investigators at La Isabela but has also been an immensely valuable colleague in resolving the many complex intellectual and logistical issues related to the project. He has provided support for the La Isabela project in Santo Domingo and, along with Francie Pou-García, has generously offered hospitality and advice to the Dominican and foreign participants in the archaeological work at La Isabela.

We have depended on the expertise of many other scholars in this undertaking. Consuelo Varela (Universidad de Sevilla), Frank Moya Pons (Centro de Estudios Avanzados and the University of Florida), and Carlos Dobal (Universidad Católica Madre y Maestra, Santiago, Dominican Republic) provided much of the historical documentation and interpretation upon which our understanding of events at La Isabela is based.

Emlen Myers and Jacqueline Olin of the Smithsonian Institution Conservation Analytical Laboratory contributed invaluable analysis and interpretation of ceramics from the site. Alan Stahl of the American Numismatic Society identified and studied coins from La Isabela, Walter Karcheski of the Higgins Armory Museum provided assessment of some of the weaponry from the site, and Patricia Muller of the Hispanic Society of America commented on items of jewelry. Robert Brill of the Corning Glass Museum gave generously of his time and expertise in the chemical analysis of glass from La Isabela. Photographer James Quine and artist Merald Clark each spent several weeks on site photographing and drawing the artifact collection, respectively.

John Masemann (South Florida Conservation Center) surveyed the artifact collection from La Isabela for conservation needs and developed guidelines for a conservation program. These have since been partially implemented with assistance from the U.S. National Endowment for the Humanities, the U.S. Department of Agriculture, and the Museo de la Atarazana in Santo Domingo, directed by Pedro Borrell. We would especially like to acknowledge the generous assistance of Francis Soto and the conservation staff of the Museo de la Atarazana for their work in conserving the materials from La Isabela.

Antonio Tejera Gaspar of the Universidad de La Laguna, Gran Canaria, offered invaluable comparative insights from his work on the Columbian contact sites in the Canary Islands, both during the time he spent with us at La Isabela and subsequently. Elena Sosa of the Universidad de La Laguna also contributed many voluntary hours in the lab.

Elizabeth Reitz of the University of Georgia provided uncounted hours in the search for faunal and dietary evidence from La Isabela, including her time spent (uncomfortably) on site. Archaeobotanists Lee Ann Newsom and Margaret Mosenfelder Scarry also made valuable contributions to our assessments of plant use at La Isabela. Margaret was stung by a scorpion under the dinner table on her first night in La Isabela, yet continued nevertheless to be enthusiastic about the project.

The substance of this book would not have been possible without the dedicated work of a number of highly competent graduate students (and now former graduate students) in historical archaeology programs at the University of Florida and the Universidad Francisco de Miranda. Ricardo Fernández-Sardina, Gardner Gordon, James Cusick, and Ed Napolean very capably supervised the fieldwork sponsored by the University of Florida. Kate Hoffman, George Avery, James Cusick, Jeremy Cohen, Mary Herron, Terrance Weik, Gifford Waters, Ann Stokes, Robin Stuhlman, Kimberly Martin, Marietta Estéfan, and Gianna Brown all spent many months both on site in El Castillo and at the University of Florida analyzing, documenting, and computerizing the data reported here. Alvira Mercator of the Universidad Nacional Francisco de Miranda provided invaluable assistance and input throughout the project, both on site and from Coro, Venezuela. She contributed significantly to this undertaking in many ways.

Lab technicians from El Castillo included Isabel Peralta, Amable Osorio, Paula Rodríguez, and Diamilde Aristide, and they provided continuity, excellent technical assistance, and steadfast companionship in the lab over the years. The current laboratory was constructed as part of the site museum by the Instituto Española de Cooperación Internacional, and we appreciate not only the much more comfortable working conditions the institute provided but also the long-term protection of the collections themselves.

Maurice Williams and Al Woods, historical archaeologists at the Florida Museum of Natural History, were instrumental in the organization, computerization, and interpretation of field and lab data throughout the project. We appreciate the dedication and enthusiasm for the program of all these participants under what were often very physically uncomfortable conditions.

We would also like to thank Miguel González of Cabudare, Venezuela, for his unstinting support of Cruxent and the generous hospitality he extended to both Cruxent and Deagan during the final stages of writing this book. He also provided secure and accessible storage facilities in the restored Convento de Santa Barbara in Cabudare for Cruxent's personal papers related to La Isabela and for copies of Cruxent's field records.

We acknowledge our intellectual debt to the many scholars who worked at La Isabela before us, and whose work we had the advantage of building upon. These include Juan Puig Ortíz, Rafael Cantisano, Fernando Luna Calderón, José Guerrero, Marcio Veloz Maggiolo, Elpidio Ortega, and Carlos Dobal.

This project would also not have been possible without the assistance and cooperation of several of our colleagues at the University of Florida. We would particularly like to acknowledge the critical input of Michael Gannon, director of the Institute for Early Contact Period Studies, who provided seed money and initial encouragement for the project. Invaluable logistical assistance was also provided by

Gene Hemp, vice president for academic affairs, Terry McCoy, director of the Center for Latin American Studies, George Scheffer of the College of Architecture, and William Keegan and Jerry Milanich, chairs consecutively of the Florida Museum Department of Anthropology during our work at La Isabela.

Valuable editorial assistance and reviews were provided by Jeremy Cohen, Bekis Suárez y Cohen, and Al Woods. We would particularly like to acknowledge the assistance of Otto Bohlmann, whose graceful way with words and steel-trap mind have made this an immeasurably more readable book.

We must finally and gratefully acknowledge the help and *amistad* of our many friends in El Castillo, who have made it possible and pleasant for us to work there by their open acceptance of us all into their community. We would especially like to thank Corina Peralta and her family for their many kindnesses to the foreign archaeologists, not to mention the many wonderful meals they have prepared over the years. Doña Corina as well as Roberto Montolio and his family have made our time at El Castillo not only an immensely enjoyable cultural adventure but also gastronomically rewarding, and more often than not, fun.

INDEX

hygiene, 148, 152, 153(f); jewelry,
159–60; horse equipment, 172,
174(f), 175; decline in America, 219,
222, 238

Jacaque, 60
Jánico, 56
Jetons, 195, 197(f)
Jewelry, Spanish, 155–56, 158–60, 159
  (f), 165, 219, 220(f), 252; Taíno, 129
  (see also rings, finger)
Junta para la Celebración del Centenario, 79,
  120

Kilns, pottery, 65, 95–97, 111, 140, 181,
  191–92, 192(f)

La Breña, 96
La Vega, town of, 214
La Isabela, establishment of, vii, 50, 66;
  historical research on, 4; Indian
  towns at, 44–45, 51, 65; present site
  of, 48–52; town plan, 54, 104–7;
  defenses, 55, 104, 105–6, 107, 167;
  governance, 58, 59, 64, 66, 67; abandonment of, 70, 199; early descriptions, 76–79; excavations at, 80,
  91–93; plaza, 107; architecture,
  110–12
La Navidad, establishment of, 14–15;
  Columbus at, 14, 165; during second
  voyage, 21–22; destruction of, 47, 59;
  influence on La Isabela, 22, 43–44,
  55, 105; near Puerto Real, 238
La Yaguana, 75
Ladrillos, 111, 181
Lanzas de Jinetas, 19, 167, 173–75, 253
Las Casas, Bartolomé de, 12, 62, 28; at
  Puerto Plata, 72, 118; as historical
  source, 233–34
Las Casas, Pedro de, 19
Las Coles, satellite settlement, 53, 57,
  76, 82; excavations at, 96–97; craft
  activity at, 180, 181, 191
Laws of Burgos, 209

Lead smelting, 187–88
León, Juan Ponce de, 19
Lighting equipment, 147–148, 148(f)
Lime and lime burning, 111–12, 122, 181
Limpieza de sangre, 224
López de Gómara, Francisco, 224
Lucayans, 15, 210
Luján, Juan de, 58
Luna Calderón, Fernando, 87
Luperón, Dominican Republic, 50

Macorijes, 26, 30, 45, 240, 241
Magdalena fortress, 60, 61, 66, 67
Magua, 59
Maguana, 59
Maímon, Dominican Republic, 83
Majolica, Spanish, 83, 142, 146(f);
  Italian, 218(f)
Manatees, 36, 133, 136, 219
Manioc, 36, 68, 134–35, 142, 144, 219
Marchena, Antonio de, 19, 164
Margarite, Pedro de, 56, 57, 58, 59, 60,
  167
María, Galadas, 83
Marien, 44, 59
Marque, town of, 68
Marriages, 28, 214, 215, 216
Marta, ciudad de, 51, 53, 97
Martini, Francesco di Giorgio, 102
Martyr D'Anghiera, Peter, 224
Mass, 50, 55, 163
Mayabonex, 44, 59
McEwan, Bonnie, 219
Medicine and medical supplies,
  151–52, 153(f)
Meillacan-Ostionoid tradition, 26
Memoria del reinado de los Reyes Católicos, 24
Mercederians, 20
Mercury, 185–86
Mestizos and *mestizaje,* 212, 202, 222,
  224
Metallurgy, 122, 185–90, 254
Mexico City, 222, 223(f), 224
Mills, 51, 52, 57, 65, 180
Miners, 63, 64, 202, 211